# Scattered, Smothered, and Covered

## A Memoir of Resilience

### Sandra Tow

Tethered Tides Press, LLC

# Contents

# Dedication

All of the love in my heart for my family, who are my world. For my mom.

# *Teardrops Fall*

I wish my mother had said she was sorry before she died. If only I had heard her say those words—but she didn't, she couldn't. Her ability to speak was taken in a surgery deemed necessary to give her a chance to live, to beat the cancer. After she was relegated to notebook communication only, even writing her regrets or apologies would've broken her apart because she was too busy fighting for her life. I was born to a single mother who loved me and made mistakes like all humans. Looking back on the past has also caused me to examine my own missteps as a mother. I wonder how often she did the same thing, but could never force herself to utter any excuses or apologies, choosing instead to remain silent.

When I turned thirty, I told her I was thinking of writing about my childhood experiences, our experiences. She took a puff of her cigarette, narrowed her blue-eyed gaze, and said, "They certainly were an adventure." I don't know if I'd classify my childhood as an adventure, but the approval I'd really been seeking with my question was answered. The answer was a firm "no." Mom had a way of voicing her displeasure with measured, exact phrasing, and I'd spent years interpreting looks, verbal inflections, and touches to gauge her emotions.

Looking back, I now understand she was my first and greatest love until I met my husband and had children of my own. I would and did do most things she asked of me until I deviated from our unspoken, enmeshed agreement I don't recall signing as a child. By the age of five, I knew she loved dropping peanuts into a glass Pepsi bottle, eating pretzels, drinking extra sweet iced tea and strong black coffee, driving fast, teaching me yoga poses, and reading romance and mystery novels. She believed in ghosts, the afterlife, white witch-craft, and in men more than she should. Mom had a wicked sense of humor and an even more wicked competitive nature, the warmest hugs, and in the rarest of times, a nasty temper always directed toward the men in her life, never toward me. And most disturbing now, as I fully examine our lives together, is that she never spoke of her dreams. Not once. Not ever.

In Mom's eyes, I was her perfect child incapable of doing wrong until I proved otherwise. And I loved her unconditionally, until I discovered a need to love myself more. This is my story, or better yet, this is our story. I wouldn't be the person I am without those experiences, without the mother I was gifted.

In the seventies, everyone I knew smoked, with the exception of my great-grandparents, whom we lived with off and on until I was five years old. Mom never smoked in their house, or at least I never recall her smoking there. I sat in my little rocking chair in front of the television and watched the actors on *Wonder Woman* and *The Six Million Dollar Man* puff sagely on cigarettes as they solved disasters and saved people and the world from imminent destruction. My mom, Ann, and her sister, my Aunt Leigh, smoked almost continuously—the cigarette dangled from either their fingers or lips, a fire-tipped extension of their persona, and while they didn't save people like my favorite actors, I wanted to imitate them.

Mom was thin, her thick auburn hair pulled back with blue or red handkerchiefs on days she did chores and falling just past her shoulders on other days. Her style was bell-bottom jeans and form-fitting T-shirts. Aunt Leigh had long, straight blonde hair that brushed her lower back only inches from the hem of the dresses she wore. Anytime Aunt Leigh visited she pulled me onto her lap and hugged and nuzzled my head and neck before releasing me to play. The sisters sat at the kitchen table, talking and pulling the cigarettes to their lips slowly, parting them ever so slightly, touching the filter to their lips, and drawing in the smoke. I was drawn to the glamor of how Mom closed her eyes with every drag of the cigarette, tipped her head back, and smiled slightly when she released a billow of white-gray smoke in a combination of ways: a single burst, smoke rings, clouds rolling like a fog bank over the English moor, and my least favorite form—through the nose. I wasn't exactly sure what the look of ecstasy was all about. Still, it sure seemed the cigarettes provided some sort of pleasure and maturity I wanted to capture. I wanted to be just like Mom and Aunt Leigh.

On a warm spring day, I was feeling overly confident wearing my favorite terrycloth green shorts and matching white and green floral sleeveless shirt—the ultimate confidence-boosting material in 1975. That outfit made me feel unruffled, and it brought a level of confidence I've rarely found in apparel since. I pranced into the kitchen to pour my bowl of Franken Berry cereal. It was the perfect morning to take my adoring imitation to the next level.

I had practiced the puff, the blow, and the exact tilt of the head when inhaling with the store-bought candy cigarettes made especially for future smokers. The candy manufacturers had to be conspiring with the big tobacco companies, because I recall the boxes of candy cigarettes sitting right next to the boxes of Lucky Strikes, Marlboros, and Salem 100s on the grocery store shelves. In those days, laws didn't prevent children from buying packs of cigarettes, and the major brands were lined along the grocery check-out lanes like packs of gum and mints are today. I had plenty of practice taking a dollar bill from Mom's hand, walking into the local convenience store, grabbing a pack of Salem 100s, a pack of gum, or a box of candy cigarettes, and still getting some coins in return from the cashier.

Since I was wearing my favorite outfit and brimming with self-confidence on the fateful day, I waited for my mother to light off in the direction of the bathroom for her morning break. Then I made a beeline for the amber-colored ashtray collecting the mountain of butts. It filled fairly quickly as my mother had a habit of sparking another cigarette as soon as she smoked one down to the filter. I picked through the collection of used butts in the tray, pushing the unmarked ones to the side with disdain. Those belonged to her boyfriend, John, and the thought of my lips touching anything his mouth touched repulsed me. I carefully plucked the one with the bright red lip creases encircling the filter. Mom must have forgotten about this one. The anticipation of finally getting to practice on the real thing had my fingers struggling to close around the cigarette without breaking it in two. There was at least a quarter of a cigarette still intact. I drew the unlit cigarette to my lips and was surprised when they tingled from the menthol. I sucked in a deep breath, full of stale tobacco and charred paper, and then tapped the cigarette against the rim of the ashtray like I'd practiced over and over in my head, precisely as my mother had done.

My body buzzed with excitement from finally feeling sophisticated and worldly. I felt infinitely older than my almost five years. I brought the cigarette to my lips again and paced the living room, my head tilted like Mom when she was surveying a kitchen before she cleaned a sinkful of dishes or before she started cooking dinner. I was mid-puff into my role-play when my mother returned. She stopped dead in her tracks at the sight of me prancing around the living room. I immediately dropped the butt on the floor and my ass onto the green plaid couch with the upholstery that scratched the backs of my legs.

I knew this would be it, the time I would finally get a spanking. I hadn't gotten one up to this point, but I'd witnessed my cousins getting plenty from my great-grandma with the switches she kept lined up against the side of her house. I imagined my mother pulling me across her knees and hitting me, my small body shuddering in fear. Tears sprung to my eyes just thinking about it because I'd never been spanked or even popped on the bottom. I was already imagining burning butt cheeks and permanent fingerprints marring my flesh.

My mother's face flushed crimson red. Her arms crossed against her heaving chest, and she glared at me with signature maternal disappointment for what seemed like hours. Finally, she pointed to the kitchen table and told me to sit down. She grabbed a green ashtray from a side table and dropped it in front of me. I wiggled in the chair, anxious and confused by the look of complete calm that had settled on my mother's face.

She continued to stare in silence. The longer she waited, the calmer my breathing became, and I felt certain I wasn't getting a spanking. But my discomfort remained, and I looked everywhere except into the displeased baby-blue eyes of my mother.

"Sandra Dawn, what were you thinking?" she demanded drawing out my middle name, the name she'd called me since I was born. Somehow the "w" never materialized and to my ears it sounded like my name rhymed with bone.

I shrugged.

Any explanation of my actions seemed stupid to me. I knew telling Mom that I wanted to mimic her and Aunt Leigh wouldn't hold much weight on the excuse meter. Even at my young age, I recalled Mom telling me she wanted more for me. She would frequently quiz me on the spelling of words. I learned to spell Rolaids before I read my first Dick and Jane book in the first grade. And she always made me watch the Wheel of Fortune nightly, nudging me to sound out or guess a word.

The hand on the wall clock clicked the minutes away in the eerily silent house as she continued to stare me down. I imagined her yelling at me the way she yelled at John during their many arguments, but she did nothing but nail me with a stern look. It was a look I feared. The CIA could've used that look as an interrogation method.

She finally turned away, and I exhaled a breath I didn't know I'd been holding. She opened the refrigerator door and pulled my carton of chocolate milk from the shelf. I couldn't believe she was going to let me have chocolate milk after what I'd just done. Chocolate milk was a luxury I usually received after cleaning my plate at dinner because of all the hungry children around the world. Angrily drawing on her cigarette and exhaling with unusual force, she placed the carton and a glass in front of me. This wasn't the glamorous picture I'd held in my mind of my first smoking experience. I was confused, and my stomach flip-flopped in fear. My mother sat down across from me, picked up the carton of milk, and poured the chocolate milk to the brim of the glass.

My stomach hit the floor when she shook two Salem Menthol 100s from her pack, the only brand she smoked until she could no longer afford them. I stared at the two cigarettes on the table.

"Pick it up," she directed with an even and calm tone. My entire body shook from fear. By this point, I would have taken a beating instead because at least the anticipation would be over. I could be back outside playing on my Big Wheel instead of sitting at that table like Wile E. Coyote waiting for the anvil to drop on my head.

"If you're determined to smoke, I'm going to teach you to do it the right way." The words were clipped, but with a slight Southern accent.

Mom was a high school drop-out who read voraciously and prided herself on speaking properly. She rarely used slang, and her words never stuttered unless she was nervous or angry; those times, she'd cease speaking until she was composed enough to finish her thoughts.

She instructed me to suck on the filter like I would on a straw. "Do you understand?" she asked me. I nodded, damp tendrils sticking against my forehead. First, she lit her cigarette, then nodded at me. I raised the cigarette to my lips. Holding the lighter to the end, she commanded, "Puff on it a couple of times, just like you see me do." I did as she said and was rewarded with a wry smile. It was the type of smile that made me want to hide under my bed if I wasn't already afraid of the monsters I knew lounged there nightly. But I told myself everything would be okay. I was going to live another day, my mother would not give me the first spanking of my life, and we would enjoy a cigarette together. I sat up straighter in the chair and crossed my legs. Her eyes narrowed. "Now suck on it like you're gulping a big mouthful of chocolate milk."

I sucked a lungful of noxious smoke into my lungs. It took nano-seconds for my body to revolt. I was seized by a coughing fit, which made me think my fire-ensconced throat would be expelled from my body like projectile vomit. I gasped for air, my nose poured snot, and I turned pleading eyes to my mom to make the pain stop. She reached for the cigarette that dangled from my fingers and pushed the glass of chocolate milk toward me. I gulped the entire glass. The cold drink soothed my throat and filled my stomach with its massive, sweet weight.

She reached for the glass and filled it once more. "Please, Mom, no," I whimpered. But instead of stopping, she handed me the lit cigarette and told me to take another puff. "If you want to smoke, you're going to smoke this entire thing." My eyes burned with tears of pain, fear, and anger. I wondered if I would die and then thought how sorry she'd be if I did. My flair for drama began early on and served me well into adulthood, passing on to my children like a surprise legacy.

My shaky hands managed to pull the cigarette back to my mouth. As hurt and angry as I was, I didn't want to disappoint my mother any more than I had already. So, I sucked another lungful of smoke. Coughing wracked my small body and nausea washed over me in waves. She suggested I take another drink of milk. I obeyed. I slurped a few more sips before nausea slammed into me like a tsunami.

I threw the cigarette in the direction of the ashtray and raced to the bathroom. Chocolate milk and half-digested cereal spewed from my mouth as I hugged the toilet bowl, my tears mixing with vomit. I struggled to reconcile her serene look as she forced me to smoke. My body shook as I rested against the toilet, stunned by confusion and anger. I couldn't make sense of the awful pain that was inflicted on me by the person I trusted the most. This was my first taste of my mother's form of logic as she attempted to mold me into a better human, unlike her.

After the sobs stopped, I rose from the floor and rinsed my face. Cupping my hands under the running water, I filled my mouth, swished and spit until the sourness was gone. When I looked into the mirror, I saw my face matched my green terrycloth shorts. I no longer felt any semblance of the self-esteem high I'd rocked earlier. I shuffled back to the kitchen and dropped into the chair to face my mother. She fixed a solemn gaze on me. "Did you learn your lesson?" she asked. I nodded my head up and down, afraid to open my mouth again. I wasn't sure anything was left in my stomach, but I didn't want to take any chances.

"Do as I say, not as I do." She squeezed my shoulder as she stood and moved toward the sink to wash our breakfast dishes, humming along with a tune in her head.

Mom loved to spout these purported nuggets of wisdom. I nodded again to show her I understood, but I didn't understand how my loving mother could turn on me, could hurt me. The life lesson she'd tried to teach me became the very first deposit in my anger memory bank.

Looking back now, I understand the reasoning behind her split-second decision and reaction; being a parent and being human must be reconciled. The reconciliation is that sometimes a parent reacts before thinking. Sometimes parents aren't superheroes like we imagine and mistakes are made. Parenting isn't taught in schools, and clearly, some parents have an innate ability to nurture more than others. My mother honed her parenting skills by doing the opposite of her parents. Given the fact she was the oldest of four children, she had been parentified and expected to serve in a role she wasn't ready to take on. I now understand the toxicity of her difficult upbringing seeped into many of the decisions she made in her life, ceaselessly drawing her back into the old trauma despite her efforts to leave it all behind.

My mother was also born to a teenage mom, same as me. My grandmother Bobbie married Ralph, a gruff man she'd met at a church function. From stories I'd heard, my grandfather lived a rough childhood in Wilkesboro, North Carolina, a place known for blue-collar roots anchored in the mountains of Appalachia. Years later, Aunt Leigh would tell me he was raised by his grandma in a small cabin, both of his parents absent from his life. The story about him attending a church event was hard for me to believe. Trolling the church parking lot trying to sell moonshine to a rebellious preacher's kid seemed more likely.

Ralph, who I didn't meet until I was four years old, was stoic and weathered with a hint of mean escaping his hooded eyes. My earliest memories were of him brooding in his chair while sipping from a whiskey glass and aggressively pulling the smoke from a cigarette, grunting monosyllables when someone asked him a question. My mother told me he was cruel. She also told me stories that would've had child services beating down their door nowadays. Still, in the sixties, when he pushed Mom down the steps and she hurt her tailbone so badly she could barely walk for weeks, domestic violence was dismissed as an accident. My mother didn't have much of a childhood as she took on caring for her younger siblings and cooking for the family since her mama was always sick. Mom would spend weekends and summers with Bobbie's parents, James and Beulah, when she needed a break. When she was sixteen, Ralph wiped out the savings she'd accrued from her job as a nursing assistant at a local nursing home. Thieving her money served as the final blow to a strained relationship, so she packed her bags and left home for good.

When my mother left home at sixteen, she moved to Conover, North Carolina, an area about an hour away from her home in Troutman, where she began working in a hospital as a nurse's aide. She told me stories years later of how she met my father while she was caring for his mother at the hospital. Mom was in a program at the hospital to train nursing aids to become registered nurses. When she got pregnant with me, James and Beulah let her move in with them since they refused to turn away their grandchild in need, even when Mom's parents refused to help their daughter in her most dire time of need. When she told me this story of her being an unwed mother, she always emphasized her love for me was greater than her desire to become a nurse.

James and Beulah, my great-grandparents, had lived in the house on Spruce Street in Mooresville's mill area for many years. Both of my great-grandparents worked for Burlington Mills, the leading employer in the area during the 1950s and 60s. They allowed my pregnant, unwed mother to stay with them, and after I was born, the most loving memories of my early childhood were made in their home. Going through my photo album revealed numerous pictures of me after I was born until around four years old, sharing their home. My mom must've taken the pictures of me sitting on James's lap being fed a bottle, playing in the middle of their living room, the black woodstove in the background. She herself was never in them. I loved the woodstove, the smell of smoke clinging to my clothes when I stood beside my grandpa James as he struck a match and lit a crumpled pile of newspaper under a piece of firewood. He left the used piles of matchsticks in a small tray behind the stove. I went through a phase around three or four where I'd snatch the used matchsticks and chew the blackened tips, which explains my love of blackened marshmallows over a fire to this day. Other pictures from that time show me posing in dresses and sitting beside my cousins who were around my age.

I loved the way their house always smelled like cinnamon apples, and my great-grandma's hugs were like being enveloped in a freshly baked loaf of bread. I would sit on the top of her kitchen table cross-legged and content, watching her mix cake batters, bake persimmon pies, and fry chicken for Sunday dinners with the family. James's and Beulah's house was where all of their grandchildren congregated. I'm uncertain if they were actually babysitting or if we were simply drawn there because it was such a warm and loving home.

All of the grandkids played tag, hide-and-seek, and Tarzan in the empty lot across the street from their house where English ivy vines as thick as my wrist hung from enormous oak trees whose canopy of limbs and leaves blocked the sky. I would spend hours sitting on the front porch swing watching cars drive by as my mother worked at a local factory as a sewing machine operator. My favorite times on the swing happened during summer thunderstorms. I watched the lightning streak the sky, and the thunder rumbled the swing chains as fat raindrops hit the black pavement, leaving behind an aroma of steamed asphalt. Sometimes, Grandma Beulah would join me on the porch, wrapping an arm around my shoulders and pulling me close as we watched the storm clean the world around us.

Mom and I lived with James and Beulah off and on during my first four years. Then my childhood bubble disintegrated when we left that warm, loving home environment and moved in with my mother's boyfriend, John, who was a prize-winning asshole. He wasn't the first man she'd dated since I was born, but he was the first man I remembered. She made it clear to me that he was not my father, like I would have ever considered such a ridiculous fact.

I immediately disliked him. John wore his hair slicked back and loved his side-zip black leather dress boots, which he kept meticulously polished. His Aqua Velva cologne was so thick the smell would cling to my nostrils for hours after he left the house. John's appearance wasn't the primary point of disgust. When he bothered to acknowledge my existence, he generally shot me a look of disdain or fixated on an imaginary point about a foot over my head. You know what they say about small children and pets seeing a person's true identity. Well, my mom wasn't asking my dating advice at the time, because if she did, I would've told her she should know better than to date her father. I went out of my way to keep a couch-length distance between us at all times unless we were eating at the same table.

His house was a small brick ranch with dark wood-paneled walls that created the dungeon of our living space, the only light streaming through a set of sliding glass doors that led to the backyard. I shared a bedroom wall with them and stayed up at night on more nights than not listening to their angry words and my mom's crying during the few months we lived with him. When I finally drifted off to sleep, I would dream of the safety of my great-grandparents' house. I would think about my favorite memories with them, like when they used to fill my sippy cup with iced coffee and let me sit in my child-sized rocking chair while we watched *Hee Haw* and *The Lawrence Welk Show*. After the last of the bubbles settled on the stage, my great-grandpa would rock me to sleep, sometimes humming and singing songs I didn't know but that soothed me.

Every house has a particular atmosphere based on the temperament of its occupants. John's place was closed off and cold. There were no pictures on the walls of loved ones, no wall decorations at all unless one would count the rough linear grooves in the wood paneling. The only decorations were amber and emerald green glass ashtrays placed in strategic locations around the room. A dark-green low shag carpet carried the weight of the dark furniture in the living room. My great-grandparents' home was filled with smells of cooking, laughing, kids' toys everywhere, and warm hugs for no reason, and I longed for the days we'd spent in that safe nest.

Some mornings, John and Mom would quarrel before he left for work. I had no idea why they argued so much. My earliest memories of conflict involved aggression, instability, and violence. Their arguments resulted in John storming out of the house and slamming the door for emphasis. I was unsure if he was going to work or leaving to get away from us. Mom would wait for him to back out of the driveway before she grabbed the closest glass or coffee mug, screamed, and then hurled it against the wall. I watched her from the living room and wondered what he'd said or done this time to make Mom so angry. Usually, after these heated moments, she'd pull me in for a hug like she wanted to ensure I knew her anger wasn't directed at me. I hated John for making her sad, and I shot him a scowl every time he looked my way. I never hid my dislike of the man.

When John was at work, Mom taught me to add and subtract numbers by showing me how to kill it at blackjack and other strategy games. I'm sure some folks would take issue with the games she taught me, but I learned how to read facial expressions at a young age and improved my skills over the years to my advantage. We'd play for hours, her smoking cigarettes and drinking glasses of orange juice after lunch, me eventually bored with card games and longing to watch *Scooby-Doo* or *Bugs Bunny*. Sometimes my aunt would come over to visit. She blew me away with her long blond hair and infectious smile. I wanted to be just like my mom when I grew up, but if I could be like anyone else, it would've been my Aunt Leigh. It would be another ten years before I'd change my mind.

Mom's physical features were only one reason I wanted to be like her. She displayed a confidence only women who'd been frequently told they were beautiful could exude when we left the walls of John's dungeon. Inside, she dimmed her light to become a fixture. When Mom smiled at me, I felt I was the most important kid in the world. I was struck by how she always appeared perfect. I sometimes sat on the side of John's green enameled bathtub and watched her apply mascara. If her hand shook and accidentally deposited a black mark on her eyelid, she'd grab a Q-tip, dab it to her tongue, and use the moistened tip to remove the mark. She walked me through applying makeup when I was four: foundation, powder, eyeliner, mascara, eyeshadow, and blush. To show I was paying attention, I nodded every time she looked in my direction.

But she was only willing to let me play grown-up to a certain extent; pretending to smoke her cigarettes was off limits. After experiencing her cruelty firsthand with the cigarette that day, I wanted to leave John's house and run to my great-grandparents' home for refuge. I needed a break. I felt I was in an alternate universe with an imposter Mom. I couldn't reconcile the woman who tucked me into bed, placing a kiss on my forehead or cheek, with this person who coldly stared me down and told me to suck in noxious smoke from a cigarette. I mean, really, I sucked in smoke every time she re-lit a new smoke stick. It was the mask removal that shocked me and I increased my observations of her to see if she was actually different or just taking on the strain of being in a toxic relationship. Maybe she was more like her parents than even she could admit.

No longer than a week or two after the cigarette incident, we sat at the table eating dinner. My relationship with Mom had returned to normal. She cleaned the house, I watched cartoons and rode my Big Wheel trike on the concrete pad, and John worked. Everything appeared fine on the surface, but I felt an undercurrent of uneasiness permeate the household like the air on a late July afternoon just prior to a crackling Southern thunderstorm. While I couldn't place the issue, I stayed quiet in John's presence and watched. I always watched him. John worked different shifts, and our luck found us sharing dinner with him after he worked a first-shift stint at a local factory. I think Mom once mentioned he was a supervisor of some sort to Aunt Leigh. But I never knew what he actually did for work, just that he left the house each day wearing a light-blue shirt and dark-blue pants. Mom would go by the cleaners and pick up his uniforms during the week.

On the night of the dinner, Mom made my favorite meal of fried chicken and mashed potatoes. I stuck my fork in the pile of potatoes, making crisscross patterns with the tines. Suddenly John yelled, "What?" breaking the comfortable silence. I hadn't heard my mom say anything and was confused about his outburst. He jumped out of his chair so fast it fell backward, clattering against the linoleum. I jumped, jerking my head toward him. A thick strand of greasy black hair was uncharacteristically out of place and flopped over his right eye. His face was a deep purple-red, and I wondered if he was going to die from a heart attack as I'd seen on television shows.

He wrapped his hands around my mom's neck and yanked her back as she braced her hands against the table. I started screaming for him to let her go, but he kept pulling at her head so hard I feared he was going to rip it right off her shoulders. Tears were streaming down her face as she begged him to let her go. I grabbed a butter knife from the table, wrapped my fingers around the handle, and stood in my chair, ready to plunge it in his face. My mom looked at me with eyes full of fear and tears, willing me not to do it. Moments later, John let her go and stormed from the house. My mom pulled me close as we cried together. The anger and distrust I'd harbored toward her for week was replaced by a trembling fear that John would kill her. I vowed to protect her from that point forward, and I took my vow seriously. She wept on my shoulder as I rubbed her back, a child comforting her mother. That was the beginning of the parent-child role reversal in our relationship. She packed our clothes into hampers and promised we would leave in the morning, assuring me John wouldn't return that night. I didn't fully believe her, so I spent the night on edge as she slept beside me behind my locked bedroom door.

The next morning, we moved back in with my great-grandparents. She told me I never had to worry about John hurting her again. I was happy she was so sure, but I didn't have much confidence. My life returned to normalcy with my great-grandparents: church on Wednesdays and Sundays, pies baking in the oven, afternoons playing with cousins and neighborhood kids, and swinging on the front porch swing. I could've lived in their home until I was grown. Mom had other ideas about what she wanted for her life, and at twenty-four, she desperately wanted to find a man who would care for her.

A month after leaving John, my mom went on vacation with one of her friends, met a twenty-two-year-old ex-convict, and married him. The year I turned five, I finally got the dad I thought I wanted. It took me the better part of a year to return his smile, because I didn't have the benefit of a father up to this point and my experience with John had soured me to all men besides my great-grandpa James. By the time I turned six, he'd convinced my mom that my great-grandparents spoiled me too much and they shouldn't be allowed to see me as often. This wedge between me and my great-grandparents would be my first lesson in Robert's manipulation. Mom's smoking lesson and every experience detailed in these pages, whether good, threatening, or horrific, became an opportunity for me to learn and grow because even negative experiences can have a positive takeaway and those experiences gave me resiliency, perseverance, and the true meaning of unconditional love.

# Loving You

The first time I met my new step-father, I thought he looked different, nothing like the men I was used to seeing. My uncles and great-grandfather all had close-cropped haircuts while Robert had long straight black hair that hit mid-back and caramel-colored skin that I wished I'd inherited instead of the white freckled skin and rosy cheeks of my European ancestors. He told Mom that he had Apache in his bloodline. While that was never confirmed, Robert did resemble images I'd seen of Native Americans in the Westerns I watched with my great-grandpa. Robert flashed a broad, toothy grin as my mom introduced him to my great-grandparents as her new husband and my new step-dad.

I test drove Robert's title in my head over and over before I ever let it touch my tongue. I'd wanted a father of my own for some time, and, suddenly, there was a new man in my mother's life. She'd chosen this man without even introducing him to me, though she claimed any man in her life had to receive my approval first. We were clearly playing by different rules now, and I didn't approve of Robert or the rule change.

"What do you think?" she asked after pulling me into the front living room of my great-grandparents' house.

"I think that was fast." One day I was playing with my cousins at our grandma's house, carefree as we played hide-and-seek for hours in and around her house, and then, my life changed.

"You'll love him like I do."

I rolled my eyes like my pre-teen cousin, Michelle. Mom laughed and nudged my shoulder, "Stop, just give him a chance."

"I'm not calling him 'Dad.'"

"When a person meets 'the one,' they just know. It can take a week or a year. Doesn't matter if you're meant to be together," she told me. "He's the one, Dawn."

I wonder what would've happened if she had dated him for a year before marrying him. Would she have seen the real person beneath the façade? Would she have still believed love was worth all the trouble? What she failed to tell me or maybe even acknowledge herself was that people change, relationships change, and I couldn't help but wonder what this meant for ours.

I finally had a dad to call mine. I used him for the title alone since I refused to hug him for months; instead, I chose to keep him at arm's length to see how he treated my mom. After the John incident, I watched for any warning signs. He hugged her frequently, always kissed her hello and goodbye, and never invoked her wrath. She had no desire to throw objects at the walls and scream in frustration with him, so we settled into a routine as a new family—I went to daycare, and they'd pick me up on their way home from work. They worked in a factory, and we lived in a small trailer park just outside Mooresville city limits.

This was my first experience living in a trailer, though far from the last. Mom and Robert's bedroom was in the very back, followed by mine, and then the bathroom. A small hallway led to the kitchen, and the living room occupied the front of the trailer. Comfort-wise, it wasn't much different than our two previous homes. The big difference I noticed was how the summer heat in the middle of the day would wrap around our skin and wring us out, a constant sheen of sweat rising from our pores. No matter how hard the fans Mom had placed around the living worked, or the window AC units ran, my head remained drenched in sweat as if I was roasting inside an oven like one of Mom's grease-excreting meatloafs she cooked at least once a week. Our trailer was pea green and off white, while the other surrounding trailers were varying shades of yellows or tan. We had a small wooden deck for a front porch, and every time I accidentally slammed the front door on my way to play in the yard, I was thankful for the stability since the trailer shook. After my first summer living in a trailer, I decided the flimsy tin boxes were not for me.

Robert was handy with mechanical stuff, and he spent a lot of time outdoors working on old push mowers and the car after work. He made friends with the neighbors, sometimes offering to help them with their car repairs also. He never seemed to spend a lot of time indoors unless he was eating dinner, watching evening television, or sleeping. For a while I watched and questioned if he was avoiding me or Mom, but then he'd come in from working and they'd gross me out by kissing with tongues and I was reassured all was okay for now since I'd never witnessed Mom acting like this with John.

I spent the majority of my time playing cards with Mom in the trailer that summer camped out on the living room floor, the wooden coffee table between us, the box fan providing a tepid breeze and sitting on a tan pile carpet that left fiber imprints all over the backs of my clammy legs. The heat and lack of neighborhood kids to play with forced me to watch game shows on television or play cards. After Mom taught me how to play blackjack, she moved on to her version of rummy. Whoever got to five hundred points first, won. Whoever had the queen of spades got fifty points. Whoever went out first left the other person holding a handful of cards which counted against them. Mom won a lot. We'd play for hours, and I would eventually slam my cards onto the table in frustration at her constant trouncing.

She would point to the cards and say, "Pick them up and finish this game."

"What's the point? You're beating me." I crossed my arms and stared at her, barely able to keep the tears of frustration at bay. "You always win."

"Nobody likes a sore loser."

I shrugged my shoulders. I hated losing. I even once had a Snoopy T-shirt with a "I hate losing" slogan across its front. Mom used to laugh and point at the picture she had of me sitting on my great-grandma Beulah's kitchen table wearing the shirt and say, "Never has there been a truer saying."

"Pick them up. One day you'll beat me, but until then, you'll play the rest of this hand so I can get a hundred and forty more points and win this game."

I picked up my hand of cards, what felt like half of the deck and almost too many to hold with my small hands, and stewed in my hatred of losing. I liked to believe my mom didn't take a perverse pleasure in always winning, but I know she did. I made it my goal in life to one day beat her at her own game. Losing made me feel small and weak, and I abhorred being at a disadvantage even at my young age. I studied her face, following her gaze when I laid down cards, looking for any sign she needed a card, like an eyebrow raise or a glint in her eyes. I studied Ann like a scientist watching a mouse navigate a maze. I analyzed her so closely just trying to figure out her tells that I wonder if these hours of card play were the early stages of losing myself.

During the first year with my new dad, one of my favorite memories was regularly eating dinner together. My new life was starting to look more like the shows I watched on television. My mom was no June Cleaver, but she was a great cook, although most of her meals were standard Southern fare with a fat dollop of Crisco and liberal dashes of salt and pepper. My favorite was her crispy fried chicken with sides of mashed potatoes and peas. The most significant disadvantage of the new dad arrangement was he seemed to think I was spoiled and didn't have enough chores around the house. I was six, for goodness' sake. In Robert's opinion it was like I was supposed to be ready to enter the workforce. I made my bed every morning. Wasn't that enough? How many six-year-olds make their beds? I didn't share his outlook and waited patiently for the reckoning Mom would give him about *her* daughter. I was used to being called spoiled by my cousins since I was the first great-grandchild of the family. I recognized my great-grandparents did treat me differently than my cousins, but this new man in my life had no right to make this accusation.

One night after having fried chicken for dinner, Robert looked at my mom and told her she'd cooked and, therefore, I should wash the dishes. I watched Mom's face for some sort of sign that she disagreed with him. I would need to be patient. I didn't realize then it would take another ten years before she would ever stand up to him. Instead, that night Mom nodded, and before I knew it, she'd pulled up a step stool to the sink. She motioned for me to try it. I raised an eyebrow in question as I stood at the sink and surveyed the pile of glasses, dishes, and greasy pans. I would've loved a dishwasher instead of handwashing dishes, but those appliances weren't available. There was nothing enticing about sticking my hand in a slimy, grease-encrusted pan.

Robert and my mom moved to the living room and snuggled on the couch, smoking cigarettes and watching the after-the-news batch of game shows. I dipped a glass in the suds and half-heartedly swirled a dishrag around the rim before dropping it into the rinse side of the sink. I slowly continued washing, paying more attention to the letters being revealed by Vanna White on the television screen than the task before me. I finished washing the dishes and had stacked them in the drying rack when Mom decided she should do a quality control check. She wiped a finger over the frying pan bottom and presented a greasy finger.

"Wash them again."

"I already washed them."

"You're going to wash all of them again because I can't trust you did a good job. If you're going to do anything, do it right the first time."

I felt the anger bubble to the surface. I blamed Robert. He'd been the one who'd talked Mom into this unlawful child labor. The tears started, and I said, "Why can't I just wash the frying pan?"

"I told you to wash all the dishes again."

I drained the sinks and filled them with hot water and tears.

"Don't take all night. We need to take showers, and I want some hot water," Robert called over his shoulder, never removing his eyes from the television screen.

I took in the stack of dishes and cried louder. I could hardly stop the sobs. I rarely cried or threw any fits as a child, but that night it seemed the boredom of the day, the heat, the frustration of not seeing my great-grandparents, and losing all of the rummy games, ignited an emotional fire I couldn't extinguish.

"Do I need to call Mr. Devil?" Robert asked nonchalantly.

"What?"

"I could call Mr. Devil to help you get those dishes washed faster."

"Nooooo!"

The fear of this mythical creature was real at this time in my life, and Robert knew how to leverage it. My great-grandparents had taken me to their church, The Church of God, since I was a small child. While there, I'd witnessed people talking in tongues and the booming voice of the preacher enact miracles with his sweaty touch. The devil and his monsters from the fiery pits of hell filled my nightmares and kept me from sleep.

"Mr. Devil," Robert called.

"Mr. Devil," my mom chimed in.

They started laughing, and as I cried hysterically at the kitchen sink, the betrayal of my mother's words and actions cut me to my core. I could see how Robert could try to scare me. He wasn't even my father. But Mom's laughter, in my mind, signaled she'd put another man before the wellbeing of her child.

After I finished the dishes, I climbed down from the step stool and turned to go to my room when she called me to her side. I sat down on the edge of the couch cushion, still too angry to get closer. She pulled me into a hug. "I'm sorry," she whispered close to my ear so Robert wouldn't hear. I knew she was sorry, but I would remember that time. I was reminded that a man can make a woman irrational, even with her children.

Right after I took on the chore of washing dishes at six, by seven, I was scrubbing the bathroom as part of my weekly duties. The first time Mom asked me to clean the bathroom, she handed me a can of Scrubbing Bubbles, a sponge, and some canary-yellow rubber gloves that were three sizes too big. I approached the bathtub and peered over the side taking in the grease and dirt layer ring that lined the tub from Robert's construction job and from working on the car. I'd watched the commercials about the cleaner. The lady on the commercial had simply sprayed the cleaner on the tub and waited for the bubbles to do the cleaning. I just had to rinse it away once the bubbles were done.

My mom leaned against the doorway and watched me with a quizzical look as she observed me perched on the toilet seat watching the tub.

"Dawn, what are you doing?"

"I'm waiting for the scrubbing bubbles to clean the tub so I can rinse it away."

Mom laughed sharply.

"Why're you laughing?"

"Oh, honey. You have to actually use elbow grease on those stains."

"But on the commercials, the bubbles erased all the dirt."

She chuckled again and said, "You're so gullible. The company wants people to buy it. They'll tell you anything."

My face reddened because it seemed I was always embarrassed about something in my youth. I found I blushed whenever I stammered over words when called on by a teacher and especially when my mother scolded me for something she thought I should know or be.

"You'd better figure it out before you get much older, or people are going to take advantage of your gullibility."

I didn't know what the word meant at the time, but I knew by my mother's tone that she thought I lacked something vital. I dropped to my knees and focused on scrubbing the stains so she wouldn't see my tears. I wished she had explained it without ridicule, without the sharp rebuke of my core nature. Knowing how sharp words gashed my feelings, I was cautious with mine and picked my words judiciously over the years, maybe even to a fault for fear of making someone feel embarrassed like I was in this situation with my mother. There was this old saying in elementary school about sticks and stones may break my bones, but words will never hurt me. Such a fallacy. Words were said that hurt me. Words have always stuck in my brain on a loop as I analyzed meanings behind them. Words dictated my behavior with Mom. I wanted her to see me as smart and not gullible, and so I tried harder to hide the naivety of youth by watching her actions and reactions to gauge a more adult response in situations.

Robert never said anything hurtful to me. He always seemed happy, a grin plastered easily on his face. It would be another year before I witnessed the cruelty Robert kept so well hidden behind that ingratiating smile. By this time, we'd moved to a small house in a section of Mill Hill in Mooresville within walking distance of What-A-Burger, my favorite cheeseburger joint, and the library. Mom took me on weekly trips to the library for her to check out stacks of books. Mom was a voracious reader, but I had yet to find my love of books. I was happy to lie on the couch or floor and watch *Tom and Jerry* or *Scooby-Doo* cartoons or dance along to *American Bandstand* with Dick Clark as opposed to reading a book. I did love What-A-Burger though. Besides doing something magical with their cheeseburgers, What-A-Burger also served my two favorite drinks: Cherry Lemon Sun Drop and a fountain drink called a Witch Doctor, simply a little bit of this and that from the fountain drinks on the menu and topped with a couple of dill pickle slices.

What-A-Burger sat a couple of blocks back from Mooresville's small downtown area comprising about a four-block area with Gibson's Furniture Store anchoring one end and the North Carolina License Plate Agency the other. In between those stores were a beauty shop, a couple of insurance agencies, a pawn shop, and a jewelry store. A movie theater sat on one of the blocks where I watched *Grease*, my first movie ever inside of a building. Mom and Robert had taken me to the drive-in with them a few times to watch action movies or the latest Cheech and Chong movie, but the experience of watching a movie full of singing and dancing where the lead character shared my name was magical.

About a mile from the downtown area was the Burlington Mill factory which employed many of the people in town, before Nascar teams or city dwellers from Charlotte drove up the prices of the real estate in the area. There were blocks upon blocks of neatly stacked, and some not so neat, mill houses surrounding the old Burlington Mills factory where so many, including my great-grandparents and mother, had worked. The mill was the primary employer in the area and as the older generation of mill workers retired and then died, these homes were either sold or gifted to the original owners' children and grandchildren. I'd had only happy memories of mill houses by the time Mom and Robert rented this particular one. The yard was small in width and long in depth like an elongated rectangle. Neighboring houses stood within ten feet on both sides, and a narrow road divided our house from the ones lining the other side of the street. Mill houses were cozy.

The house we moved into looked cute enough; bright yellow paint on the exterior extended a welcoming, cheerful glow. Within a day of settling into my room, I had turned the sloping backyard into my personal slip and slide haven. I spent hours throwing myself down the soap-slicked plastic sheeting at breakneck speeds and breathlessly running up the hill to do it again. Mom and Robert sat in folding aluminum chairs drinking iced tea, smoking cigarettes, and watching me fly down the hill without reservations. There are moments in life where everything seems perfect and right, like the moment should never end. On that afternoon the sun streamed through the branches of the oak trees baking the Palmolive-covered black plastic, and I basked in the cheers of my parents, feeling like I was a star. Look at me, I was Sandra D.

One afternoon when my mom had taken our car to the grocery store, Robert asked me if we had any pinto beans. At first, I was confused as to why he was asking me since Mom did all of the cooking. I told him I thought there were some in the cabinet. He instructed me to get a paper lunch bag and the beans. When I returned to the front porch with the requested items, he had rubbed the neighbors' tabby cat into a pile of fur at his feet.

"Pet the cat for a minute."

I reached over and stroked the cat's back as she purred and rubbed against my legs.

"Hold the cat still while I tie this on its tail."

"Why? What're you doing?"

"Just watch."

I will forever be sorry for my part in what happened next. Robert tied the bag holding the dried beans to the cat's tail and then slapped the bag causing the beans to rattle. The cat meowed loudly and ran across the road, simultaneously screeching and pawing at the bag on its tail before running out of sight.

Robert rolled all over the porch laughing while I ran in the direction of the cat.

"Get back here," he shouted between his sick laughter.

"I have to get that off. The cat is scared." I was scared. Scared for the part I played in some sick prank Robert found funny and I found horrific.

"It'll come off by itself. Now, wasn't that a funny sight?"

"No."

He shrugged and went back inside the house. I waited on the porch for Mom to get home, ashamed of my part in scaring the neighbors' cat. I vowed that day never to harm another animal on purpose. I now wonder why I ever trusted him again after those instances with the cat and Mr. Devil. I suppose it was because his smile was broad and warm, and he never seemed as serious as Mom. He'd established his status as the fun parent over the past two years. It was while living in this house that I found out he'd been in prison before he married Mom. On a day she kept me home from school to hang out with her, I used the alone time as an opportunity to tell her about the cat incident.

"I'm sure he didn't hurt the cat."

"But it meowed and ran."

"He likes to pull pranks. You know that."

I squinted and shot her a side eye. She laughed.

"Your face is going to end up like that if you don't stop."

I stopped the rebuke on my tongue, thinking better of breaking the confidential tone of the conversation.

"He went to jail when he was seventeen because he egged some cars at a car lot and took one of the cars for a joyride."

I nodded and processed the new information. The way she made it sound so innocent like it was a common error of youth to be brushed off like a stray hair didn't raise any warning signals in the moment. In hindsight, I wonder how much she looked past to have a companion by her side, to no longer be an unwed mother raising a daughter alone in the 1970s. I guess we both had a way of being swayed by a disarming smile.

In light of this new information about Robert, I also discovered the house had ghosts. Yes, you heard me right; I said ghosts. I could never arrive at a better explanation for all that happened in that house in all of my rationalization over the years. There are plenty of ghost hunter shows on television, and I think most of those shows are pure bullshit. There's a ton of money being made based on people's love and fear of the unknown, and the specialized cameras and audio devices claim to pick up the appearance and voices of the dead. The ghosts in our house hovered, knocked, and watched us sleep without the benefit of the fancy equipment.

My bedroom was at the front of the house with a window that looked onto the front porch. My mom and step-dad's bedroom was on the other side of the house facing the backyard. I awoke to the prickly touch of a woman's long fingernails sliding down my cheek. The screaming started when my eyes opened, and I saw a woman sitting on the edge of my bed, staring at me with saddened eyes. She had dark hair reaching her mid-back and wore a white nightgown. She ran long fingernails down my cheek once more before moving her hands to her lap and studying me. The scream turned into one continuous wail for Mom. I squeezed my eyes shut so I wouldn't have to see the ghost anymore; I screamed and screamed.

I know this was not the nightmare of a child because I had experienced night terrors until about the age of five. Mom would hear my screams, rush into my room, and throw her body across mine to stop me from hurting myself as I thrashed. I could never tell her what the terrors were about. They were gone as soon as I awoke. The visions in my nightmares disappeared when my eyes opened, leaving sweat-drenched locks and terror of ever closing my eyes again.

That's not what happened the night I met the woman in white. That night, her touch on my cheek awakened me. She didn't disappear when I opened my eyes. She touched me and then studied me. I could feel her weight on my mattress as though my mother was sitting there. She only disappeared when Mom's footfalls reached my doorway.

When Mom raced into my room to comfort me, I told her a witch had scratched the side of my face. She held me close while I sobbed uncontrollably. A witch was the only description I had to give based on the woman's long dark hair that fell to her waist and the long fingernails on weathered hands that had touched me and then returned to her lap as she studied me when I jolted awake. It was the only word my seven-year-old brain could conjure to describe the woman.

I believe this was my first fearful ghost experience, but it was far from my last. I asked for a nightlight in my room after this event. The glow of the streetlamp through my window was no longer adequate to illuminate the dark corners of my room. I developed the habit of switching on a light before entering a dark room. To this day, I despise the dark.

The incident with the witch woman changed me and opened new doors of perception in my mind. I wondered if ghosts were just hanging around waiting for me to acknowledge their existence after that night. Every unexplained noise had me peeking around corners, cautious yet mostly curious about a potential spirit. I wondered if the stories my great-grandma told me of miracles and demons fueled what Mom deemed an overactive imagination. My newfound fears also left me cautious, almost to the point of being paralyzed. I refused to go outside in the dark unless an adult was with me, and I hated being alone in a room after dark. My mom and step-dad first tried to make light of my fears of the dark as though joking would miraculously cure me. When joking failed to work, they scared me at every opportunity. I'm not sure if this was some amateur attempt at aversion therapy to work through my fears, but it only served to piss me off and scare me even more.

I would be in the bathtub, and they would scratch on the wall outside the bathroom and wail like a ghost from the *Scooby-Doo* cartoons I loved watching, except this wasn't nearly as entertaining as watching the gang uncover bad guys posing as ghosts. I shook and shivered in the tub—wet, cold, and clutching my knees to my chest, too afraid to move. I screamed for them to stop because even though I knew it was them, it didn't make my fear subside.

Eventually, things escalated. When I wasn't overcoming my fears the way they thought I should, Mom and Robert decided to abandon the wall scratching and calling on Mr. Devil for more traumatizing scare tactics. I'm unsure why they found such pleasure in scaring me. I have to imagine they were also recipients of such tough love in their own childhoods and forgot that it was traumatizing, not empowering. Whether they truly thought they were helping me or were only trying to entertain themselves, I'll never know.

One night, they tied my mom's white nightgown to some fishing line and pulled it across the dark living room as I walked into the room. I had a meltdown right there in my mom's arms. She saw my terror and thought maybe they'd crossed the line, perhaps I was permanently broken. But I wasn't broken. I was angry. A wave of deep burning rage swept through me toward my mother, the one who was supposed to love and protect me, for abusing my fear so carelessly.

This was the tipping point when my fear was eclipsed by resolve with which I vowed never to torment my future children. I learned to hide my fear with a mask of anger and indifference because if I refused to give my parents a reaction, they eventually stopped trying to scare me. Their torture was my first lesson in powerlessness. I could only endure and persevere.

Following the nightgown incident, they no longer tried to frighten me with their shenanigans, and the devil references and scratching noises ceased. Instead, I think whatever spirit was residing in the old house decided it was time for some payback. I was never visited by the lady with the long dark hair again. Still, my mother had nightly visits from a white cloud, as she referred to it, that would hover over her bed and wake her from a deep sleep. I never saw the spirit, but its presence unnerved Mom deeply. I'll admit some part of me took a small amount of pleasure in seeing Mom's discomfort as she rubbed tired eyes and drained the coffee pot the mornings after the visits.

The incident that caused us to move from that house within a day was when our furnace, which wasn't on because it was eighty-five degrees and smoldering hot in the middle of a North Carolina summer, started spewing flames. I was coloring in my room when I heard Mom shout from the living room.

I opened the bedroom door and yelled, "What's wrong?" I waited for a response.

"Dawn, I mean, Sandra, come here."

Mom still slipped into calling me Dawn when she was flustered even though I'd told everyone I wanted to be called by my first name. This change was a result of starting first grade with a new identity, leaving behind the dreadful nickname my family had dubbed me with, Dawny Boney.

I shuffled slowly to the hallway by Mom and Robert's bedroom. Mom was peering at the thermostat on the wall.

"Can you tell if the heater's on?"

I must've given her a sideways eye, because she said, "Just look."

I stepped on tiptoes and peered at the round thermostat. "It's off."

"Come outside and look." Mom grabbed my hand and led me out the front door and into the middle of our street. She pointed toward the chimney. "What do you see?

"Smoke coming out of the pipe."

"Yes! I knew I didn't imagine it."

Mom sat at the kitchen table until Robert got home from work, while I went back to coloring, not giving much thought to her odd questions.

When Robert got home from work that evening, they huddled in the kitchen talking. By the next weekend, we moved to another trailer park, this one a step up from the first one we'd lived in just after they were married. At my young age, I was already able to identify the caliber of trailer park by the lot size and the size and type of porch/steps attached to the front and back doors. Our new home had a full deck on the front and wooden steps with handrails at the back door, not the unattached and wobbly metal steps we'd had at our previous trailer home.

Gone were my parents' cruel shenanigans. It was as though our fresh start reset their parenting buttons. I have to remind myself they were in their mid-twenties at this time, and this was way before parenting manuals were a thing. I'm unsure if their adjustment had anything to do with Mom's ghostly retribution or the fact they realized they were adults picking on a child. Either way, the elaborate scare tactics ceased, and I didn't see my step-dad torture any more animals. We settled into a more traditional family dynamic: work, school, family dinners, card and board games, and fishing on the weekends. I embraced this normalcy like a child attached to the leg of their parent on the first day of kindergarten, until the summer I turned nine.

# Silver Threads and Golden Webs

The thing about my mom was that she never exercised, ever. She must've had an aversion to sweating. She didn't do any sort of yard work, but give her a badminton racket, and she turned into damned Chris Evert. Much like cards, she tried to annihilate me every time I picked up a racket and faced her across the net. It was a trait passed along from the women in my family—competitive badminton games are still our go-to summer sport. Early May of 1979, Mom and I had just ended a game of badminton before dinner. I felt exhilarated because I almost beat her with a respectable score of 21–14.

Sam, our two-year-old Siberian Husky who thought he was Mom's seventy-pound lapdog, watched us from the porch. Sam was the only dog we owned when I was a child. Mom was never a fan of "slobbery dogs," but she loved Sam. I think it must've been because they shared the same color eyes, so looking at him was like looking in a mirror. Sam's gaze reflected unconditional love. I don't know what my mother saw when she studied her reflection under the yellow light of the bare bulbs in her bathroom, but I doubt it was love.

We joined Sam on the porch steps that day to cool down with a glass of sweet tea, and it was at this moment that my mother sprang the news. She was always the one giving me "the news." Maybe she still didn't trust Robert with parental duties after nearly four years or perhaps she staked a claim to sole duties as my biological parent and bearer of all information regarding my future. Regardless, she asked me if I was okay leaving North Carolina for the summer. Robert had gotten a new construction job that required him to travel, and he wanted us to come with him. The idea of seeing other states intrigued me, but I had reservations.

"It's just for the summer?"

"Yes, his boss says we'll be back to North Carolina in time for you to start fourth grade."

"What about Sam? Can he go with us?" I put an arm around the dog and eyed my mom from under his chin.

"No. Sam has to stay. Traveling with a dog isn't possible." Mom assured me it would all be okay. "Sam will stay with your grandparents in Troutman until we return in a few months."

"They agreed?"

"We have to ask them."

I nodded. Grandpa Ralph and Grandma Bobbie were trying to be better grandparents than they were parents the few times we visited since Mom and Robert married, but a part of me never trusted them fully. Call it the whole disowning their daughter for being an unwed mother in the early seventies and not really welcoming me into their home until Mom married Robert thing.

"Can we go visit Grandma and Grandpa?"

"Yes, we'll go visit this weekend and ask them about watching Sam."

"No, not them. My other grandma and grandpa." The last time we'd visited my great-grandparents, I'd been sick with a high fever for days and only remembered falling asleep on their couch while coloring a picture and drinking a grape soda.

"Of course, we'll go see them before we leave."

We never did visit them at their house, and when I did see them again, it was too late.

I asked her about school. She assured me we'd be back in time to start fourth grade at the same school I'd attended since first grade. I loved South Elementary School. I had a large group of friends, the teachers loved me, and I was in an advanced reading class. A story I'd written in the fall about a bloody hand chasing an evil man around a barn had been placed on a board for everyone to read. Even Grandpa Ralph loved the story, and there wasn't much that brought a smile to his grouchy stubble-covered face.

I told her how much I loved my school and friends. What I wasn't saying was, "You've upended my life a few times before. I'm happy here. Please don't do it again."

She assured me once again that we'd be back. But assurances are the kissing cousin of excuses and hold even less merit. In the naivety of early childhood, I was still learning this tragic truth about the world. I loved and trusted my mother's word, so I agreed to our next big adventure, both of us pretending my opinion held some sort of weight.

One week before third grade ended, Mom and Robert signed me out after lunch like it was just another day. Little did I know, it was for good. As soon as my butt hit the back seat, we left for the first stop on our summer road trip, South Carolina. Robert's new job was working for a construction company that installed sprinkler systems at golf courses, and the first job was across the state line, only three hours from my great-grandparents. While we seemed so far away from home, I took comfort in the fact that we were a short drive from them. My great-grandparents were a consistent source of comfort for me then and now as I look back on pictures of them hugging me or letting me drink iced coffee as a four-year-old. If I think hard enough, I can still feel the warmth of Grandma Beulah's hugs smashing my face to her ample bosom and the sweet scent of pies and cakes baked into the cotton fibers of her housecoats. Some might consider home a place, but for me, my great-grandparents were my home.

In South Carolina, Robert and Mom rented a trailer in a small park next to a bustling laundromat, just down the road from a noisy railroad that screeched through the middle of town. There were maybe four other trailers, all with metal steps in the front and back. *Moving back down the trailer park hierarchy,* I thought as I carried my bag of clothes into the stifling dark-paneled interior.

During the day, Mom and I would hang out in the trailer, her watching morning television shows that turned into talk shows, and me with my nose in a Nancy Drew or Trixie Belden book. I didn't like reading much until that summer. People sometimes say those who hate reading just haven't found their genre, and that was certainly true for me. Boredom and isolation drove me to the pages of my books, where I discovered a love for mystery and adventure. I wanted to solve crimes and go spelunking in dark caves because my summer break was plagued by monotony unless I was reading.

Robert worked ten- to twelve-hour days and took the car to work, leaving us stranded at the trailer. Our options for any sort of adventure were limited. Staying home with me was a major transition for Mom as she had left behind her self-sufficiency she garnered from working as a seamstress after marrying Robert. Once, before Mom quit her job, I overheard Robert complaining that too many of her male co-workers gawked at her. I had to go into school the next day and ask the teacher what that word meant. Ms. Adams eyed me for a minute before asking, "Where'd you hear that word?"

"While watching TV," I smiled, turning on the charm.

"Well, let's see. It means to look at someone for too long."

"Thank you." I turned away from Ms. Adams and smirked all the way back to the reading circle. I'd watched Marilyn Monroe in *Gentlemen Prefer Blondes*. I now understood what gawking meant. Robert was jealous. I benefited from her staying home during those formative years, so I didn't complain. Mom baked cookies for me, kept me company, and helped me with my homework, sometimes more than I would've liked given her penchant for making me re-write any cursive she pronounced too sloppy.

The only problem with us being in that little trailer in South Carolina was we were both bored, and when we were bored, we turned antsy. We could only play so much rummy and blackjack before we both tired of looking across the table at one another. We'd already run through the stack of books we'd checked out from the local library, and Mom had perfected deep cleaning every inch of the trailer in less than two hours a day.

We spent our days hot and bored with ninety-degree cross-ventilation breezes provided by a fritz-prone window air conditioner in the back bedroom, a box fan in the kitchen window, and a rickety front door propped open with a jagged piece of cinder block. The heat and humidity were so intense that when I stood, I would have to peel the cotton underwear from my ass crack before moving. Sweat collected on the ends of the bangs Mom had given me for my third-grade spring pictures. Having shorter hair was easier, but the humidity made the thick hair of my bob cut expand to twice its size. I resembled a real-life picture of an animated figure after sticking their finger in a light socket.

One afternoon when we'd reached our limit of staring at the trailer's wood paneling and each other, Mom and I sat on the front steps trying to catch a breeze cooler than the one sputtering from the window unit when a stray kitten strolled into our lives. The kitten was a solid black fur ball, barely bigger than my fist. My mom ran inside to get the kitten a can of tuna from the never-ending supply she kept in the cupboard along with some powdered milk. We named him Smokey for apparent reasons. Smokey spent much of his day curled up on my shoulder, occasionally licking the back of my neck while I devoured the latest mystery novel. I found his licks disgusting and oddly comforting at the same time.

Life went on like this for a couple of weeks, the kitten providing a much needed distraction until I began to notice Mom's unhappiness. I guess the many years of studying her expressions and body language made me insightful. I have no clue how I became so observant and in tune with other people's emotions at such a young age. I suppose I was an emotional intelligence savant or it was a trauma response. I studied my mom a lot as a child, early on because I loved and adored her, and later as I tried to understand her actions. When she was really anxious, she smoked about three packs of cigarettes a day. She'd also clean every surface of the house until everything I touched left a lemon scent on my skin. If she was relaxed and unconcerned, she'd play cards, read a book, or pull a crossword puzzle book from a stack she kept on the end table.

In South Carolina, her long stares off into the distance, the tapping of her foot on the floor, and her polishing, removing polish, and re-polishing her nails multiple times a day clued me into her frustration at our new situation. As soon as Robert got home from work, she'd grab the keys and breeze out the door, saying she needed to grab a carton of milk even if we had a half gallon still in the refrigerator.

Mom had worked in factories as a seamstress before she married Robert. She had worked off and on as a nursing assistant over the years, but in South Carolina, she was fully entrenched in her role as a stay-at-home mom without the comfort of being able to visit her sisters or friends. I'm not altogether sure she liked playing the part since she loved talking to people and staying active. Mom could strike up a conversation with just about any stranger in a grocery line, and within minutes of meeting, they'd tell her their entire life story. Her conversational skills saved our asses down the road, but most of the time, I just wanted her to blend in like the other moms. What I wouldn't give now to hear her talk endlessly to a complete stranger, to have the time to appreciate all of her idiosyncrasies that used to drive me crazy. Grief and time make for a potent what-if stew with maybe more woulda, coulda, shoulda's thrown in for good measure.

I don't know that she ever had the luxury of finding herself before becoming a mother and wife. Though some people can be soul snatchers, and many might argue Robert was exactly that, Mom gave hers away freely, piece by piece, to every man she ever took as a partner. So, I grew up believing that love meant relinquishing identity and independence, doing whatever it took to keep a man happy and satisfied.

That summer in South Carolina, my books and Mom's music served as a backdrop to our long, drawn-out days. My mother loved Linda Ronstadt's music. In those few sweltering months, I listened to Linda Ronstadt belt out "Silver Threads and Golden Needles" to a bluegrass tune a hundred times a week as Mom and I sat on the steps of the trailer, the one place where we could watch the world around us. I wondered why she listened to such a sad song. She'd only been married to Robert for a few short years. I hoped her sadness didn't mean she was dumping him. I had grown accustomed to us as a family, and I feared being without a dad again.

Linda Ronstadt was an indication of mom's depression meter that summer. Music reflected the state of my mom's psyche like a giant roadside billboard displaying giant words against a cloudless sky. Robert must have noticed, because after an especially long week with Linda on repeat, he finally took us to the golf course one Saturday for a family outing. We raced around the greens in a rented golf cart, making revving engine noises and flying over hills, giggling as our stomachs dropped out. I remembered how Mom and I used to drive around country roads with the windows down singing about Pina Coladas, hair blowing wild and free in the breeze. It was always me and Mom. But on that day, I was glad we had Robert too. We felt more like a family again after the excursion, stopping for a rare cheeseburger meal out at a local curbside diner.

While Robert worked, my mom smoked her long menthol cigarettes, brows furrowed above the shades that hid her eyes, and I wondered when we would finally leave that flat, mosquito-infested state. At night, the trucks would spray for mosquitos. The glow of the street lamps illuminated the insecticide, and the poisonous fog wafted through the open windows, searing my nostrils. I longed to return to Mooresville, where the air smelled sweet like honeysuckles and wisteria during the summer. I missed seeing Sam and playing at my great-grandparents' house. I could feel my boredom and frustration growing each day we remained in the tin-walled hellscape. I turned nine in South Carolina and celebrated with a German chocolate cake, my favorite. The only thought that kept scrolling through my mind was *When will we go home to North Carolina?*

*When can I go back to school?* It was almost the Fourth of July. Time was moving simultaneously slowly and rocket fast.

Robert usually worked long hours at the golf course, but one night, he got off early and announced one of his co-workers was coming over for dinner. We had fried pork chops because that was my mom's second favorite food to fry in the depths of Crisco. She always instructed me to let the grease get hot, but not too hot. Mom told me to test the oil by dropping a pinch of flour into the oil. If it sizzled, the oil was ready. I nodded along like I was paying attention, not having the heart to tell her I hated the way the lingering oil settled on my skin and clothes or the way it coated the roof of my mouth, causing me to incessantly run my tongue over it to remove the slimy film. I kept my mouth shut or else I might have been disowned given the amount of Crisco that flowed through Southerners' veins.

This was the first time a man had come to our house without a wife or girlfriend. Even to my childish instincts, it seemed off. I helped my mom wash the dishes while Robert and the man talked about work.

After cleaning the kitchen, the three of them sat at the kitchen table while I grabbed my Nancy Drew book and flopped into my reading chair in the living room.

"Sandra?"

I looked up from the page to see her standing in front of me. I had been so absorbed in Nancy's rescue from the cold, dark basement, I didn't hear her approach.

"Yeah, Mom."

"We're going to the bedroom to smoke a special cigarette."

"Okaaay."

"Don't come back there. Okay?"

"Got it. I'll be right here reading my book."

Of course, my curiosity was piqued. They always smoked cigarettes in the house and around me. The entire situation felt odd, but again, what options did I have?

I was still unraveling the hidden staircase mystery when my mom raced into the living room. Her face was flushed and hair askew, eyes darting around the kitchen looking for some unknown object. She finally grabbed some ice cubes, placed them in a towel, and raced toward the bathroom.

I returned to reading my book because I didn't know what else to do. Mom used to tease me about how the world could be falling down around me, and I wouldn't notice because my head was stuffed too far into a book. I loved imagining myself as the heroine of my favorite adventure stories, diving headfirst into danger and saving the day. This was a relatively carefree time in my life, before I became aware of every anxious thought striking the inside of my head like fat raindrops mushrooming against a windshield in a thunderstorm. Thankfully, fiction had a way of preserving my sanity through those early years and allowed me to stay child-like for a little while longer. I was unconcerned by whatever was transpiring in the back bedroom.

The next day we sat on the steps and watched a woman lumber into the laundromat, clutching two overflowing clothes baskets against each hip. She snarled like an angry giant, screaming at her two young children who were steps behind her to open the laundromat door. I wondered why this woman would yell at her children that way. My mom hardly ever raised her voice toward me unless she was calling me for dinner. I could see her shaking her head out of the corner of my eye. She also disapproved of the mother's actions.

She turned to me and nonchalantly said, "Your dad experienced a reaction to something he smoked last night."

"So that's what happened."

"I was worried. Your dad's eyes rolled back in his head, and when he came to, he said he'd seen 'the light.'"

I knew all about the light, the devil, and people speaking in tongues from my early years attending church with my great-grand-parents. I grew up hearing stories about how God could enact miracles or smite people for sinning depending on his mood. I knew this meant Robert thought he saw Jesus, but I was smart enough to know he'd gotten sick from some tainted pot and had probably hallucinated so badly that he thought the bare-bulbed bathroom light was the other side.

Even though I was only nine, I knew about the things adults did for pleasure like smoking pot and drinking. My parents took me to the drive-in movies, where I watched Cheech and Chong light up bongs and blunts and talk about being wasted. I was a quick study in human nature and was fascinated by the pot-smoking and suggestive dancing I saw in movies. I was concerned for a while because my name was Sandra D. like the girl in the song from *Grease*, and asked my mom what it meant to be "blousing with virginity."

"It means not letting anyone touch your mootsie until you're an adult, Sandra." I blushed in embarrassment. It wouldn't be until the school-sponsored sex education classes in the seventh grade that I'd understand the proper names for female genitalia, but Mom was always quick to tell me to never let anyone touch me down there.

As we sat on the steps of the trailer and Mom promised me she'd never do anything like that again, I realized I was her confidant. I suppose I had always been her confidant, friend, and, later on, mother. We leaned on each other because when things went bad, we knew we could depend on the other. Looking back, I wonder if the reason for my existence was solely because Mom needed the unconditional love she'd never received.

The week after Robert's tainted pot trip, we packed our few belongings: clothes, a few books, Mom's electric skillet, and our cat Smokey and his litter box into the boxy, green four-door sedan and put South Carolina behind us. Our next stop was Gallup, New Mexico for another golf course job. I was excited to see what it was like out west. Mostly, I was thrilled to be out of South Carolina and hoping the next stop would be more interesting. We headed northwest, weaving through backroads until we reached our entry onto I-40 and joined the line of trucks and cars venturing west. Once the signs for Nashville appeared, Robert flipped the turn signal and took an offramp for a road leading to the downtown area. I leaned my head against the windowsill peering upward toward the tall buildings dotting the skyline. I'd never seen anything like this city in my life. I'd spent ten years in a small town, encased in the familiarity of one-story brick buildings and the railroad track that ran the length of the town. The brightest lights I experienced to this point were from the glow of the Harris Teeter sign illuminating the front of the grocery store at night, nothing close to the electric glow of the flashing lights on Broadway. Excitement forced me to question something I knew was non-negotiable.

"Can we stay longer?" My breath and my lip caught between my teeth. I couldn't pinpoint the excitement I felt other than the city felt like magic.

Mom looked toward Robert. He shook his head from side to side. "We need to reach this side of Memphis by tonight."

As we pulled onto the interstate once more, Robert called out, "Be sure to keep your eyes peeled for a Motel 6 or Red Roof Inn as we get closer to Memphis." I was being given a job I had no interest in performing. If we couldn't stay in Nashville, I wanted to stretch out across the back seat and read a book or simply study clouds, not look for a motel room.

The first day we pushed through Tennessee. By the next day, we stopped at a museum just across the Texas border that boasted real memorabilia from Billy the Kid. I had no idea who this person was, but I was impressed by the black-and-white pictures of a dark-haired, handsome man with a boyish grin and a dangerous twinkle in his eyes. I studied exhibits of guns, bullets, and pictures of the towns he'd frequented. I felt immersed in the late 1800s wild west, feeling like I had been transported inside the westerns I watched with Robert. The next stop was a mega truck stop where semis lined one side and cars like ours filled gas tanks for under one dollar a gallon. Robert pumped the gas while Mom and I went inside to use the bathroom.

Once finished, I walked the aisles of the store, fingering leather key chains adorned with colorful beads. Mom scooped up a blue T-shirt with "Texas" written across the left chest area with a set of cow horns emphasizing the name of the state. I pointed toward the rows of brightly colored cactus jelly.

"Can we get some?"

"What do you think it taste like?" Mom scrunched her nose as she studied the picture of a spiny cactus on the label.

"Don't know, but I'd like to try it."

Then Robert walked up and stood behind us. "What are we trying?"

"Cactus jelly, can you believe they make this from real cactus?" I pointed to the label.

Robert smiled, "I think they make just about anything." He ruffled my hair and smiled, "Why not?"

Robert had settled into his role of step-dad, and as each day went on, I relaxed, pushing the memories of him scaring me, terrorizing innocent animals, and isolating us from our family into the recesses of my mind. I never forgot the transgressions; I simply wanted our family to be more like the perfect families I saw on television and less like what I'd witnessed so far in my young life. I fantasized about a reality in which we were a normal family shopping at the truck stop, buying things we wanted, not needed, and talking about what we expected from Gallup, New Mexico. I didn't allow myself to think about the fact that normal families don't live out of boxes and bags and stay in motels. I'd nearly forgotten about starting fourth grade with my friends in North Carolina as I convinced myself of our normalcy.

After we made our purchases, I settled in the back seat once more. I spent most of the trip sprawled across the back seat, alternately reading, pumping my arms to get the passing truck drivers to blow their horns, and watching the clouds form animal shapes with which I had full, deep philosophical conversations. My mother always told me I had a good imagination; what she really meant was that I had an *overactive* imagination. The way she said the words, it almost seemed as though it was one of my flaws, but I saw it as a strength.

The trip across the country felt like an adventure straight out of the pages of one of my books, and I suppose that's initially what made the trip fun. Mom and Robert laughed and sang along with the radio the entire way there. I grinned at their silliness and gagged when they stole kisses in the front seat. Leaving New Mexico less than five months later would be a much different ride. My mother never referred to that return trip as an adventure.

# Wasted Days, Wasted Nights, and Boredom

It took about a week to reach Gallup, New Mexico, but once we did, we didn't live in a trailer; instead, we shared a room in the Motel 6. Our new home consisted of a room with two double beds, a miniature refrigerator, a television that was almost as large as the dresser it sat atop, and a small bathroom where Smokey's litter box resided in the space between the toilet and bathtub. Motel living was initially fun and different, but after the second week of trying to block out Mom and Robert's active sex life when they thought I'd fallen asleep, I would've given anything to be back in that hot, cramped trailer in South Carolina where I at least had my own room with walls and a door. When I started asking for a brother or sister, they told me they'd work on it during their Sunday afternoon nap time. I finally understood what they were doing in there every week.

An unexpected bonus of living at the Motel 6 was I didn't have to worry about Mom critiquing my cleaning skills. I no longer had to change my sheets or clean toilets, though I was still expected to make my bed every morning. A lovely woman stopped by every Monday to take care of those things. She didn't even tell management that we had a cat in our room. Knowing what I do now about these types of motels, I'm sure our cat was the least offensive secret she found while cleaning rooms. Mom chatted with her while she cleaned, making sure to call her by name and thanking her profusely for her help. Mom turned on her Southern charm when speaking to strangers, leaving out the sharp tone her voice took on when she was stressed; that tone she reserved for her family. Watching her, I learned about the masks adults wore in public when they were expected to be nice and accommodating. I found myself jealous of this cleaning woman, that she, a complete stranger, somehow received Mom's unconditional kindness, but I had to earn it.

I soon adjusted to the boredom of watching morning television, studying the local newscasters and then playing along with *Hollywood Squares*. Mom never watched soap operas, choosing instead to read from mid-morning to lunchtime. During these moments, I took the rubber ball we'd bought at one of the truck stops in Oklahoma and bounced it off the stairwell wall, the only place I'd found that was cool in the middle of the day. Once, a boy about my age with blond hair and glasses asked to join me. We took turns bouncing the ball, and I asked him what he was doing at the motel, curious to see if his situation was similar to mine. He told me his parents were in town for a rodeo and that they'd leave in a couple of days. When he asked when I was leaving, I could only shrug. Words were inadequate to describe my crippling fear that I might never escape the nightmarish monotony of living at the Motel 6.

When I returned from bouncing the ball and walking laps around the two-story motel, Mom coaxed me into playing Yahtzee until it approached time for Robert to return from work, watching her cook dinners out of her Swiss Army pot, also known as the Presto electric skillet. The skillet had deep walls and could accommodate a meal of Tuna or Hamburger Helper or buttered and fried toast with a side of fried eggs for breakfast on the weekends. She was a connoisseur of every flavor of Hamburger and Tuna Helper during those Motel 6 days, the starchy and cheesy flavors of each variety tasting eerily similar. Even after we no longer used motel rooms as our primary residence, she swore this kitchen appliance was indispensable.

In Gallup, my step-dad worked all day, just like he'd done in South Carolina. He left before seven o'clock and got back to the room around dinnertime covered in a fine layer of dust. He'd shower, eat, and then stretch out across the bed to watch television. I once found a picture Mom had taken on her old Polaroid camera of me and Robert wrestling like Rick Flair or Hulk Hogan. Robert would jokingly grab my forehead with "the claw" and I writhed and wriggled, acting like I was suffering under the fake pressure until we were both laughing at our antics, Mom shaking her head at our silliness. I'd sometimes catch her sad looks and possibly a flash of jealousy when we wrestled because she and I didn't have that type of roughhousing relationship.

The motel did have a pool, small and rectangular, flanked by a four-foot fence. When we walked past the pool to the KOA with our laundry, the smell of chlorine, sunscreen, and the scent of hot, dusty Gallup air assailed my senses.

"Mom, when can I go to the pool?"

"You don't have a swimsuit."

"I can wear shorts and a T-shirt," I offered, refusing to give up on my dream of diving under the cool water.

"No, you don't know how to swim."

That was a true statement. I'd never learned to swim. I couldn't stand water in my face, and I'd always struggled to swallow pills of any sort. I just knew if I could splash around in the water, my days would improve. I pushed instead of backing down like I usually did when Mom shut me down.

"I could just stay in the shallow end."

"Sandra Dawn, I said no, and I mean no! Do not ask me again, or you will never step foot near that pool."

For the first time that I could remember, I let the anger sit on my face instead of letting it go to appease her. My feelings mattered. When my mom went to the KOA section that housed the washers and dryers, I stayed in the store and surveyed their collection of stones and turquoise necklaces. I occasionally glanced out the window and watched the sunlight dance off the pool water. I rationalized I could talk her into letting me go swimming if I could find the right angle. I never got the opportunity to take a dip in the inviting Motel 6 pool, but I did have what was my first, but not last, brush-up with my mom. Fortunately, the thrill of standing up to her carried into my adolescence. It's easy to be an obedient child, but I learned I didn't necessarily appreciate easy.

Our life continued in this same holding pattern until around mid-August. It was then that my step-father unexpectedly parted ways with his employer, telling us he'd been shorted on his paycheck and that his employers had abruptly left town. I didn't know the real story but was vaguely aware of a pattern in Robert's employment history. He changed jobs a lot, and according to him, it was usually because of the stupidity or ineptitude of others. Once again, we were on the move.

We migrated the hour or so to Albuquerque and a squat, brick motel even more questionable than the one in Gallup. It housed about ten rooms and sat right by a busy four-lane road in the middle of town. Robert seemed to think he'd find a better job in a larger city. It was now late August, and we definitely weren't going to make it back to North Carolina in time for me to start fourth grade with my class. Instead, my mom bought a homeschool kit because she didn't want me to attend Albuquerque's public schools. I was a nerdy child, and I felt giddy when the school books arrived at the motel room door. I had a distraction, something to fill my days besides watching television, playing handball against the grubby brick motel wall, and wondering how many more times they would argue about when to return to North Carolina. My mother wanted to leave as soon as possible; Robert wanted to wait.

In North Carolina, we had the support of our extended families. In New Mexico, we knew no one, and Robert seemed to prefer it that way. At the time, I didn't understand why he wanted to keep us separated from our family. As an adult, I now know abusive relationships aren't always physical. Many are psychological in nature, making the abuse harder to detect, especially with all of the mask-wearing adults perpetrate. Even the vilest antagonist has redeeming qualities. Robert, in his need to control every aspect of Mom's life, vilified my great-grandparents, then moved us two thousand miles away. He assured my mom she needed to be a stay-at-home wife even though she enjoyed working and being around people. This ensured we had no extra money to get back, much less leave Robert should it come to that. We relied on him for everything.

Robert settled into his parenting style during our New Mexico adventure. Before this time, he kept a mostly hands-off approach with me. He would smile or ruffle my hair, but most of my daily interaction was with my mom. Mom took care of the discipline, which usually meant grounding me from reading my precious books when I hit her with a sassy tone or rolled my eyes. Robert became the fun parent of the duo. If I wanted to watch *Tom and Jerry* or *Bugs Bunny* until my brain bled, he'd let me. At the shitty motel in Albuquerque, he bought me a gold-plated Bugs Bunny pin from a door-to-door salesman, even though money was tight. He knew how much I loved that cartoon character. I'd like to think he loved me, although I don't ever remember him saying the words.

I wanted so badly for us to be a stable, tight-knit family that I ignored the warning signs. I clung to the idea of him being my dad for so long, I convinced myself he cared. It would be later in my life, after I was an adult, after he borrowed money and borrowed a car without ever returning it, that his propensity for smiling one minute and stealing indiscriminately the next really registered. I felt so gullible for believing he ever cared. What did that say about my ability to read people? There are always pieces of a person that can never be known, and if the person is really charismatic, the unknown is even more difficult to uncover.

September and October in Albuquerque were rough. Robert struggled to find work and we were homesick for anywhere with trees and green grass. By early November of 1979, we piled back into our car and started the trek east toward North Carolina. This time, the mood in the car wasn't one of excitement and adventure like six months prior. Mom and Robert had fewer snuggle sessions in the month before we left. Gone were the little treats I looked forward to, like eating out and ice-cold sodas from gas station refrigerators. Robert smiled less, frown lines deepening along the corners of his mouth. I had become pretty adept at reading moods and situations during my nine years, particularly since I'd spent many hours studying my parents' behavior in those tiny motel rooms. I heard them talking about how much money they had for gas to get them back to jobs and family safety nets in North Carolina. I kept quiet in the back seat as we left the snow-covered Sandia Mountains in the rearview mirror. Smokey curled up beside me on the seat as I scanned the gray sky for fluffy clouds or a hint of sunshine but to no avail.

While I was concerned about where we might live next or how it might affect our family, I was also happy to be returning to North Carolina. I hoped to see my great-grandparents, my cousins, or even Mom's parents. I wanted the security of my past, for all those memories that kept the homesickness at bay to become a reality once more. But our shared experiences on the road had changed us, had changed me, and there was no going back to the way things were. While I wanted to be the carefree child running around my great-grandparents' house playing hide-and-seek with cousins, I was different. I was older and even more aware of the cracks in Mom and Robert's relationship and in the realities of the world. I sometimes felt more responsible adult than child, sliding in and out of the role like a chameleon, adjusting to what Mom needed.

Our time on the road and in those motel rooms defined my role as comfort-giver and people-pleaser. I once thought I lost what remained of my childhood in my teens. In actuality, this is when I started to believe my worth was determined by how happy I could make everyone around me, especially my mom. As a response to my unstable upbringing, I turned this misguided sense of responsibility for the adults in my life into a superpower. I found it easier to focus on the one thing I could control versus all of the things I couldn't like retaining my childhood innocence and wonder.

# Heart of Glass

I watched New Mexico, Texas, and Oklahoma's flatlands flash by from my perch in the back seat. I'd run out of books to read, and instead, I fantasized about where we'd live next. I hoped for a house—not like the haunted one we'd lived in on Mill Hill, but a modestly sized one. And I definitely didn't want to ever live in another motel room. I'd had enough of those to last a lifetime. I wanted space. I wanted my own room again. I didn't want to hear my parents argue or do all of that heavy moaning that would wake me in the middle of the night. I wanted a bright room painted light blue, or really any shade of blue since it was my favorite color. I wanted a soft quilt on my bed, not like the ones on motel beds, the scratchy, polyester material that barely felt thicker than the tarps I used for my slip and slide. My house and room fantasies went on and on.

Robert had driven for hours without stopping on the trip back East, his face set in a grim line. I knew it was futile to ask how much longer because I'd heard Mom say it was about 1,600 miles to North

Carolina according to the Rand McNally map stretched across her lap. I couldn't comprehend miles, but I remembered how many days it had taken to get to New Mexico. I read the white signs that showed 55 MPH and groaned. Yes, highway speeds during the seventies were turtle speed slow. I wanted to be out of that car so I could stretch my legs and pee. I scanned the roadside for a rest area or Stuckey's truck stop sign. I tried to not focus on my full bladder, but trying not to focus on something has a way of doing the exact opposite. The green sign we just passed said the next rest stop was sixty-two miles. I knew I couldn't wait another hour. Smokey wouldn't have appreciated me using his litter box, but I eyed it and considered the benefits.

"Mom, I need to pee."

"Can't you hold it?"

"I've been holding it. I can't anymore."

She looked at Robert, and he shook his head.

My mom bent over, and I heard rustling. She handed me a large Styrofoam cup she snagged from the floorboard. I grabbed the cup and shot her a quizzical look.

"How am I supposed to use this in a moving car?"

"You squat down in the floorboard and hope your dad doesn't hit a bump."

"Why can't we stop along the side of the road? I'll go like we do when we're fishing."

"No." I suppose our mission to return to North Carolina in as few days as possible was more important than my basic needs. Or maybe it was the fact it was pitch black without the benefit of moonlight or street lamps along this desolate part of I-40.

It was either pee in the cup or on myself. Neither option appealed to my senses. I pushed my jeans off my hips and squatted down on the floorboard, steadying one arm on the back of Mom's seat and the other against the back seat. I perched over the cup opening and froze, stuck between the urge to release my bladder and my brain not relaying the message that it was okay. It wasn't as though I hadn't relieved myself outside of a conventional bathroom before, mostly behind trees during fishing trips to backwoods ponds. I'd perfected the rocking motion to get the last droplets of pee to shake free. The car bounced along the highway as I finally concentrated my attention on urinating into that disposable cup, filling it almost to the top. It was funny because I couldn't remember putting that much liquid into my body, but it was definitely coming out.

I juggled the cup of urine in the dark of night and asked, "What now?"

Mom directed me to roll down the window and pour it out. Again, stopping the car would've prevented the accident potential in this situation, and yet, this wasn't an option. Not even for a few seconds.

I held the cup in my left hand as I rolled the window down, willing Robert not to hit any bumps. Mom kept her eyes forward as she encouraged me to hold the cup upright until she gave me the word. Waiting felt like hours as I gripped tighter to the cup of urine, my arm perched like a seagull clutching its prized catch.

"Tilt the cup toward the rear of the car and let the wind do the work."

She made it sound easy, like the wind was some sort of pee fairy. I wondered how much experience she had in this type of situation. I don't think she realized my true inexperience in pee-dumping from a vehicle doing sixty miles an hour down Interstate 40 in Oklahoma. You see, she didn't specify which end of the cup to tilt. I was adept at following instructions even at nine years old. I tilted the bottom of the cup toward the rear of the car and not the opening. As one can imagine, the force of the wind caught the cup. I dropped the cup the instant my warm pee splashed onto my hand.

"Oh no!"

"What happened?" my mom asked.

"I dropped it. I'm so sorry." Tears spiked my lashes. I was quick to cry and sometimes wished I hadn't been born so tender-hearted, as Mom liked to say.

"Don't apologize to me. I'd be worried about the poor animals that come across that mess."

I would now like to think she was smiling when she said this. However, with Mom, there was really no telling.

"I said, I'm sorry." I cried louder as I held my pee hand in the air. "How can I clean my hand?"

"You'll have to wait until we reach the next rest area."

"How much longer?"

"About another hour."

*Forever, then.*

I stretched out across the back seat holding the offending hand off the edge of the seat. I studied Mom's profile and looked for a sign she wasn't mad at me. I never wanted to be the reason she was upset. By the time we reached the rest stop, my hand was dry of course, but I scrubbed it under the hot water before I went into the stall and relieved myself again. I made a mental note to limit my liquid intake from this point forward on a road trip. That night, we slept in a rest area parking lot, Robert holding the shotgun he'd bought in New Mexico across his lap. I felt my own fear spike as a result and had a hard time closing my eyes, choosing instead to watch the headlights of other travelers dance around the roof of the car as they pulled into the rest area.

The next night we slept in another rest area just outside Nashville. And by the third day of traveling, we arrived in Tennessee's mountains with an empty gas tank and no cash to fill up or eat. I only knew this because I heard my parents discussing our plight in what they thought were whispers in the front seat. Robert pulled into a grocery store parking lot, and my mother handed me a dollar in paper food stamp money. We'd needed groceries when we'd first arrived in Albuquerque and they'd been given an emergency supply. Mom had hoarded them even after Robert started working at a hardware store, which apparently didn't pay as well as the construction business because the books of paper money kept coming.

Mom instructed me to buy a ten-cent pack of gum with the one dollar of food stamp money and bring her the change.

She looked at me intently and said, "You remember the time I sent you in the store for Kotex pads, and you came out with a box of Q-tips?"

I nodded vigorously, angry that she'd brought up this moment from last year. I hated being wrong or making mistakes, and I hated being reminded of them when those memories were already filed away and easily accessed when I needed them. Mom had laughed when I'd returned with the box of Q-tips, actually doubled over and laughed that I'd gotten the wrong item. I vividly remembered my embarrassment when I had to return said Q-tips and asked to be directed to the sanitary pads. My anger at Mom for not going inside and buying them herself waged war with the embarrassment I felt for looking like a dumb kid. The grocery store lady graciously helped me find the right box of sanitary pads for my mother, who had an aversion to running her own errands. The clerk's warm smile made up for my mom's laughter.

I folded the fake green paper money in half and shoved it in my front pants pocket. I walked quickly through the parking lot and into the store, avoiding all eyes as I tried to appear nonchalant in my meandering. I did a quick drive-by of the lunch meat section looking longingly at the packages of bacon and sausage, my mouth watering at the thought of eating bacon, cheesy grits, and buttered toast with strawberry jam. I swallowed hard and made my way to the front of the store where they kept the rows of candy and gum next to the cash register. I studied the gum before choosing a pack of spearmint. The checker smiled as she told me it'd be ten cents. My hand shook as I handed her the crumpled piece of fake money. Her smile never wavered as she dropped the real money in my hands. I mumbled a "thank you" and bolted out the doors afraid a store employee would call the police for my actions.

"That wasn't so bad, huh?" Mom asked when I opened the car door and plopped onto the seat.

I dropped the change into her outstretched hand and crossed my arms over my chest choosing not to speak.

By the third store, the change I received from each exchange equated to roughly three gallons of gas, enough to fill our gas tank so we could continue this crime spree on down the highway to North Carolina. My face felt permanently scorched with shame and anger, and I worried it would remain that shade forever. I hated the looks I received from the other patrons when I pulled the paper money from my pocket, that cross between pity and outrage. I hated those looks as much as I hated being put in a position that felt dishonest. I wanted to shrink away until I was invisible to the naked eye. I assumed the grocery store clerks at these stores knew what I was doing, that someone would call the cops or pull me aside to question me, but all that happened was I was given the ninety cents in change and told to have a good day. We made our way through a handful of stores in the adjoining towns we hit along the way until we had enough change to fill up the gas tank. With the leftover change, Robert bought a Coke and a Snickers bar, smiling like some sort of hero when he presented them to Mom. I scowled as I assembled bologna and cheese sandwiches in the back seat, my purchase from the last grocery store we scammed.

I handed Mom a sandwich, and she pointed toward the stacks of spearmint gum packs on the seat beside me, "You have plenty of gum to chew after you eat."

I stared at the seat beside me. I didn't touch a piece of that gum, and to this day, I never chew green spearmint.

The shame I felt stuck with me for years, like I'd done something illegal, but mostly because I'd been used as a pawn. I realized being used to do the dirty work of others left a curdled milk taste in my mouth that I couldn't wash away. Some may say Mom and Robert were just thinking outside the box, creatively finding a solution to our money problems. I felt powerless and used, outraged that they dumped the burden on a child's shoulders instead of carrying it on their own. The dynamics of my relationship with Mom shifted after our little family scam. Robert was likely involved in the decision to use me, hoping to deflect whatever scrutiny they wanted to avoid, but at the time, I placed all the blame on Mom. The shame and guilt I felt made me doubt the depth of my mother's love in a way I never had before. I studied her reflection in the rearview mirror as I rubbed Smokey's ears and nibbled on the corners of my sandwich, my stomach still too knotted to have much of an appetite.

The tank of gas from our food stamp hustle allowed us to roll into a truck stop on the outskirts of Statesville, North Carolina. We were within twenty miles of my extended family. I wanted to see Sam, and I recall even missing my mom's parents in all their crankiness. Robert put the car in park among a set of tractor-trailer trucks. I read the names on the doors and didn't recognize any of them.

Robert opened the car door and shoved the shotgun under his jacket. I hoped he wouldn't consider robbing someone for money. Nothing I'd witnessed in his character would lead me to this conclusion, but I was witnessing a different side of my parents and felt anything was possible. He slammed the door and disappeared around the cab of a truck.

"What's he doing?"

"Getting some cash for gas and a place to stay."

"With the shotgun?"

"Don't worry. He's just selling it."

"Do I have to go into any grocery stores with the food stamps again?"

"No."

Mom had a hard time apologizing or admitting wrongdoing—ever.

In 1979, I knew she was sorry by how she said the word "no." There wasn't a barbed-wire sharpness to the word such as those times I asked for more books after finishing one in a few hours. There were the times she wouldn't let me watch television, the word sliding off her tongue like an echo. There was also her joking "no" when we had tickle wars and I went after her feet. It's funny how monosyllables can carry so much real or perceived meaning, or maybe, it was what I wanted to hear in that word. Her "no" that day at the truck stop was soft, almost imperceptible like a leaf floating on a fall breeze. I put a hand on her shoulder and without turning in her seat, she placed an always cold hand over mine.

She always told me cold hands equated to a warm heart. I never doubted Mom's love for me, I felt it in her hugs, her smile, her need for me to spend time with her like when she kept me home from school so I could hang out with her for a day of swinging at the park and trips to the library capped off with a visit to the What-A-Burger for cheeseburgers and cherry lemon Sun Drop. Yet over the last several months she seemed to be shrinking inside herself. She no longer asked me to play Yahtzee or cards with her after dinner. Instead, she withdrew into her romance novels, the covers either covered in shirtless muscled men or rakish cowboys. A part of me was concerned, but the other was happy anytime Robert took me to a local flea market or coin shop to hunt for foreign coins, the allure of discovering unique coins adding to the mystery and adventures playing in my head. Mom was likely unhappy or depressed at our situation after New Mexico, but I didn't have the language to understand that then. Neither did she.

That day at the truck stop, Robert sold the shotgun before Mom's hand had a chance to warm over mine. He filled up the gas tank, bought a newspaper, and rented a room in a six-unit motel next to a dairy farm. While he circled jobs in the classifieds, I sat beside him at the table and studied the field of black and white cows outside our window. The stench of cow pies made me question my love of fudge ripple ice cream and milk. Spending three months next to one should've been enough to turn me off dairy for a lifetime, but I never tired of fresh milk with the cream still on top that we bought from the dairy farm.

I finished fourth grade and started fifth grade at a school in Statesville, but partially through the school year, we moved once more. I wondered at the time if I would ever start and finish a school year with the same students. I thought I had found my place at Mount Mourne Elementary. I'd been elected to the student council by my peers. There was a duo of Hannahs that'd proclaimed to be my best friends, and we would spend recess swinging and trying to figure out which boys had crushes on us. I thought it was frivolous, but I enjoyed the camaraderie more than the topic of boys.

By ten years of age, I'd learned to expect instability and adapt to change or be left behind. We moved to an apartment complex in Charlotte in the fall of 1980, and I started a new school once more. I can't remember the name of the school. Amnesia from too much change is something I experienced throughout my early years when it came to changing schools, like a sort of self-preservation tactic. I now know the official psychological term for this phenomenon is selective memory. The brain's ability to remember pleasant events more readily while suppressing unpleasant or traumatic ones. For many years, I felt I lacked real connections. After all, I couldn't remember the names of close childhood friends or favorite teachers because I had very few memorable memories. Some people can rattle off names and gush about the person's impact on their lives. Instead, I recall the unforgettable places I've lived. I imagine when a child has a stable home life and lives in the same house for years, they can focus on relationships. In my formative years, I moved so much, I just wanted to find a stable place to call home. The apartment in

Charlotte lasted until the end of my fifth grade year, though much of what I learned and the people I met were a blur.

Robert was working at a local hardware store. By the summer of 1981, we moved to Monroe, a suburb of Charlotte, and my life finally felt calm and normal. The new neighborhood consisted of one-level ranch style homes that'd been built next to cornfields as far as I could see, and the neighborhood kids played in their yards or rode bikes along the streets, dawn to dusk. Because it was such a dramatic shift from my earlier years, it stands out in my memory as a time of peace and stability, what I saw as normal through my lens of television families. I had a two-parent household and my own room, although my mattress was supported by the heavily worn and scratched oak floors and not a bedframe for months. Life seemed perfect. I allowed myself to release the fear I'd been harboring that we'd have to move back into a dingy trailer or questionable motel. As each day passed in our new neighborhood, our new suburban life, I unfurled the fear until it was so far from my mind that I was able to ignore the rustling of unrest in the air in the coming years, attributing it to my imagination instead of the reality of living in the calm eye of a category five hurricane.

# Feels So Right

I sat on the edge of my neighbor's bed and took in the multiple posters of the country group Alabama plastered all over the walls. I half-heartedly listened to the siblings' conversation, a boy and girl who'd knocked on our door just after breakfast and asked if I wanted to play. This offering of childhood friendship was new to me. I mean sure, I'd made friends at school, but my sole companions had been my mom and step-dad for the past two years. I'd met kids at the motels we'd lived in. I'd talked to classmates at three different schools I'd attended since we returned from our trip out west, but never had anyone outside of my family requested I come play with them. I was awkward in my pre-teen body. I'd let my thick brown hair reach my shoulders, but my thin frame felt child-like next to that of an already developing girl sitting in front of me on her brother's bed.

I wasn't sure how to proceed in the conversation. I hadn't listened to much of Alabama's music, and that seemed to be the topic they most loved. I was more of a rock and pop music fan because country music seemed too hokey and slow for my musical tastes. Give me Blondie or Quarterflash instead. I nodded along, doing the whole fake-it-till-you-make-it routine. I hoped they would overlook my Alabama ignorance because I suddenly wanted them to invite me back, not because they were interesting conversationalists, but because I felt like a normal child in their presence.

Looking back, I marvel at my awkwardness in trying to fit in with kids my age. I suppose my ability to converse with adults left me with little knowledge of how to communicate with kids my age. I struggled to connect with my peers for the remainder of my childhood.

Back at my house after hanging out with my new friends, I walked into our den. The little brick ranch felt like what I imagined the perfect television families' homes were like. The den was off the kitchen down a couple of brick-lined steps. One wood-paneled wall was lined with built-in bookshelves, and Mom had already started filling them with used books she purchased from yard sales and the Book Nook, a discount bookstore she found. Cookbooks and paperback mysteries and romances shared the shelves. A small television set sat perched on a wooden shelf in the corner, and most nights we spent time after dinner watching the news, game shows, and then shows like *MacGyver* and *The Rockford Files*. That afternoon when I returned, Mom was snuggled in Robert's lap in the recliner. My heart warmed.

"How were your new friends?"

"Good, I guess. They love Alabama. It was all they talked about."

"Why are you turning up your lip?" Robert asked.

"I just don't like country music."

Mom got up, went over to the tape deck on the shelf, and pressed play.

The music started playing. My mom extended an arm, and Robert took her hand and stood. He pulled her close and started swaying to "Feels So Right." I watched them dance and laugh from my perch in the doorway until I couldn't take the lovefest anymore.

"Sandra, come back and dance with us."

"No, thanks."

I retreated to my room smiling and turned on the radio I'd been given last Christmas. It was tuned to my favorite pop station out of Charlotte. I stretched out on my bed and sang along to "Bette Davis Eyes" to keep the country drivel at bay. It would take a few more years before I experienced heartbreak and the real healing powers of country music. The melodies and lyrics that connect deeply with loss and pain would escape me until I experienced those feelings firsthand.

During my sixth-grade year, I learned the meaning of being a neighborhood kid. We moved in packs of three or four, roller-skating down uneven sidewalks together, and took turns watching movies at each other's houses. Mom was in her element when we congregated at my house. I didn't realize until this time how much she loved cooking and hosting. It may have been all of the compliments she received from the neighborhood kids, her face lighting up with the praise. She shoved plates of chocolate chip cookies in front of us as we sprawled in front of the television in the den and then she sent me with plates of peanut butter cookies the next day when I went to another friend's house.

Making friends in the neighborhood also helped me make friends at school. My shyness and uncertainty around kids my own age was slipping away as I was accepted like no other place I'd lived. Friendship and socialization sparked my transformation, and the awkwardness I felt being the new kid disappeared. My love of Sun Valley Middle School would be an understatement of grand proportions. I'd found my place. The teachers were supportive and kind, and I no longer wanted to play hooky with Mom to play cards all day. I wanted to go to classes, see my friends and learn.

It was also at this school that I discovered my love of writing when I won a science essay contest. In seventh grade, I was asked if I wanted to join the school newspaper. The past two years of travel and upheaval were fodder for my writing, and I took to carrying a journal with me everywhere. Toward the end of my sixth-grade year, we moved out of the neighborhood. I was devastated to leave the neighborhood crew behind, but I still saw them at school waving and smiling in the hall. We rented a brick ranch house in the Sun Valley district, where Robert could more easily commute to his job as manager of a hardware store in Charlotte.

I didn't mind moving to another house because it wasn't a musty motel room or a rundown trailer. Our new home didn't have as many neighborhood kids, and we were flanked by retirees on one side and a dilapidated, revolving door house of occupants on the other. Mom and Robert had plans to grow our family after years of my begging for a sibling and years of trying on their part. The house was another brick ranch with a huge yard filled with oak and pine trees. I settled into my room and became comfortable in our new home. We were a family like I'd always envisioned. Mom greeted me when I came home from school, the bus dropping me off in front of my driveway every day. The only missing part of my perfect family fantasy was the fact that Mom did not drive me to and from school. I longed for her to do so, but I abandoned that dream since she no longer drove anywhere, allowing Robert to do all of the driving.

Mom gave birth to my baby brother in April of 1983. He was a whopping eight pounds, a fact Mom regularly lamented as she sat on sitz baths for weeks after his birth. I really had no idea what she meant when she mentioned tearing with his delivery. I was afraid to ask for fear of getting more information than I wanted. We soon discovered my brother was a lactose intolerant baby with a penchant for bouts of puking, screaming, and explosive diarrhea. This point in history did little for advancing formula choices for new mothers. Only Similac and Enfamil lined the shelves compared to the numerous hypoallergenic options now available to desperate mothers. I'm uncertain why Mom wanted to use cloth diapers, but it was as though my brother's bottom only deserved the best. I couldn't help but wonder if she was trying to do a better job with him than she did with me when she was nineteen.

Since Mom was determined to give Jacob only the best, she was continually washing diapers and doing laundry in general. She refused to put him in Pampers, even though Robert told her it would be easier given the baby's explosive bowel habits. I didn't know what she was thinking with this continued choice, but she soon got tired of rinsing poopy diapers. I swooped in with an offer to charge twenty-five cents for every three diapers I rinsed out. That's the unadvertised bit concerning cloth diapers versus disposable. I made quite a piggy bank full of coins from this endeavor. I used the poop money to pay for trips to the movies with my friend John, who lived a few houses down from us. If books and music were my top entertainment choices, then movies were a close third. John and I had seen *The Lady in Red*, *Arthur*, *Cujo*, *Leigh*, and my least favorite, *Halloween*. I refused to go to another horror movie after *Halloween*. I watched a brain crack like a runny egg on the big screen and subsequently refused to eat once-loved over-easy eggs for years.

One Saturday when Jacob couldn't have been more than several months old, Robert knocked on my bedroom door, opened it, and asked, "Do you want to go to the mall?"

I envisioned going to Waldenbooks and getting a new Nancy Drew book or a new notebook to write stories. I'd taken to writing a story for the school newspaper involving ghosts. Ever since my run-in with one at our house on Mill Hill, I'd developed a keen interest in trying to understand anything paranormal. The topic had become the one thing I could talk about with Mom; she'd become withdrawn since Jacob's birth. She was always up for talking about ghosts or letting me read her palms after I picked up a palm reading book at the flea market and decided I could predict her future. I now wonder if she actually thought I had that kind of power or maybe she was simply hoping I did.

"Can we go to the book store?"

"Maybe, you'll have to ask your mom."

I weighed the idea of just asking to stay home. I was thirteen now and I felt I could watch myself without burning down the house.

"Can I stay here?"

Robert shook his head no and laughed. "You know your mom won't let that happen. You're still her baby."

I rolled my eyes and then my body off the bed. Once we arrived at the mall, Robert carried Jacob in his carrier in the direction of some benches and Mom linked arms with me and we walked toward the JCPenney.

"What are we looking for?"

"I need some new jeans."

I shot a look at the ones mom was wearing looking for the tell-tale signs of wear like holes or the even worse problem of having high water legs on pants. I thought she still looked great for just having a baby not so long ago. I thought she looked gorgeous all the time, but she rarely went too long past her second cup of coffee in the morning without makeup and never left the house without wearing some.

"Why?" I guess the word must've escaped my mouth sharper than intended because she stopped and shot me a scathing look she usually reserved for Robert when he got home late from work and missed dinner.

She turned away from me and searched the table of Levi's for the right pair. "I've gained weight since having Jacob, and I only have one pair I can fit now. Watch what you wish for."

The warning sounded like she had some regrets. I found that hard to believe based on the way she snuggled Jacob's neck or affection-ately blew raspberries on his stomach as she lifted him from the crib. I'd once asked her about my real dad when I was around seven. She told me he was smart and handsome and he asked her to marry him when she found out she was pregnant. Mom said she was in nursing school when she found out she was expecting, and she had to leave the program. She must've seen the concern brought on by the unspoken question.

"I never regretted having you, Sandra Dawn. You're the best gift ever in my entire life."

I never doubted the truth in her words that day years before, but the day we were looking for jeans, I was stunned by the sadness of her tone. Mom went on to purchase two new pairs of size eleven jeans from the juniors section and we returned to the parking deck, our family of four.

We'd just reached the car when Robert said, "Jacob had another blowout."

"You didn't change him?"

"Nope."

"He's been sitting in this for how long?"

"Don't know."

Mom peeked in the carrier at Jacob's diaper and groaned. She then exhaled loudly and said, "I need to change him before he develops a bad rash or gets a worse rash since you let him sit in it."

"Me? What have you done to make him do this?"

Tears filled Mom's eyes before she blinked them away. His words hurt her and I looked away from her pain afraid I'd start crying. The entire silent car ride home I pressed my face to the cracked window to avoid the stench of the dirty diaper wrapped in a plastic bag and to inhale fresh air from a car interior drenched in oxygen-depleting tension.

\*\*\*

In the early fall of 1983, the owners of the hardware store where Robert worked invited us to join them for the weekend at their house in Myrtle Beach. I figured these people were rich because they had a vacation home at the beach. We'd only recently been fortunate enough to be renting a house, and they had two. We packed into our car, and for the first time ever, we went away for a weekend vacation. I could hardly find the words to describe my elation over going somewhere just for fun, just to see something new. Though a short one, this was a real live vacation, not a move to another suck-filled location.

We left on a Friday after Robert got off work. The mood in the car was anticipatory and upbeat with the exception of my brother. He was always attached to Mom's hip. I had the unfortunate luck of sharing the back seat with him. Jacob kicked his feet against the car seat and screamed for the first fifteen minutes of the drive as I plugged my fingers into my ears and hummed along to "Gloria" by Laura Branigan playing in my head. I noticed my mom smiling at Robert in the front seat, something she hadn't done in a long time. My brother's birth had created a new dynamic in our family. Mom and Robert were used to a self-sufficient thirteen-year-old. Then my brother arrived, a ball of colic, and they were catapulted back into newborn land. Lack of sleep and a demanding newborn changed our evenings. We no longer watched television together. Instead,

Robert or I gave Jacob a bath and Mom went to bed early most nights.

When Jacob was born, Mom suddenly had no free time and was faced with that kind of extreme tiredness new mothers face. She transitioned from always having her makeup on to pulling her hair back with a headband and letting the blackish-purple undereye bags announce her sleepless nights. We all know that look on a new mother's face. I wonder now if it was the first stage of a breakdown in their relationship. After my brother was born, Robert would take me to the coin shop to search for the foreign coins that I loved to collect. Other times, we'd go to the flea market on Saturday mornings and leave Mom and Jacob at home. I felt guilty for leaving her at home, afraid she'd think I was betraying our relationship in some way.

I felt a push and pull between them around this time, like I was their moderator or the one they wanted as their little buddy. The only problem was that after months of this, I had grown tired of the struggle and wanted to be my own person. I wanted to hang out with my friends, not be the glue that held them together.

That night as we got closer to Myrtle Beach, I inhaled the salt air, and the scent called to me like a siren. I stuck my head out the window and took three or four deep breaths until it flooded my senses and filled my soul. "Tainted Love" played on the radio, and the night sucked the words from my mouth as I closed my eyes and embraced the wind. We pulled up to a seafood restaurant for dinner, it being long past our regular 6 p.m. mealtime. In a sure sign of more financial stability, we'd been eating out more recently. This was a welcome change from our regular rotation of Tuna and Hamburger Helper when money was tight.

Robert ruffled my already messy hair as the hostess led us to the table. I took in all of the colorful mermaids, boats, and fish painted on the walls, the thick ropes and buoys hanging from the large nets draped in the corners of the room. I scanned the menu and asked Mom what it meant by popcorn shrimp. I loved popcorn, but I wasn't sure about the shrimp.

My mom shook her head, perplexed, and looked to Robert to answer.

"They're like baby shrimp. They're kind of sweet and taste good."

I nodded as I ran my finger down the laminated menu and saw fried fish, shrimp, or clam strips. There was an occasional blackened item, but it could've been a fried menu from my mom's kitchen.

I didn't want fish. I decided this would be my first time trying baby shrimp. I was feeling bold and adventurous. I wanted to do things I'd never done before. I'd already envisioned my profound journal entries about the trip when we returned home. We didn't know Myrtle Beach was a filthy tourist trap sometimes referred to as "Dirty Myrtle," a place that the locals avoided like the plague. It was the crusty mall Santa of the Carolina beaches, and we couldn't wait for our turn. Even if we had known, we wouldn't have cared. This was our first beach vacation, and it was going to be epic.

Mom always ordered the fried flounder if it was on the menu at a restaurant. If flounder wasn't available, she went to perch, the back-up fish, but she never in her lifetime tried any other seafood. She scrunched her nose at foods that deviated from the mainstream chicken, pork chops, meatloaf, or fried cube steak. By the time I left home, I craved any food beyond traditional southern mama fare. Strangely enough, I didn't have Mexican food until I was eighteen.

During our second day at Myrtle Beach, we went for a walk on the boardwalk. Mom and Robert took turns carrying Jacob since he refused to stay in his stroller without screaming loudly enough to be heard over the crashing waves and conversations of passersby. At the same time, I devoured the sound of waves hitting the shore, the taste of the salt air on my tongue, and the gleeful sounds of laughter and electronic joy spilling from the arcade next to the fishing pier. I rode the Scrambler and the Tilt-A-Whirl multiple times. I begged to return that night to see the fireworks show I'd heard announced over the loudspeaker while throwing Skee-Ball. My mom looked to Robert again, and he nodded confirmation.

We went back to Robert's boss's house, and the adults napped while I played with Jacob. I was too amped to do anything other than dream about what an actual firework show would be like. I was positive it would be way cooler than the smoke bombs and sparklers we got every year around the Fourth of July. My body tingled in excitement the entire way back to the boardwalk that night. I kept shooting glances at my parents to see if they were as excited as me since we were rarely out as a family after dark. The crush of the crowd added to my anticipation, the collective buzz of conversations pulsing like a speaker turned to max volume.

We found a spot along the pier railing, and I pressed against the weathered wood, listening to the rock music blaring from the nearby arcade. I stared skyward at the stars, waiting. I jumped with the first pop and crack of fireworks that lit the entire night sky; vivid reds, greens, and blues against the backdrop of crashing waves. I pressed my body against the wooden railing like I could get closer. Jacob squealed with every pop, fireworks crackled, and I exchanged grins with my parents. Robert wrapped his arms around our shoulders and pulled us in for a hug, and I stretched my arms around their waists like my grip could hold us in this moment in time for an eternity.

# Changes

My life imploded on a typical night, a night that changed my trajectory and stole what innocence remained. I sat with my back propped against the spit-up stained blue velour couch, legs outstretched to accommodate Jacob building a tunnel of blocks over my right shin. Mom answered the phone with a catch in her "hello" that reminded me of the Lionel Ritchie song playing incessantly on the radio. I studied Mom from my vantage point on the living room floor as she paced the dining room. She leaned against the yellow Formica countertop and wrapped and unwrapped the nicotine-stained phone cord along the length of her index finger as she puffed her cigarette to a nub. Mom had an uncanny ability to do just about any task while smoking a cigarette, and the speed with which she smoked one matched her mood.

"When will you be home then?"

Emphasis on "when," the word drawn out like a tightrope walker's net laced with knives.

Mom's mouth turned downward, and her eyes narrowed. She turned away, but unmistakably her mood charged the room's atmosphere like a humid summer night, and imagined or not, I struggled to catch my breath. I expected lightning strikes and thunder to shake the house to its foundation any second. She alternately popped a hip on a wooden bar stool for a second before she jolted to her feet, leaned against the counter, and stretched the full six feet of the coiled phone cord to its max. I was certain the line would snap any second.

The day had started normally enough. Normal meant Robert drove to his job as manager of a hardware store five days a week and every other Saturday. He was home from work in time for us to sit around the dining room table and discuss our days. Normal meant Mom stayed home and cared for my brother. My normal meant, for the first time in my young life, I attended the same school for three consecutive years, staying long enough to build real friendships. I was dreaming of graduating eighth grade and starting high school with my friends in the fall.

"You don't know?"

Mom turned to look out the dining room window. I wondered what she saw in the low light of dusk. Her shoulders sagged and hunched forward as she said, "I love you." She dropped the phone in the cradle and continued to stare outside.

Nothing good ever came from an unexpected phone call. I learned this the hard way. My body tensed as I remembered the deep grief that accompanied the last unexpected phone call. A few years prior, I was unexpectedly called to the school office. I assumed I was in trouble. It didn't matter that I was new to the school and I wasn't sure any of my teachers even knew my name. My Aunt Rosie's voice relayed that my beloved great-grandmother Beulah was dying of intestinal cancer. No precursor, no niceties, simply, "Come see your grandma before she dies." At the time, I couldn't tell if I was more shocked that my aunt tracked me down after we'd bounced around more motel rooms and trailer parks than I could remember. Or that I was facing the loss of a woman I may have loved even more than my mom, a woman who was a combination of mother and grandmother for my first seven years of life. I got off the bus that afternoon and told Mom the news. In a rare moment of bravado, I demanded I be taken to the hospital in Mooresville so I could visit my grandmother.

The next day, we dropped my step-dad at work and drove over an hour to see her. The irony of the situation was dumbfounding; in the same hospital where I'd been born, my grandma Beulah's life was vanishing. Standing in the doorway of her room, I didn't recognize her cancer-ravaged frame. I stumble-walked into her room and buried my head in her chest. Her scent was no longer fresh-baked bread, honeysuckle perfume, and persimmon pies as I'd so loved. Despite gagging from the bitter smells of bleach and the powder found at the bottom of a bottle of Tylenol, I burrowed deeper into her bosom. I wept for the time I missed with her. I crammed the bitter resentment toward my mom and step-dad for keeping me away from her for the past three years into a shard of my shattering heart. I wanted to stay cuddled in her weakened but warm embrace until she died. Tears of disbelief, love, and grief escaped closed eyes and stained her light-green hospital gown.

After what seemed like seconds but was in reality closer to thirty minutes according to the wall clock, Mom and Aunt Rosie laid their cold hands on my shoulders and lifted me from her chest. I didn't want to leave her side, although my aunt said she needed her rest. I stood propped against the door frame, wiping my face with my T-shirt as Mom hugged her one last time. I sobbed harder weeks later when Mom told me Grandma Beulah died and handed me the obituary she'd clipped from the local newspaper.

I could feel the familiar heaviness of death hanging in the stale grease and smoke-filled air of our small brick ranch that day. Mingled with the smells of our fried chicken dinner and Mom's chain-smoking, I sensed a shift happening that would rock our worlds. It seemed my step-dad wouldn't be home. My stomach fluttered, and a coldness radiated from my core with the certainty that my step-dad was one of those men who went out for cigarettes and never returned to their families. I didn't think he was capable of such vile abandonment until that moment, but this wasn't my first life lesson in the unpredictability of humans.

Robert had been in my life since I was five; I incorrectly assumed he loved us too much to do something that unfathomable. My mind raced with possibilities for his absence. I wondered if he wouldn't be coming home because of the new baby, or maybe being a dad to a teenager was too much for him to handle. And then I remembered something from a few weeks ago that didn't seem important at the time but came back into sharp focus in my mind now. I wondered if the phone call was related to the visit from the lady in the sharply creased pants.

That afternoon, I'd gotten off the bus like every other day. Except on this day, there'd been an unfamiliar car in the driveway with a circular emblem on the door declaring it belonged to the Union County Health Department. I prided myself on being a top-notch detective given my love of mystery novels and an uncanny ability to read people's moods. Channeling my inner Nancy Drew, I slipped into the house as quietly as possible. I pretended to get an after-school snack and ignored the woman in the navy-blue pants and white collared shirt sitting on our couch with the official-looking clipboard. I opened and closed a few cabinet doors for good measure and crept closer to the living room. With my head against the wall, I could hardly make out the indecipherable voices.

Shifting closer to the living room entryway, I could just make out my mother making excuses for Robert. The woman's responses dripped with pity, alternating between "I see" and "Mmhmmm."

"He told me the spot on his penis was due to an unfortunate zipper accident," Mom told the woman, recognizing her naivety even as she spoke it out loud. I took a deep breath and peeked around the corner for a better view. The woman shook her head, made a note with her pen, and informed my mother otherwise. I didn't recognize the word she used, but the sympathy on the woman's face was unmistakable as she held eye contact. Mom's tone changed from confused disbelief to controlled rage with each clipped syllable she uttered. I couldn't tell if her anger was directed at Robert or at this woman for having the audacity to take that tone with her. How dare the woman pity her? Southern women rejected pity about as much as they rejected a gallon of sweet tea made with less than a cup and a half of sugar.

"The Health Department requires we notify all sexual partners and suggest you go for testing."

Mom sat board-like in her rocker recliner, her slipper-covered feet scuffing the oak floor as she rocked, gripping the arms of the brown chair that were stained with baby formula. She lifted her hand and ran it through phantom tresses, her thick auburn locks having been lopped off a few weeks ago in a makeover attempt. Mom's face transformed into a serene mask, her narrowed sky-blue eyes the only indicator of internal hurt and rage. Mom agreed to come in for some testing the following week as she ushered the woman to the front door. I slipped back to the kitchen and gave the peanut butter cookie and glass of milk my full attention as Mom entered the room. I wanted to ask her if she was okay, but she averted her gaze and grabbed the package of hamburger from the refrigerator.

Mom made small talk and asked about my day as she prepared a meatloaf for dinner. She kneaded and mixed the meat in a bowl, absently adding chopped onions and green peppers as her eyes took on a blank, faraway look. We later sat at the table and ate dry, overly peppered meatloaf and salty mashed potatoes as we took turns telling each other about our day. Dad talked about the store customers and the clueless kind of people with no business being in a hardware store because they couldn't tell the difference between pliers and vise grips. Mom relayed Jacob's baby achievements, and I told them about picking classes for high school.

We appeared a normal-looking family on the outside, structured and playing our roles perfectly. Yet I wondered when Mom would ask him about the Health Department visit. I imagined her anger was past the point of control, and I couldn't reconcile this calm Mom version with the Mom who once threw cups and plates at the wall when she was angry. She didn't raise her voice with Robert like she'd done with John all those years ago. I kept waiting for the knockdown, drag out fight that was surely inevitable, but it never came. The only indication they were fighting was when Mom went to bed early for the next week, leaving us to watch television in uncomfortable silence. I couldn't think of anything to say to Robert that wouldn't show I had eavesdropped and had knowledge of marital issues I had no business knowing.

The night of the infamous call, my imagination kicked into hyperdrive and I considered all the possibilities of why he wasn't coming home other than the one nagging me in the back of my mind—there was another woman. He loved Mom too much to cheat on her. Surely the car had broken down. There was a wreck, which closed down the roads blocking his paths home. A UFO had stopped him—like Richard Dreyfuss in *Close Encounters,* and he spent the last three hours at a diner making mashed potato mounds like a madman. Judging by Mom's tone, it didn't have anything to do with aliens and everything to do with his poor decisions. I'd watched enough soap operas in my great-grandma Beulah's living room to know men were lying, cheating scoundrels. I didn't want to believe the same was true of Robert, my dad, but a visit from the Health Department with lab results about his genitals screamed otherwise.

My stomach churned and flip-flopped. I desperately wished for more information about what was going on. Mom had signed a permission form for sex education the previous year, during which, much to our horror, my seventh-grade class learned all about sexually transmitted diseases and changing bodies. I had a nagging suspicion this wasn't about the car. My stomach gurgled and threatened to empty its contents at the first inkling of uneasiness or conflict. The only thing worse than a nervous stomach was my ability to flush red as a ripe strawberry with the slightest hint of embarrassment.

"What happened?" I asked as Mom left her perch on the stool and braced herself along the living room door frame.

"Your dad didn't go to work today."

It would take years for me to get up the nerve to ask him what happened that night, only to be disappointed in his response of, "I don't know," the true cop out phrase of children and adults alike when the truth is too hard to verbalize.

"Oh," I said, hoping Mom would elaborate. After a long pause in which she stared trance-like past me out the large front window. "And?" I prompted.

"He decided that instead of going to work to provide for our family, he'd rather go out drinking and wreck our only car."

Jacob cooed in the background. My heart pounded in my ears as I processed what I feared moments ago. He wouldn't be home tonight, but wrecking our only car threw an entirely new set of problems into the situation. The "why" and "how" questions ricocheted in my head, but under duress, I was incapable of finding the right words until hours later when I was alone. Only then did the questions and rebuttals form coherently. I rose from the floor and moved to embrace Mom, but she withdrew by sidestepping my arms and bent to pick up Jacob and squeeze him tight before depositing him next to his pile of toys. I swallowed my hurt and hid my tears by turning away and walking to the kitchen for a drink of water. I grabbed a kitchen towel and hurriedly wiped away tears.

She called from the living room, "I'm taking a bath. Give your brother a bottle and put him to bed in a little while." I quickly learned my grief and sadness was individual, isolating, and all mine to bear. When we could've bonded, my mother disappeared inside herself, leaving me outside looking in. That night she pushed me, her little buddy since the beginning, away.

The bedroom door slammed on my reply. I returned to the living room and sank to the floor, the oak hard on my bony bottom as I stared blankly at the television screen. Hot tears dripped from my face and rolled off my bare legs. I played cars with Jacob and wondered how I would make it through more end-of-year testing tomorrow. My world had seemingly fallen apart, and I had to go to school like nothing happened.

I wanted my old Mom back, not this brooding former shell of a woman. The old version smiled, hugged me all the time, played board games, took me to the library and to What-A-Burger so I could get a cheeseburger and my favorite drink, the Witch Doctor. During my elementary school days, she let me play hooky. We went to the park, clambering out of the car and racing to the swing set, challenging the other to swing higher. I coveted those better days. At my worst moments, I wished my brother wasn't around. I begged for a brother or sister for years, but by the time thirteen rolled around, I was long past wanting a sibling. I was too accustomed to the benefits of being an only child. But now that Jacob was a part of my life, I wanted him to experience the fun-loving, carefree version of Mom, not this imposter who hid in the darkness.

I carried Jacob to his crib in the corner of my parents' room and nestled him among the blankets. I tucked his blue train-covered blanket around his hips as he turned on his side and stuck a thumb in his mouth. I wondered how Robert's absence would impact Jacob. He loved Mom and me, but he adored his dad the most. Every night around dinnertime, Jacob perched on the back of the blue couch watching the driveway. When the boxy green sedan pulled in, he jumped from the sofa and ran toward the door. Jacob would shout his favorite word "da-da" in a sing-song voice as he jumped up and down. Dad would open the door, lift Jacob from the floor, and envelop him in a hug. As a family, we'd laugh with joy and pride at what we considered Jacob's genius baby speech development and clap with delight when he jabbered his phrase of choice all day. He was only one, but Jacob's grasp of speech had me convinced he would be using complete sentences in the next six months. After Robert's exit, Jacob wouldn't speak another word until he was three years old. He never said "da-da" again.

That night Mom was asleep with the covers pulled over her head. The hallway light illuminated a full ashtray and a couple of empty beer bottles on the nightstand. Since the Health Department visit,

Mom drank a beer or two before bed to help her sleep. The last time I remembered her drinking was about eight years prior, right after she married Robert. She usually stuck to coffee in the morning, sweet tea through mid-day, and a cup of coffee to cap off dinner. The reintroduction of alcohol as a nightcap was an ominous sign.

I again considered hugging her, more for me this time than for her, but my inner voice warned me not to wake her. Instead, I tiptoed from the room and closed the door behind me. I shut myself in my room, welcoming the quiet of my space, turned on my alarm clock, and laid out my clothes for school on top of my dresser. Exhaustion made my muscles heavy as I fumbled for the power button on my radio in the darkened room. If she had a beer to help her sleep, I needed Benatar, the Wilson sisters, and Huey Lewis. Music and books brought comfort and fueled my imagination. Most nights I combined both before I fell asleep, not to dull noise from the outside world, but to dull the noises in my head concerned for our future.

As I relaxed in bed, I reflected on how much life had changed at our house in Monroe and what it meant if Robert never came back. After years of waking in cramped motel rooms or single-wide trailers with no personal space to speak of and morally questionable, nosy neighbors, the memories we'd created at the house in Monroe brought us together as a family unit, the only real family I'd known. The house we rented sat well back from the road, buffered by hundred-foot oak and pine trees that provided adequate shade. Our first autumn in the house, I remember raking the leaves into fluffy piles under those massive trees, taking running jumps into the center of them, then raking them all back up again. After the initial joy of leaf jumping was replaced by torn, calloused hands and a sore back, I soon grew tired of raking. Our neighbors were retirees who spent every afternoon sitting on their porches, watching the world change for the past ten to fifteen years.

After a week of Robert's silent absence, Mom was well into a deep funk. In what I know now was a clinically depressed state, she functioned during the day out of necessity, caring for Jacob while I was at school. But once I stepped off the bus, she handed him off like a hot potato and retreated to her darkened bedroom with a beer or three.

Mom's use of alcohol to buffer Robert's abandonment was concerning. She told me too many stories over the years of her alcoholic father turning physically abusive during her childhood for me to take this lightly. Mom had only spanked me once or twice as a child, and they were halfhearted spankings at that. She had an aversion to causing me any physical pain. I feared if she continued drinking excessively to cope, she might follow her father's addiction path, activating the destructive, abusive DNA.

I remembered the days of visiting my grandparents, Ralph and Bobbie. They had a never-ending drink in hand by mid-afternoon and most conversations consisted of the actors' lines on the television shows. Mom told me her parents came from hard beginnings, like that was some excuse to explain shitty parenting. I didn't want Mom to turn into her parents. I feared whatever road she was walking down would change her.

While she slept in her darkened bedroom one afternoon, when I could no longer take the oppressive darkness permeating our house,

I took Jacob outside to play. The house was stifling and reminded me of the time I played hide-and-seek in my grandma's attic, the heat and dust constricting my throat. I wanted to escape the occasional sob leaking through the wall that the television couldn't drown out.

Our elderly neighbor, Jim, was sitting in his carport rocking as he did most afternoons, watching the traffic zip by on the highway. Everyone had these carports in our neighborhood, but no one seemed to use them for their actual cars, opting instead to treat them as covered porches open on three sides. He waved me over. I threw up a hand in greeting. Jim had been to our house a few times for burgers on the grill, and I'd seen Robert talk to him after work on multiple occasions. He beckoned again, and I slowly walked to the edge of his carport.

"Hello, sir."

"Call me Jim."

I said nothing and adjusted Jacob on my right hip.

"Is everything okay? With your mother?"

"Sure, everything's fine. Just getting ready for eighth grade graduation soon."

His eyes were unrecognizable behind his thick glasses. I had a habit of judging a person's intentions by their eyes, and not being able to analyze his momentarily concerned me. The absence of my step-dad's car in the driveway was likely gossip fodder between Jim and the elderly neighbors that lived on the other side of his house.

Jim motioned me to an empty rocking chair. I weighed the options and decided sitting for a few minutes was more favorable than returning to the mausoleum that was our home. I remembered that Robert said Jim's wife had died several years ago, but I never asked him how. Though Jim seemed old, I was sure he couldn't be older than his mid-sixties. I lost my great-grandparents in their late seventies, and my alcoholic grandpa had suffered a fatal heart attack a couple of years prior at fifty-four. Still, I never quite reconciled my feelings about death. I tended to avoid the subject and any feelings associated with it. It may have had something to do with my great-grandma Beulah taking me to view one of her church friends at the funeral home when I was four or five. Seeing the waxen figure in the casket startled me so much that I scream-cried until my great-grandpa James carried me outside. But whatever Jim wanted to talk to me about didn't have anything to do with his dead wife.

"I haven't seen your dad in a while."

"He's visiting his family in Albemarle."

"Oh, I see."

*Do you see? Did he tell you something in your talks?*

Jacob squirmed out of my lap and settled on the concrete to play with some loose gravel. His absence felt strange.

"Have you seen my granddaughter over here playing?"

"I think so."

"She's turning ten this Sunday, and we're having a small family party for her. I thought maybe you and your brother would like to come over for some cake and ice cream."

I rocked and tried not to respond too quickly. "I'll ask my mom."

"There'll be ice cream."

I wanted to remind him that he just said that, but instead I bit my tongue, Mom's voice rattling in my head telling me to cut the sass and always respect my elders. I wondered where the exception to the rule began? It felt like respect was something to be earned, but that's not what adults told or showed me.

"Okay, I'll ask." I picked up Jacob and trudged back across the driveway, curious how my birthday would be celebrated next month. It likely wouldn't be with Robert, or with cake and ice cream for that matter given the current state of their marriage. I wondered what my mom had done to make him want to leave. I was the perfect daughter and always did what my parents asked of me without too much attitude. I made the A/B honor roll every semester since the fifth grade. I mowed the yard every weekend without complaining. I even pre-soaked my brother's stinky cloth diapers without too many dramatic gagging moments to emphasize the nastiness.

During this time of upheaval, I missed Mom's laughter the most. Gone were the cookies she often baked for me when I got home from school, my favorite being the chewy chocolate chip. Gone was "tell me about your day" over a glass of milk at the bar, and in its place, my greeting was silent, darkened rooms and empty Michelob bottles on the nightstand.

I mourned the loss of our routine, our family unit. I assumed I'd start high school with my friends, but that felt unlikely now that it seemed Robert had no intention of returning. He'd only called twice since that first night, each call ending with Mom staring out the window, then telling me he didn't know when he'd return. Robert leaving meant we'd have to move yet again. I didn't know a lot about our bills or money, but I knew someone needed to work to pay them.

I needed one of them to act like a responsible parent because, while I wanted to help, I was only a child. Anger coursed through my body, unable to find an outlet for its release. Music, books, and writing did little to relieve it, so I compartmentalized the anger to use at a later date, unsure which parent I was angrier with. I vowed to never forgive Robert for putting us in that situation, a state of existence that would only worsen in the coming months.

# Still Standing?

The day my Aunt Leigh showed up early on a Saturday marked nearly two weeks since my step-dad vanished in some unexplained thirty-something male crisis. Mom and Leigh huddled over coffee cups at the dining room table while I hushed Jacob, trying to catch their words.

I heard Mom say, "My license lapsed."

Though I heard the words, I didn't know what they meant. I wondered what had lapsed that led to my mother's low-hung head and Aunt Leigh's concerned and confused look.

Leigh shook her head, "Ann, how could you?"

Mom shrugged, "I don't know. I didn't renew it after Jacob was born."

"How're you getting to the grocery store?"

She nodded. "The neighbors give me rides."

Her driver's license. I should've known. Little good a driver's license would do us anyway since Robert wrecked our only car.

"What about money? Is he sending any?"

"No," Mom looked up from her coffee cup and focused in my direction.

I averted my gaze and stared at Jacob's chubby toes. I ran a jagged-edged fingernail along a toenail that needed clipping.

"I'll take you for groceries after I take Dawn to get her hair cut for graduation."

*Sandra, not Dawn.* It was jarring to hear her refer to me by my middle name. I hadn't been Dawn since I was six years old and decided my middle name was too childish.

I forgave the slip. Aunt Leigh was one of my favorite aunts, followed closely by Aunt Rosie. They both gave tight, warm hugs that left no doubt their hearts were full of love.

Mom nodded and said, "Thank you," followed closely by, "Sandra, stop listening and get ready."

I blushed and rose to my feet. I ducked my head in embarrassment for getting caught eavesdropping, hoping Mom wouldn't comment on my reddened cheeks that further enhanced my guilt. Getting ready consisted of slipping on my tan Reebok tennis shoes, the only pair of shoes I owned. I had hoped to ask for two pairs this year when ordering my school clothes from the Sears and Roebuck catalog. But all of my plans were garbage as soon as my father figure walked out of our lives. As I tied the laces, panic crept up my spine and threatened to paralyze my fingers. I didn't want to see it before, but overhearing the conversation brought it home—we were broke, with no car, no income, and no plan. What were we going to do?

Aunt Leigh piled me into her car, and off we went for a graduation haircut. She'd treated me to hair appointments for the past couple of years for my birthday. She usually brought me new makeup palettes of eye shadow, blush, and occasionally lip gloss. While Mom showed me how to apply makeup last year, I rejected her so-called war paint. When she called it that, I learned to associate makeup with the mask she needed in order to face the world. I wanted nothing to do with makeup for many reasons. I didn't share her need to hide behind a costume or play a role. I also straight-up hated the feel of foreign substances caked on my face. Makeup hid dark circles, pale lashes, and blotchy skin, but I felt like a dispirited clown any time I wore it. Sometimes, I put it on to appease Mom so she thought I valued her input. After what we'd been through, I wanted nothing more than for Mom to smile once more.

Leigh asked me about school as she pulled her car onto the road. I loved Leigh even more in that moment because she didn't question me about Robert or Mom. She turned her full attention to my needs, something my mother was incapable of recently. Leigh made me feel more like an adult than a child. Though her preoccupation with my looks had me wondering if she thought my hair or face were lacking, I let the thought slip away and presumed that she treated me to these things because she loved me. I seized her offerings like a drowning person latching on to a float. Since Robert left, my position in the family consisted of babysitter and gopher of coffee, slippers, and beer. I wanted to scream whenever Mom asked anything of me, but instead, I obeyed quietly and seethed inside. I wanted her to smile once more and tell me everything would be okay.

I wanted to remain a child, but I felt like that phase of my life had been eradicated when Robert left us.

We arrived at a strip mall housing a pizza joint on one end and a hair salon on the other with an insurance agency and dry cleaners squeezed in between. The smell in the salon reminded me of the time Robert tried burning a brush pile and instead caught his shirt sleeve on fire. The gasoline he used to start the fire whooshed and engulfed his arm. He ran away from the brush fire and dropped to the ground extinguishing the flames, but the damage was done, melted fabric stuck to his arm like a second skin. I couldn't eat hamburgers cooked on charcoal for months after the accident. I shuddered and gagged as I took a seat in the salon chair taking care to breathe through my mouth.

Leigh directed the stylist to cut my hair to my shoulders and add layers for more body like she understood exactly what I needed. My relationship with my hair bordered on hate/hate most days; the long tresses frequently rebelled in the humidity, and the locks spent the greater part of warm weather months contained by a ponytail. Adults told me how much they loved my hair, but I cursed the thick brown curly strands that either stood on end or ensconced my head like a hair helmet, depending on the length.

I watched Leigh and the stylist in the mirror, awed by the assertiveness of my aunt as she directed the woman. I wanted to be like Leigh. I wanted Mom to be more like Leigh as she once was. Mom changed herself so much to accommodate Robert over the last few years that she became a shell of her former self. Mom gave up driving, gave up working, and relinquished her independence for a man who couldn't find the strength to come back and be an adult. She allowed Robert to direct how she should act to only find herself abandoned by the spineless puppeteer. I now wonder what kind of woman Mom would've been and what her life would've looked like if she'd realized at twenty-four that a man should be a complementary color and not a primary color on her wheel of life.

After the salon visit, Leigh stopped at the local DMV and picked up a driver's license handbook for my mom while I considered the effects of humidity pulling the ends of my hair to the bottom of my ears in the side mirror. I hated the cut. I would never tell Leigh I hated the haircut, but I vowed to never get my hair cut again unless I gave the stylist directions.

Leigh handed me the book when she returned to the car. I wondered if Mom would even crack it since I hadn't seen her read anything lately. Before Leigh left that afternoon, I watched her pull Mom close for some last words I hoped would motivate her to snap out of her stupor. We waved from the front porch as Leigh roared out of the driveway, kicking gravel dust in the wind.

Mom ran her hand down my hair and said, "It'll grow back. With a little makeup, you'll look beautiful on graduation day."

I blinked back tears. She hated my haircut as much as I did. "Will you be there with Jacob?"

"I'll try."

"I want you there."

"I said, I'll try."

Her words fell flat, the voice in my head telling me not to hold out hope. I was a quick student of reading people's hidden intentions behind their words; the summer of 1984 with Mom fine-tuned my skills. Even though I attempted to communicate my needs, I was too enmeshed with my mother's emotions and believed I was responsible for her happiness. My needs largely went unmet just so I could keep the mood light, or at least neutral. But nothing I did or said could pull her from the dark hole of her depression. I had foolishly thought the wellbeing of her children would be enough.

On the day of eighth-grade graduation, I sat in a metal folding chair in our humid gymnasium alongside my classmates and pondered life after graduation. The excitement I'd felt surrounding the greatest achievement of my life so far had been replaced with cold dread. How could I take pleasure in graduating from eighth grade when I was clueless about where we'd be when school started in September? Would we stay in Monroe? Would Robert come back? Would Mom really try to come to my graduation like she said, or would her words prove yet another lie? I squeezed my eyes shut and leaned forward. I wished my brain would stop spiraling, but when I opened my eyes and scanned the bleachers, all I saw were strangers. I lost myself in a daydream of Mom in the bleachers holding Jacob in one arm and a congratulatory sign with my name in the other. But that didn't happen, and I accepted my eighth-grade diploma to a spattering of required polite applause.

My daydreams seeped into my everyday life, blurring the line between fantasy and reality. The false scenarios I created in my mind saved my sanity by imagining the life I wanted instead of the reality I was living. Initially when my step-dad left, I dreamed my biological father would swoop in and save me from leaving my school and friends, and even this house. While leaning over to grab my arm and place me on his white horse, he would profess his undying love for my mother, who needed it more than I did. Then I'd remind myself she didn't need a man to save her; that's what got us into this shitshow in the first place. She needed to focus on being a mother, not a wife, not an accessory. If only she could tap into the woman she'd been who'd summoned the courage to leave home at sixteen and strike out on her own. Even in my alternate reality, I couldn't fully let myself dream.

Once the principal read all the names, the group of rising ninth-graders filed out of the gym in ant-like procession, absorbing the wild cheers of friends and family celebrating our collective milestone. I skirted the crowds of hugging families and sought out the talkative school counselor who insisted on transporting me to and from the event. The counselor offered to also bring my mom and Jacob to the graduation ceremony. Mom refused her offer with plenty of invalid excuses, such as she had nothing to wear and Jacob would cry the entire ceremony. I knew her reasons hid her embarrassment. No one at my school would've recognized my mom or our situation because she never went to any of my school functions. Her insecurities and social anxiety prevented her from experiencing much of life in those days as she watched the hours pass by like living her life was a spectator sport.

"How'd it go?" Mom asked from her position on the couch when I slammed the front door.

"Fine." I fought back anger and tears. I hated how easily I cried, tears spilling over my cheek's way too quickly most of the time. It was something I wished would change along with my boyishly thin body, thick, frizzy hair, and the gap between my front teeth large enough to hold a quarter.

"I'm going to change now." I pulled at the itchy collar of the button-down shirt my mom picked from the Sears catalog months ago in preparation for the event. She ordered all my clothes this way. I took a pen and circled the clothing I liked, mostly T-shirts and jeans. Mom's choices ranged from ruffled and collared button-down shirts with khaki and blue slacks to round out the boarding school look she preferred and I abhorred. Since she wrote the check, I was forced to wear clothes that were kryptonite for my self-esteem. My only relief was a single pair of jeans and a couple pairs of shorts I wore after school and on the weekends.

After changing into shorts and a T-shirt, I left the ruffled shirt in a bunch on my closet floor. I returned to the living room.

"Our neighbor, Jim, invited Jacob and me to his granddaughter's birthday party tomorrow."

"Jacob and I." Eyebrows raised.

She tried to forever correct my grammar and every time she did it, I seethed.

"He invited Jacob and I to her party. Can we go?"

"May Jacob and I go?"

"May we go?" I slowly drew out the words, keeping my tone even, while my body flushed hot from anger.

She studied my face. I kept it neutral because the slightest perceived attitude would ensure I wouldn't be allowed to attend this party. I wasn't entirely sure I wanted to go anyway. The only reason

I even wanted to go was to get a reprieve from the gloomy house and to have some cake and ice cream—the food alone made up for the pity invite.

"I suppose you can go for a little while as long as you take your brother with you," she said, handing me a sleeping toddler as she retreated to her darkness.

I didn't usually pray, but I prayed that day for my mom to smile again and for our life to return to normal. Mom's mouth remained either pursed or frowning, and she never asked me to play rummy with her anymore. She loved thrashing me at cards, and I would've gladly let her that summer if it brought back a smidgen of her spark. I failed to comprehend then why she withdrew from her children, but I now realize that grief and depression robbed her of the ability to function, as those emotions tend to do.

On Saturday afternoon, Jim's granddaughter celebrated turning ten. I kept my brother attached to my hip, partly my shield and my excuse. For as long as I could remember, I struggled with debilitating shyness around new people. It would take me another twenty years before I would completely understand the idiosyncrasies of being an introvert. In that moment at the birthday party, I took comfort in watching the action around me, knowing I was primarily unseen leaning against the door jamb leading from the kitchen to the living room.

Jim's living room was full of what I could only assume were relatives and elderly neighbors. The couple two houses down from us had given us vegetables from their garden in the weeks since Robert left and taken Mom to the grocery store. Their kindness ensured I ate plenty of tomato sandwiches with Duke's mayonnaise and a sprinkling of salt and pepper for lunch most days. They smiled and waved at me. I threw a hand as I continued holding up the wall and observing the activities.

Jim's granddaughter sat on the floor surrounded by stacks of pastel-colored gifts. Even during the best years in my family, I never received the number of gifts this girl did for turning ten years old. I watched as she unwrapped baby dolls, board games, books, and a Barbie-pink bike with blue and white plastic tassels adorning the handles. The girl let out a sharp squeal when she unwrapped the last present, and soon her grandpa carried the bike outside for her to ride. I wanted to slip away while everyone's attention was focused outside. Instead, I stayed long enough to mouth the happy birthday song and share a slice of cake and some ice cream with Jacob.

"Back so soon?" my mom asked, looking up from a book of crossword puzzles. The afternoon coffee she used to drink had been replaced with a Michelob.

*Soon? I was gone almost two hours.*

"Yeah, Jacob was getting sleepy." My brother said nothing because he was only fourteen months old and too young to grasp how much his presence supplied excuses for adults. I tucked Jacob into his crib and retreated to my bedroom, where I stayed until Mom called me for dinner. I wanted to escape the boredom and uncertainty of my life, so I cracked open a paperback Mary Higgins Clark book Mom had handed down and lost myself in the mystery of a fictional character's life.

The day after the party, I perched on the carport's low brick wall, writing in my notebook, toying with a new idea for a mystery inspired by the Queen of Suspense. Jacob played with cars on the concrete pad, stopping occasionally to gesture for me to play. I ignored him and continued to write when I heard Jim call my name from across the yard. I looked up from the page. He waved me over. I reluctantly shut my notebook, clipped the pen to the cover, gathered Jacob in my arms, and approached. I feared he'd ask me to attend some other family function of his, and I had no intention of socializing with strangers again anytime soon.

"Good afternoon, sir."

"I have some leftover ice cream from my granddaughter's party if you and your brother want some."

I hesitated. My intuition was on alert that something felt off today even though I'd been inside his house the previous day, milling around with strangers who shot me real or perceived expressions of pity. But my love of ice cream outweighed my sense of unease. I followed Jim through the side door that led from the carport into his kitchen. I'd never been inside his home before yesterday, and then, I'd arrived through the front door and stayed glued to the living room area. I pulled Jacob tighter to my right hip, his chubby little legs gripping my waist.

The kitchen oozed gloominess even though the sun shone brightly outside the single window over the sink. The walls were wood paneled, adding to the dungeon-like feel. His home was colder than my house. Mom cut the AC off except for the small window unit in her room to save money. To me, any temperature below 82 degrees felt cool. Jim opened the freezer door and removed two popsicles, one orange, one purple, not the Neapolitan ice cream he served for his granddaughter's party. I adjusted Jacob to my opposite hip, using my brother as a shield. Jim was blocking my exit to the carport door, so I backed toward the door leading to the backyard. My gut screamed for me to leave, but my brain rationalized that this man had been friendly with my family for over a year and this illogical reasoning prevented my legs from running.

He stepped toward me with the popsicles, and I felt frozen to the spot in the kitchen while electricity coursed through my body, urging my legs to run. His eyes glittered unrecognizably behind thick glasses, his mouth twisted into a lopsided smile. I searched for his intent while trying to calm my racing thoughts. I needed to think clearly. I had limited experience sussing out the intentions of men, but my instincts had served me well in the past when I felt uncomfortable in their presence. Though I wasn't experienced in dealing with men, my body certainly carried its own intelligence. I now felt the same tension electrifying my muscles and bones as I'd felt in the past when I'd been alerted to the insidious nature of dangerous men.

When I was three or four, every time my uncle visited, I crammed into the space between the toilet and bathtub in my great-grandma's Beulah's bathroom to avoid his unwanted hugs and kisses. But on those days when I couldn't run fast enough, he'd scoop me into his arms and hold me too close, rubbing his scruffy face along my cheek and down my throat. I screamed and pushed away until he put me down, laughing and telling my grandma his beard must be too rough for my liking. Even as a child, I knew my aversion to him went far beyond his aggressive affection or sandpapery facial hair. He died a horribly painful death in his forties, and I felt no remorse for his demise.

There was another time a man followed me home from the school bus stop in Charlotte. The bus pulled up next to the bench where it let people on and off near the townhome community where we lived. I got off at the bus stop like every other afternoon, but when the noisy, yellow vehicle pulled away in a cloud of exhaust, the hairs on my arms stood on end. I sensed someone watching me. I swiveled around and took in my surroundings. Across the street was an empty field where a blond-haired man in mirrored sunglasses stood motionless, watching me with focused attention. Everything about the scenario screamed danger.

I turned and walked toward the grassy incline leading to the townhome parking lot. I looked over my shoulder and saw he had crossed the street, following the direction of my trail. I broke into a full sprint until I reached the front door, yanking it open and slamming it shut behind me. I locked the deadbolt and slid the chain, gasping to catch my breath. Not long after this incident, the news reported a little girl had been abducted from her bus stop in Charlotte and killed. Who knows if it was the same man. But I was forever grateful I trusted my gut that day.

Finding myself standing in Jim's kitchen with no one else around but my infant brother, I wished I'd listened to the warning signs clanging in my head before I stepped into his house. Jim's hand extended with a popsicle, and Jacob reached for the sugary treat before I could intercept it. Jim stepped forward and shoved the wooden stick, the kind with the jokes printed horizontally, into Jacob's waiting hand. Jacob tried to push the popsicle into his mouth with the paper wrapping intact. While I used my free hand to remove the wrapper, Jim reached over and grabbed my right breast, barely larger than a plum. He squeezed a couple of times like he was testing fruit for ripeness. I momentarily stood frozen.

I want to think I shouted, "NO," but I think the screams were only in my head. I turned, fumbled with the lock on the back door, shoved it open, and ran back to my house, fearing he would follow me. Once inside, I slammed the door and locked it. I leaned against the frame, realizing Jacob was still holding his goddamn popsicle. I considered ripping it from his hands and throwing it away, worried that Jim's evil intentions had somehow leaked into the popsicle just waiting to infect my little brother. But I was more concerned his cries would wake Mom, so I let him keep it. I walked through the living room scanning the windows facing his house, unlatching and relatching the front door lock just to be sure.

My body shook uncontrollably as I crossed the living room and entered Mom's bedroom. I sank into the rocking chair at the end of her bed. I rocked furiously, the floorboards creaking in protest as Jacob slurped at the popsicle. My body shifted back and forth from hot to ice-cold until it settled on cold, leaving me tremoring in the stuffy, dark bedroom. I could barely hold onto Jacob as my muscles convulsed like I'd been abandoned without clothing in the middle of a blizzard.

I wanted to wake her and tell her what had happened. I took in her darkened shape in the bed, asleep during the middle of the day, and wondered what the outcome would be if I told her. Would it break her for good? Who would believe a fourteen-year-old kid over the word of a World War II veteran? Jim would likely say he accidentally touched me when he tried to hand me the popsicle. But I knew the truth—he lured me inside his home to grope me for his twisted sexual gratification. I vacillated between shock, anger, fear, and shame.

I rocked in time to my racing thoughts and emotions. My skin felt bloated in order to accommodate the hollowness and hatred coursing through my body. Then I began to question myself over what seemed so obvious just moments before.

*How could I be so stupid going inside with him? Did I provoke him in some way? Why would he touch me? I'm just a skinny child. Why must Mom sleep so much? How could she not protect me? Has he done this to his granddaughter also? Was I an easy mark? What does that say about me? Why, why, why, just fucking why?* The questions raced through my mind as I tried to process what happened. And then the cold fingers of fear clutched at my very bones. With a full body shiver, I realized *it could've been so much worse.*

I put my sleeping brother in his crib, tiptoed over to Mom's closet, and eased open the door. I grabbed the BB gun tucked away in the recesses. Robert had shown me how to shoot the BB gun the past

Christmas. I backed out of Mom's bedroom and carried the BB gun through the house, checking the windows and doors. I stopped in the kitchen, pulled a wooden-handled pocket knife from the drawer, and moved my weapons to my bedroom.

The knife went under my pillow, and the BB gun went into my closet. I stretched out on the bed, burying my head in the pillow that still smelled like the coconut shampoo from my pre-graduation haircut. After weighing my options for hours, I once again made a decision that was best for my mom, not for me. I would bury the secret and pretend it didn't happen so Mom wouldn't irreparably break. I needed her to return to us, to be the mother I recognized. I now realize I should've told her. Instead, I chose to push my fear, shame, and guilt into a special compartment because our life was already messy enough. There simply wasn't room for my pain. I convinced myself that I could handle this dark secret on my own, but of course I was wrong. I was a child, who'd already faced too many traumas, acting like a damned adult.

When I turned fourteen, I became the full-time mother in our family, and my mom allowed it to happen. Taking control was easy since she welcomed the role reversal. However, my decision, made out of a child's desperation, resulted in dangerous consequences for me and my future relationships. I did what I had to do to take care of Jacob and my mother, but I hated her for allowing it to happen. I stoked and stored that anger and resentment like the Exxon-Valdez pipeline, and we all know how that ended. Any time I felt sad or fearful, I could call upon those seemingly endless anger reserves to power me and protect me through any situation. Anger can be beneficial and a fuel for change, but my unresolved rage, resentment, and misplaced shame began to choke my happiness and settle into the dark recesses of my soul, where it would reside for years leaking toxic sludge and polluting my thoughts and relationships.

# Breaking Stride

S ince the Jim incident, it felt like a piece of my innocence slipped
away every time I thought about what happened. While I griev-
ed my losses, my mother seemed ready to finally move on from hers.
She threw open the curtains and trashed the last three Michelob
beers in the refrigerator. I had no clue what snapped her out of
the depression she experienced during the previous month, but I
didn't care. To have even a semblance of her former self back thrilled
me. She could've given up, stayed closed up in the dark bedroom;
instead, she chose to go on. Even as a teenager, I recognized that her
ability to claw her way out of a depressive episode and put down the
alcohol was impressive, given her family history of substance use.

Mom repeatedly warned me from around the age of nine or ten
that alcoholism ran in her family. Specifically, her parents struggled
with it as evidenced by the bottomless whiskey glasses in their hands
each time we visited. She'd follow up her tales of ancestral baggage
with a warning to never let alcohol ruin my life. I now believe she

woke up one morning and didn't want to be like her parents anymore. After that summer, Mom only indulged in the occasional recreational drink now and then. That is, until her demons returned years later. Inevitably, they always return if left unresolved.

Mom's first task in her newly resurrected life was to get her driver's license. She asked the neighbor lady to drive her to the license bureau and returned a few hours later triumphant, waving her license and dancing around the living room like that piece of plastic was our ticket to a better life. Her smile was infectious, and Jacob and I joined her dance, holding hands and dancing in a circle until we collapsed on the floor laughing. The dancing and joy felt like old times when we played Ring around the Rosie until we were dizzy and weak from laughter. Maybe all of the sleeping reset her brain because the woman giggling and hugging us felt a lot like the old Mom that had disappeared several years ago, the one I'd been begging to return.

Mom informed me that we were having a yard sale over the weekend, and all the furniture was going. I made cardboard signs and placed them by the road. There was nothing like a yard sale sign to attract a bunch of bargain-hunting vultures in the South. The day of the yard sale, I carried end tables, a coffee table, dishes, lamps, Jacob's crib, and an assortment of mixing bowls. Every time space opened in the front yard, Mom sent me back inside for more items. The only items not for sale were clothes and bare necessities like Mom's Presto electric frying pan. The yard sale netted about $600. The following Monday, Mom rolled into the driveway with a newly purchased white 1972 Cadillac. The car resembled a chrome monster with sharp curves that billowed smoke when she cranked the engine. But it was a way forward, our way out.

A few days later, we stuffed a couple of black garbage bags with our clothes, Mom's trusty electric skillet, the Mr. Coffee machine, the BB gun, several Corelle plates and bowls, a few glasses, and some silverware in the trunk. My ten-speed bike I'd received for my thirteenth birthday even fit in the cavernous trunk. The boxy 32-inch television that took both of us to lift went into the back seat beside Jacob. I gingerly placed my prized radio/double cassette player on the floorboard behind the passenger seat, ruffling Jacob's curls and smiling. I assumed my spot in the front seat, a place I occupied over the next several years, sometimes driving, sometimes riding shotgun, but always next to Mom as her trusty co-pilot, just like the old days.

We made the two-hour drive to Troutman to see my grandma Bobbie and ask for help, something Mom never liked doing. We needed someone to let us live with them until Mom got a job and saved some money so we could rent our own place again. Monroe was where we settled with Robert, but Troutman and Mooresville would always be our home. My grandmother still lived in the house she'd occupied with my grandfather before his premature death in 1982. He'd dropped dead from a heart attack, too young by any standards but not surprising given his devotion to drinking whiskey and chain-smoking cigarettes. We'd attended Thanksgiving dinner that year after he died. I recalled my grandma sitting with her head down like the day's weight was too much for her to endure. Aunt Leigh and Mom did most of the work around the kitchen while I eyed my aunt's new husband, who smiled too broadly and wore an offensive amount of cologne that assaulted my senses.

That Thanksgiving had been the last time we'd visited my maternal grandmother. Over the past few years, I'd overheard Mom call her a few times on the phone, but their conversations never seemed to last long. It's as if the normalcy between Mom and her mother had been tainted by past turmoil, making it challenging for them to build any kind of positive relationship. Mom told me stories of how her father was physically abusive, and her mother often feigned sickness, making my mom the de facto caretaker to her three younger siblings. Though Mom never said this, I always felt she blamed her mother for not coming to her rescue. She needed someone to take care of her, just like I did. I didn't expect her to be a perfect mother, because an ideal mother is a misconception, but I did need Mom to break the cycle and protect my brother and me.

The afternoon we pulled into my grandma's driveway, I saw my grandfather's orange pickup truck sitting by the shed. My grandma kept his stuff like he might walk through the front door again one day. I realize now that holding on to a deceased loved one's belongings means there's probably too much unresolved grief preventing the person from moving forward. I did not understand her continued grief because I failed to appreciate her love for the man. I found him gruff and unapproachable when he was alive.

My grandpa was the exact opposite of my great-grandfather James, his wife's father, and in my opinion, my only grandpa. My great-grandfather not only rocked me and fed me bottles when I was a baby, but handed out hugs to all of his grandchildren like the peanut M&Ms he kept in the chest pockets of his blue coveralls, which he wore every day except Sunday when he donned his suit and tie for church. According to the numerous pictures Mom had taken during the first five years of my life, my great-grandfather rocked and held me as a baby. She hated being in the pictures, but she must've taken hundreds during that time, documenting the love shown by my great-grandparents. I held those memories and pictures tight, using them to comfort me when I felt my worst.

My grandma opened the door after the second round of knocks. We followed her bent and shuffling frame into the living room. I remember thinking she appeared old even though she couldn't have been but in her early fifties. I couldn't avoid the unblinking eyes of my grandpa's stuffed deer head still hanging on the wall. I despised that deer head. My earliest memories of the deer head involved my grandpa Ralph lifting me up and telling me to rub the muzzle. I did so cautiously as he laughed at my shudder when my hand scraped the rough, rubbery snout. Only then did he put me back on the floor, but I imagined the deer's glassy eyes following me the rest of the day, blaming me for its predicament as a wall ornament instead of a majestic wild creature.

The house smelled like a musty ashtray mixed with the sweet aroma of my grandma Bobbie's honeysuckle perfume and whiskey breath. We followed her to the kitchen and took seats on either side of her at the table that took up much of the kitchen. Jacob crawled out of my lap and teetered off toward the living room. I stuffed jittery hands under my legs. I feared her words because I already knew the answer. I could read it in her downturned face, much like the time she informed us they'd had to get rid of our dog Sam when we'd left for South Carolina because he needed more room to run. I wanted to tell Mom not to ask, not to put herself in that position to get hurt because that's the only way Grandma Bobbie operated. Mom took a big breath, her chest rising and falling, put aside her pride, and asked if we could stay for a couple months until we could save money and find a new place.

My uncle Junior entered the kitchen around that time and placed both hands on my grandma Bobbie's shoulders. My uncle was tall and gaunt, hereditary black circles encasing blue eyes. Mom's only brother was named after her father, a junior who never met the expectations of the senior. I found myself uncomfortable around him, fearful of his permanent scowl and clipped gruff words. He was the epitome of a loner right up until the day he died. Mom once told me he was booted from the Army on account of illegal drug use. She never had a close relationship with him, most likely because of how similar he was to her father.

My grandma Bobbie's head remained bowed, Mom's request hanging in the air.

Junior squeezed an answer from her shoulders.

"I can't," she said.

*More like won't.*

Mom nodded with narrowed eyes.

"I can hardly take care of myself. There's no money left from the insurance. I don't have much."

She refused to look Mom in the eyes, instead boring holes into the cigarette-burned tablecloth. I looked around the table. It held the sadness and anger of generations of our family's women. If only it could absorb all that sorrow so it wouldn't continue manifesting in substance abuse, broken relationships, and codependence on men who had forgotten their duty to protect the family.

That summer, my grandma Bobbie was still in the throes of her grief, or at least that's what I later told myself to excuse her actions that day. Grieving beyond our comprehension and unable to care for herself, she refused to let us stay with her. Sadness washed over me as I realized our hopes were dashed by the person who was supposed to love us when we needed her most. Instead, we added her to the list of people we couldn't rely on, especially hurtful since she was family.

The day she rejected us, my mom grabbed Jacob from the living room floor, and we left without another word.

"What now?" I asked once we were back in our tank of a car.

My mom squared her shoulders, narrowed her eyes, slapped a pair of oversized shades over them, and said, "We're headed to Pageland, South Carolina."

"Pageland?"

"Yep."

She answered quickly, too quickly. I wondered how this geographical location was chosen on the old Rand McNally map. I imagined her doing the same eenie-meenie-miny-mo decision-making tactic she took when selecting a bag of her favorite pretzels from the grocery store shelf.

Mom backed the car onto the dirt road leading over the old wooden bridge I feared would buckle under the weight of our car. The mood on the ride here had been somber, but now, Mom's mood felt lighter. Her sky-blue eyes gleamed as we pulled away from the family who raised her, and I caught a glimpse of the girl inside who went streaking down Main Street, rode motorcycles with bad boys, practiced white witchcraft, and sped recklessly down back roads in her Ford Mustang. Mom's self-reliant energy fostered hope in me that we would survive this together. We could build a new life without Robert, without grandma Bobbie—just the three musketeers on a grand adventure.

"What's in Pageland?" I asked, hardly able to hide the anticipation in my voice.

She gripped the wheel tighter, her eyes laser focused on the road. "I don't know, but we're going to find out."

And find out we did.

# *A Warrior?*

A looming, shadowy figure chased me through dark woods. When my legs wouldn't run anymore, the hooded demon crept forward and pinned me on the precipice of a craggy cliff. Panting and panicking, I toed the edge. Should I fight this omen of death head on? Or do I flee by jumping over the edge into the dark abyss? Before I could decide, a hand jostled me awake. Startled and disoriented, I rubbed my eyes and tried to clear my head. Sweat beaded on my nose and upper lip from the chase scene in my dream or possibly from the oppressive heat in the tin box of a trailer we were living in.

Mom's breath tickled my ear as she whispered urgently, "Someone's at the door."

I shook my head and sat upright in the bed we shared in the one-bedroom trailer we rented in Pageland, South Carolina. We found the trailer the same day we left my grandma's house while sitting in a Hardee's eating cheeseburgers and scouring the local classified section of the paper. We'd been there for a little over a week.

My first fear was that Robert had found us, part of me excited by the idea and the other dreading the prospect. This scenario was unlikely, though. We couldn't afford telephone service. We barely had enough money to rent the trailer and buy some groceries each week. By groceries, I mean bread, off-brand cereal, milk, peanut butter, a block of Velveeta, and a couple of boxes of Tuna and Hamburger Helper.

I shook my head again, still hazy from my dream, only to find reality was no less terrifying than my nightmare. The door handle rattled. We held our breath and listened intently in the dark bedroom. Whoever was on the other side of our door was an intruder, not a visitor.

I reached under the bed and grabbed our only weapon to defend ourselves. Robert taught me to shoot the BB gun in the backyard last year, aiming at the cardboard target leaning against the tall pine tree. He'd clapped me on the back and called me a natural sharpshooter when I hit the target's inner circle multiple times, but this situation was much different. A BB gun might slow an intruder, but it wouldn't stop him if he intended to harm us. I cursed not having anything better for protection. Mom had pawned the remainder of Robert's fancy pocket knife collection that didn't sell at the yard sale, though I didn't think I had the stomach to cut someone and would most likely pass out at the sight of blood.

Anyone trying to break into our trailer must have evil intentions since we had no money or possessions to speak of. I crept from the bedroom, the BB gun clutched across my chest like a shield. Kneeling next to the kitchen table in the middle of the trailer, I settled the plastic butt into my shoulder. The trailer was small, with the living room in the front, the kitchen/dining room in the center, and the small bedroom and bathroom at the back. It was more of a camp trailer than anything resembling a home, and by far the worst and smallest trailer we'd lived in yet. The only door was next to the living room, mere feet from my position. A sliver of light showed through the little window over the kitchen sink, but fear prevented me from peeking out to see who might be outside.

The entire scene reminded me of the suspenseful movies I used to watch before we pawned the old television in order to rent our luxurious accommodations. The intruder was on one side of the door listening to us, gauging our movements, while Mom crouched behind me in the darkness. I wondered if and when they'd burst through the door. I questioned why none of our neighbors responded to the noise or came to our defense. I realized if I needed help, I would have to do it myself. The possibility of anyone coming to my rescue, be damned!

Robert's voice played back in my head, telling me to pump the gun until it was too hard to pump anymore, ensuring the most power from the weapon. If the intruder got into our house, I had one shot before I had to use precious seconds to pump it again. Mom's hand squeezed my shoulder, and I was unsure if it was out of support or fear. Where could I aim to do the most damage—the eyes or the groin? Or would I aim for the face and kick him in the balls while I pumped the BB gun? How was a fourteen-year-old supposed to protect a grown woman and a child?

The doorknob rattled again, this time causing the door to buck its hinges allowing moonlight to peek through gaps at the top and bottom of the threshold. It sounded like the intruder was trying to pull the door off the hinges. I begged the metal to hold as I furiously pumped the gun again, trying to put more air in the chamber. The aluminum strained, and I crooked my sweaty forefinger across the trigger. Let him step one toe through that door, and he'd regret it. I clenched my jaw, my whole body tensed for action, when finally the rattling stopped. There was nothing but silence.

My breath stuck in my throat, and I waited, tilting my head and listening. Hardly daring to breathe, I imagined the person on the other side contemplating their next move like climbing through one of the windows. With eyes that finally adjusted to the low light, I glanced at the clock on the wall. It was just after midnight, the witching hour, when nothing good happens in a trailer park in the middle of sand-flat-nowhere. We remained crouched until my knees ached and my muscles quaked.

"I think he's gone," Mom said after a few minutes of silence.

I nodded in agreement, my voice still strangled by fear.

We silently rose and returned to the bed where Jacob was sound asleep and oblivious to how close we'd come to an entirely different kind of night. We didn't talk about what had just happened; instead, we lay on either side of Jacob, silent with our thoughts. My heart still raced, not from fear but from the adrenaline of facing danger. I equated the experience with an adventure like one had by Nancy

Drew or Trixie Belden. The situation didn't warrant action, but I was ready if it had. I laid the BB gun beside me and listened as my heartbeat retreated from my ears and returned to my chest. After too many minutes of replaying the could-have-been's, I drifted off to sleep, hugging the plastic stock against my torso. I had asked Mom what was in South Carolina on the trip here, and I guess I now had my answer.

My mom found a sewing job at an upholstery factory in Pageland within a couple of days of arriving in South Carolina. Since she had never finished high school, her work experience was limited. Having previously worked as a sewing machine operator, she was eligible for the exhausting, back-breaking minimum wage jobs. I babysat Jacob while Mom worked, alternately reading books during his nap and playing cars or blocks with him when he was awake. The days dragged endlessly, accompanied by South Carolina's sweltering July temperatures.

When Mom got home from work around 3:30, I waved a greeting over my shoulder before escaping to the sand-covered asphalt roads flanking the trailer park. I cherished my time alone while Mom relaxed until she started dinner. I unlocked my bike from the metal steps and walked along the dirt road leading out of the trailer park. There must've been over fifty trailers dotting the landscape. Most trailers in the park had no AC, judging by propped-open doors and all age ranges of women sitting on stoops fanning themselves. At the slightest noise from outside, the occupants, usually a woman or a child, leaned out the door, surveyed what the other tin-dweller was doing, and ducked back inside to make assumptions about their neighbor's business. Unlike my neighbors, I covertly spied. Since we were without a TV, I imagined mysterious lives for them, jotting ideas in my notebook to pass the time.

I climbed my bicycle, perched on the hard seat, and pedaled to the only road with an incline of any substance. I inhaled humidity-laden air, akin to a sauna, and pushed on the pedals. I pumped my legs as fast as possible, the soles of my tennis shoes glued to the pedals, the wind lifting sweaty tendrils from my forehead. Occasionally, I took my hands off the handlebars and stretched my arms to embrace the air, reveling in the freedom of soaring like a bird. It was in these moments I knew there was more to life than what I was experiencing. I hit my brakes and put my hands back on the handlebars a split second before my front tire started wobbling. I reached the stop sign signaling the intersection of the fifty-five-mile-per-hour country road where people always went faster than the posted speed. This game of chicken with the stop sign continued until the sun dropped low in the sky, my shirt sweat-drenched, and I slowly biked home for dinner.

The day after the attempted break-in, we sat at the small kitchen table, Mom drinking her morning coffee while I scooped spoonfuls of knock-off Froot Loops in my mouth.

She took a deep breath and finally looked up at me. "We're not safe here."

I nodded in agreement, a drop of milk running down my chin. I wiped it off with my hand and onto my shorts. Being poor meant using a pants leg for a napkin.

"What are you going to do?"

"I'm thinking on it. Maybe it'll come to me while we're at the laundromat."

She gathered our dirty clothes in a trash bag, and we set off to do our Saturday morning routine. I would be a millionaire if I had a dollar for every time we went to the laundromat or a park during those four years after Robert left. Mom used these two locales as meditation temples. There's something to be said for watching clothes tumble, the garments taking turns free-falling in the drum. It became a game I played. Mom's nightgown, my Snoopy T-shirt, Jacob's tiny shorts; would the red T-shirt be next? Instead, it was the white towel with the splotchy dye stains from when Mom went more reddish than her natural auburn shade.

That Saturday in Pageland, my mom went outside to use the pay phone while our clothes tumbled in an industrial dryer and ate quarters like the slot machines at a casino. I was uncertain who Mom was calling since she pretty much disowned her mother after she turned us away. The remaining options left Robert or her younger sister, Aunt Leigh, who lived near Mooresville. She'd called Robert on a few occasions since he left, asking him to help financially, but I don't think she ever asked him to return home, and he never sent money to help. No matter how hard I tried to eavesdrop, I failed to hear their conversations. Their communications ended with Mom slamming the receiver, anger burning in her eyes and frown lines framing her mouth for hours afterwards.

I surveyed her through the laundromat's front window as I held Jacob up to the Pac-Man game he thought he was playing. She appeared younger now than she had in years, her auburn hair pinned back. She wore her blue Texas T-shirt with the longhorn over the left breast, cut-off jeans shorts showing tanned and toned legs, and a pair of wedge sandals. Mom pretended to ignore the gawking men who passed by, but I knew the attention filled her self-esteem tank. She blinked her eyes and flirted with men in the grocery store as only a self-assured, attractive woman could do. She continued to rebound after Robert's emotional bankruptcy and returned to the smiling, vibrant Mom I remembered.

"Who'd you call?" I asked, hoping it wasn't Robert.

Mom lifted wet clothes and deposited them into a metal rolling cart to transport them to the dryers lining the back wall. "Leigh."

"And?"

"She said we could stay with her for a bit."

*Bit, what's a bit? A day, a week, a month?*

I chose not to ask about a timeline. All I cared about was leaving the South Carolina flatlands and that cramped trailer I no longer trusted to keep us safe, locked door or not.

We packed the car and headed to Aunt Leigh's house the next day. Mooresville had a sentimental spot in my heart. It was my hometown, my birthplace, the land that held my best memories of my great-grandparents, Beulah and James. It was the town in which I spent my first nine years of life before Robert dragged us west, from one dismal motel to the next until we reached North Carolina once more. Mooresville was my warm and fuzzy place, and for a short time, I hoped we would settle there permanently. I wished for the familiarity and normalcy of life in this town I loved. Of course, by the time I turned eighteen and had moved back and forth on multiple occasions from this town, I was ready to leave it for good. Bad memories have a way of spoiling paradise.

The day we arrived at my aunt's home she shared with her second husband and young son filled me with warm nostalgia. Hope jockeyed for a position in the darkness I had carried since Robert left. I spent the first few days dreaming of starting high school in my hometown next month. There was a chance I could have classes with my cousin I grew up with in my great-grandma's house, an exact month separating our birth dates. She used to squeeze the life out of me when I was younger, but I loved playing hide-and-seek and riding Big Wheels with her nonetheless.

My premature dreams hit a snag about a week into our stay when I picked up an undercurrent of tension between Mom and Aunt Leigh. I wished I was wrong for once, and I hated being wrong. They were sharing the same space cordially at first, and even though I'd witnessed no arguments, the atmosphere reminded me of the heaviness between Mom and Robert before he left. Trying to ignore the possibility of what this meant for me, I spent my days playing with my brother and my six-year-old cousin. I cycled through child-like abandon, giggling with delight while playing Tarzan by swinging from rope-like vines in the woods, and feeling agitated and alone because I was too old for those games. I'd gone through too much in the past few months to consider myself a child any longer, though part of me wished to savor the carefree innocence of play a little longer.

By the end of the second week, the tension between the sisters reached its climax. It filled and strained the dark-paneled walls of the trailer, with neither one talking or making eye contact when in the same room with each other. It was a Saturday when we loaded our few possessions into the car, once more homeless. I didn't fault my aunt because I knew even then some people shouldn't cohabitate. Aunt Leigh pulled me close, hugged me, and whispered she loved me as she held me. Mom refused to look in her direction; instead, she buckled Jacob into his car seat and adjusted her sunglasses for the umpteenth time. Mom never verbalized her unfathomable hurt. She clutched it to her chest like the emotional pain wasn't real if the words remained unspoken. That summer, when Mom's feelings were trampled by the people she needed the most, she hid her hurt behind thin-lipped smirks and razor-sharp retorts.

"Come on, Sandra. We need to go if we're going to find a place to live."

I pulled away from my aunt's arms, feeling like a traitor because part of me wanted to stay. Getting in the car meant my dream of living a life in my hometown was over. Our life reminded me of a pinball bouncing off the bumpers before racing toward a black hole.

I opened the passenger door and slid along the seat, the white, sun-cracked vinyl searing and pinching the back of my thighs as I buckled in. I avoided Mom's stare and focused my blurry gaze on unfulfilled expectations. This time I didn't have to ask her where we were going. We took off in the only other direction we could, toward a town and a man unprepared for the imminent onslaught of an angry mother and jilted wife.

# I Want a New Life

We left Aunt Leigh's house and drove the hour and a half to my step-dad's hometown, once again following road signs to the unknown. Robert told Mom a few days prior he'd help financially if we moved closer to his family. I guessed Mom knew the end was coming for our stay with Leigh and her family, but I think she held out hope the sister bond would prevail. As it turned out, blood relationships don't always withstand life's traumas, and it would be thirty plus years before I saw my favorite aunt once more.

Mom had a way of cutting people out of her life when she felt wronged or slighted, which was much easier in a world before the internet or cell phones. The woman could hold a grudge, and not surprisingly, I picked up on her habits. She used to say it was my astrological sign of being a Cancer or my inherited stubbornness that combined to make me too sensitive with the memory of an elephant who wouldn't let anything go, however slight or large.

But I'd argue my penchant for stubbornness and holding grudges against people who slighted me was due to being Ann's daughter. The sensitive part was all me though, hard shell and soft interior, my outer shell being toughened by each experience we had. Most recently, leaving Aunt Leigh's house had left my shell cracked. The anger and hurt filled the fissure, leaving a bumpy ridge like calcium surging and pooling around the break in a bone, the body rallying to fortify the spot.

While I questioned and second-guessed Mom's decisions during those years, I stood by her side because I became the constant she needed when all other support was lost. The day we made the journey to Robert's hometown, I sat shotgun as the pine trees flashed by. The Carolina blue sky, colorful wildflowers, and canopies of trees mocked my reality, which seemed more like the furious tail of a tornado whipping random objects into its spinning vortex than a bright and happy summer day. I squinted and pushed my forehead against the passenger window. My vision blurred, mirroring the uncertainty in my life—no rhyme or reason, no clear plan on what felt like another journey toward self-destruction.

When we got to town, the hotel Robert set us up at occupied a section on Wadesboro's downtrodden Main Street that had long since been abandoned. We parked in a back lot adjacent to the hotel that shared space with a junk shop that proudly displayed second-hand toys and garish, flowery dresses only a grandma on a budget would buy. The hotel was a two-story brick monstrosity taking up about half a block. I carried Jacob, his head tucked in the space between my neck and collarbone, while Mom walked a few feet ahead along the mold-tinged sidewalk.

Upon entering, the twelve-foot tin-paneled ceiling and marble floors immediately caught my attention, though they belied the subtle seediness that permeated the atmosphere. An array of middle-aged men loitered in the lobby chairs while another leaned against the banister of the stairs leading to the second floor. A man with a bulbous nose and bespectacled eyes on the steps leered at us as we approached the desk. I held Jacob tighter and stepped toward Mom until our hips touched. She shifted and met my gaze. I silently communicated my discomfort, and she wrapped a protective arm around my shoulder. The clerk gestured to a large sign behind the counter displaying hourly, daily, or weekly rates. Mom started with a week. I swallowed my bitterness over selling my beloved bicycle so we could stay in this dump. She'd given me the option of my bike or my radio cassette player, my only forms of freedom left in this circumstance. I let the bike go knowing if she took my music, I might lose my mind.

The clerk put us in a room on the second floor, and when Mom opened the door, I was outraged by how we'd been ripped off. The room looked more like a large closet, barely big enough to fit a full-sized bed, small bathroom, and a squat three-drawer dresser with a television perched on a cigarette-burned top. I squeezed around the end of the bed to reach the compact mini-refrigerator that bumped against the dresser every time the door opened. There were bars on the windows like the establishment was afraid occupants would jump if given the chance, or worse, to keep predators from entering. I peered out the window and saw the beer can–littered tops of the shorter buildings along the block. How sad was this town that locals had nothing better to do than drink beer on top of these shitty buildings? Then again if I had to live here longer than our allotted week, I might be inclined to join them.

After changing Jacob's diaper, we ventured out by walking to the small grocery store a few blocks away. The gas-guzzling Caddie was running on fumes when we parked her, too depleted to be of much good. And low fuel wasn't our only concern. There were oil spots pooling when we parked anywhere for too long, making me question how long the old girl would keep running. I couldn't think about the car breaking down on top of everything else or the spiral of damning possibilities would overwhelm me. We had enough money left for my mom to buy a loaf of bread, a plastic container of chicken salad with more mayonnaise and celery than chicken, some off-brand peanut butter, and a carton of cigarettes. I had started to hate those cigarettes as much as our predicament.

Back in the no-tell hotel, Jacob and I shared half of a chicken salad sandwich that first night. Mom sat on the bed absently watching *Wheel of Fortune* and smoking cigarettes for dinner. I could've devoured two whole sandwiches by myself, but Mom said we had to make the food last a week. I shot a gaze toward the loaf of bread and wondered how three people could possibly survive a week on those three items. Exhaustion saved me from the gnawing and growling in my stomach as I hugged the time-warped, cigarette-yellowed wall to avoid Jacob's foot in the small of my back.

The next morning, I found Mom chain-smoking from her position on the bed, and I questioned her about our next move. She eyed me through a blue-gray cloud, then dropped her gaze and studied her fingers, fidgeting with the sheets before admitting, "I don't know."

I knew she was as weary of answering the question as I was asking it.

"I'm supposed to start high school soon."

"Cut me some slack," she huffed. "I'm working on it."

What she meant was that she was waiting for Robert to drop off some money, which he did later that day. I was shocked he actually kept his word. Mom met him downstairs in the lobby, leaving us in the room. Maybe she was using us as bargaining chips, refusing to let him see us to punish him. Perhaps she didn't want us to bear witness to her shame. Whatever the case, we were able to fill the gas tank, buy a few more groceries, and head to the laundromat to wash a load of clothes since Mom had thrown our dirty ones in with our few sets of clean ones when we left Aunt Leigh's house.

Lots of people take for granted having a washer and dryer at home. If you've never been poor enough to have to do your laundry in a money-sucking laundromat, consider yourself blessed. Sunday morning was the best time to hit the laundromat—fewer people and more machines available. There were these metal rolling carts to transport clothes from the washer to dryer and then from the dryer to the folding tables. Jacob would jump on the side of one of those carts and point for me to push him, squealing with laughter as I raced around the laundromat making race car sounds. The only blank wall in the laundromat was reserved for a machine with single use boxes of detergent sold for a dollar. Hard plastic chairs lined the area in front of large glass windows. A dollar bought the use of a washing machine and a quarter bought ten minutes in a dryer.

Mom was adamant that we presented ourselves in a certain manner, ensuring we didn't look like we were scraping by with just a few dollars to our name. Despite our dangerously low finances, she consistently managed to find the money to keep our clothes clean. Many Sunday mornings were dedicated to feeding quarters into laundry machines to maintain a polished appearance. She never met a stranger she didn't like at these places. Two of the most important women in my story walked into our lives at a laundromat.

Joy was a woman Mom met in a laundromat that Sunday. One minute, I was pushing Jacob around the laundromat, and the next, Mom was talking with a short, plump woman with kind brown eyes and big eighties hair teased and falling to her shoulders. I have no clue how Mom had a way of striking up conversations with random strangers, but it was a knack. Joy had two kids, an eight-year-old girl and a twelve-year-old son, who relied on her skills as a single mother. As soon as she found out where we were staying, she offered us her home despite her own meager income as a factory worker. We learned from Joy that the old hotel was only for drug addicts, perverts, and prostitutes. My suspicions confirmed, I fueled my resentment toward Robert for setting us up there. I wondered if he even cared about the safety of his family. In hindsight, I realize he only truly cared about meeting his own needs.

Joy and Mom became fast friends, bonding over deadbeat husbands, single motherhood, and card games. Joy converted her dining room into an extra bedroom for us. I didn't ask why she had two twin beds in her dining room, but I was content to sleep in my own bed instead of sharing with Mom and Jacob. Within a week, Mom enrolled me in the county high school. It was certainly not the one I envisioned a few short months prior, but rather a sprawling set of buildings in the middle of a former, and possibly current, cow pasture. The campus of the high school reminded me of the dairy fields outside the run-down motel we'd stayed in when we returned from New Mexico several years ago.

Joy helped Mom land a job at the factory where she worked and coordinated childcare for Jacob. Joy even encouraged Mom to pay a visit to the local child support division of Social Services to force Robert to pay child support for his son. I held a squirming Jacob in my lap as we sat in front of a gray-haired woman with a kind smile who asked questions and wrote answers on a stack of papers. The Social Services worker pointed to me and asked, "Is this his child too?"

"No, she's mine."

Three words said so forcefully and defiantly in response to the innocent question. Mom didn't want Robert to claim any stake in me, but I wasn't sure I wanted to be claimed by anyone. I was mine. At one point in my life, I would've beamed with joy at her words, but something had changed since Robert walked out and with everything that had happened to this point, I bristled at her claim. We left the squat government building with the knowledge that Robert would be told to pay child support for Jacob or else the state would take him to court. Mom smiled as she drove us back to Joy's house as though she was happy to force Robert to do something he should've been willing to do for months without the state getting involved.

Joy's house offered safety the hotel never could, though it was drafty and unclean, at least to my standards. I made an effort to ignore it and refrained from judging her too harshly, despite the fact that she used her back porch to accumulate stacks of black trash bags as high as my waist instead of utilizing garbage cans or going to the dump. The bags seemed to occupy the entire space, and every time I entered the kitchen, I couldn't help but wonder how the trash situation had spiraled out of control. Thankfully as autumn approached, the cooler morning temperatures masked the odor of rotting garbage. The trash bags remained on the porch during the three months we stayed with her. I guess country living didn't involve a trash truck service.

My first few months of high school were a blur, and though I was physically present, my mind struggled to engage with what I was learning. I picked classes so meticulously when I thought I was going to high school with my friends in Monroe, but here, the office stuffed me into classrooms wherever space was available. Home economics was not my idea of a good time. *Fuck sewing* was my mantra for many years after high school. I refused to mend a hole in anything, choosing instead to throw it away and buy a brand new item of clothing. The county high school was simply a placeholder school until we inevitably moved once more. I didn't bother to learn classmates' names or put any effort into participating in the classes. I simply sat in the classroom desks like a placeholder student.

I was saved from riding a bus because Joy's nephew, Mike, gave me a ride to school most days, a wad of dip the size of a peach pit stuffed into his lip. Mike was a junior in high school and already on his way to fulfilling the country hick persona I found disgusting. A grimy Mountain Dew bottle used to collect Mike's spit rolled back and forth between us on the truck's bench seat. The half-full, tobacco-stained spit bottle rolled against my hip as the boy raced around curves, but I dealt with it. I was just glad to avoid riding the bus every day, even if it meant trying to keep my breakfast down on the nauseating ride.

We settled into a routine of sorts in the fall of 1984. Joy and Mom took turns cooking dinner during the week. I babysat the younger children on Saturday nights when they'd go to the local bar to relax after a long week. Mom hadn't drunk any alcohol since she ditched the last of the Michelob beers in Monroe. She chose instead to people-watch and listen to music on the night out. We kept our distance from Robert and focused on trying to find a new normal, whatever that was. I wondered what our next move would be while my mom seemed content in the moment. I was unsure if she thought we could just keep doing the same old shit, but my patience in that limbo was wearing thin. I felt like I was treading water in a murky, rain-swollen river.

Soon Halloween rolled around, and I was invited to my first party in the basement of one of the neighbor's houses. Boys and girls packed the musty space; some played pool while others talked and listened to music. Mike escorted me to the space and then made off in the direction of a group of girls huddled around a stereo system in the corner. I held up the cinderblock wall and scanned the room, true to my introverted nature. A boy I recognized from school struck up a conversation. He was decent looking with gentle brown eyes, a clear complexion and dark hair, though it was hard to tell if it was black or brown in the lighting. I didn't know his name—he didn't offer, and I didn't ask. He was a few inches taller than me and checked all my boxes for a boy I'd like. My gut told me he was kind, though I had no proof.

We talked about classes—*yuck*, plans for Halloween—*none*, and our favorite musical artists like Huey Lewis and the News, Corey Hart, and Prince. After noticing almost everyone else in the basement was lip-locked, he asked to kiss me. I'd been kissed by a boy twice in my life so far. Once, I was in daycare when a blond-haired boy on the mat beside me planted a corn breath kiss on my unsuspecting mouth during nap time. Mom freaked out when I told her, pulling me from the daycare the next day. The second time was at an eighth-grade dance with a boy who held my hand in the halls and wanted to be my boyfriend. He nervously pressed cracked, dry lips to mine, and I smiled in response like I thought I was supposed to.

On that night in a neighbor kid's basement, I looked around and noticed the only other boy in the room resembled a pimply-faced child. For whatever reason I didn't understand at the time, I nodded my consent, curious and hungry for the attention. As our lips touched, his tongue pushed my lips apart, filling my mouth like a water-logged kitchen sponge. At first, I didn't move my tongue. My senses were shocked by having a stranger's tongue inside my mouth that only an hour earlier had been filled with a cheeseburger.

I shut my eyes, avoiding the proximity of his face to mine. After a few seconds, I opened them to find his eyes tightly closed. I darted my tongue in and around his, engaging in a dance of parries. He steadied himself against the basement wall, placing his arm on the top of my shoulder. My heart raced, not fueled by lust or desire, but simply because in that moment, I recognized my newfound power over the opposite sex.

He kept space between our bodies. He never tried to touch me anywhere else, though I sensed if I had given permission, he might have taken it farther. The kiss went on for an entire song before he disengaged his tongue from my mouth and went back to playing a game of pool. I snagged a Coca-Cola from the cooler to wash away the garlicky pizza taste he'd left behind. I hung around for a few more songs, watching from the basement corner, physically present but as detached as a stringless helium balloon.

My first real kiss, a French kiss, was with some guy whose name I couldn't or didn't care to remember and had no real significance. I crossed a milestone off the teen girl list that night, but on the walk back to Joy's house all I could think about was the sensation of power I gained in those moments. After feeling so powerless for so long, I flexed my female strength in the light of the moon. I wondered if this was what Mom felt like when she caught men eyeing her wolfishly and would purposefully add an extra pop to the sway of her hips. Was she filling her female prowess tank? It all felt foreign to me, and not something I felt comfortable exploring just yet. I was still a fourteen-year-old girl with a boyish frame and barely budding breasts. Yet I caught myself grinning at the knowledge that I could exert my power if I desired.

The next evening, I stood outside after doing dishes, enjoying some fresh air and space from my baby brother's constant demands to play with him, when a car crept down the dirt road and approached Joy's house. I could only identify human shapes in the windows, made more difficult by the darkening sky, but I could feel mysterious eyes clearly watching me. I went inside and told my mom a strange car had driven by very slowly, too slowly. She accused me of having an overactive imagination from reading all those mysteries and thrillers I still consumed. Mom dismissed it as someone who was lost, but the house was off the beaten path, making her flippant logic improbable. Less than five houses lined the dirt road we lived down, and I didn't recognize the car as any of our neighbors'. Plus, the tingly sensation along the nape of my neck was enough to tell me something wasn't right.

Less than fifteen minutes later, we were sitting in the living room watching the news when three to four ear-piercing pops erupted from the front of the house. I'd never heard gunshots before, except in Western movies. I thought it sounded like fireworks, like a crack of lightning tearing through the air. Mom hissed for me to take Jacob to the back of the house. I scooped him up and rushed to the kitchen, stopping short of the door that led to the garbage porch. I pressed him into the space next to the refrigerator and told him to stay put. Racing through our makeshift bedroom, I saw Mom peeking through the curtains hanging over the front door. I don't know what I thought I could do in that moment; I just knew I needed to protect Mom.

Time slowed, the wall clock in Joy's dining room the only sound as it ticked off seconds that rolled into minutes. Mom finally stepped away from the front door and made a beeline for the kitchen. She jerked the phone receiver from the wall, punched in some numbers, and paced in a circle waiting for an answer on the other end of the line.

"You tell Robert his kids were here just now. He shot a gun near us." Her lips pursed in a thin line, eyes narrowed. "No, none of the shots hit the house. He's crazy for shooting in the air. You tell him he better stay away from us."

"Are you okay?" I asked after she slammed the receiver down.

"Yeah. Just pissed. What was he thinking?"

I shrugged. I had no idea what the man was thinking. Most days, I vacillated between sadness, anger, and hatred toward him for putting us in this situation. When he first left, I wanted him to return more than anything I ever wished for before. I had no real knowledge of the depths of his depravity, and compared to the man who'd come before him, he was a prize in my eyes in those early days. But I was starting to understand the maneuverings of the adult world. Any man who tried to scare his wife with gunfire because she sought child support through the legal system was clearly unhinged.

"Who'd you call?" I asked my mom, still a little shaky from the adrenaline. She'd called Ted.

If anyone could set him straight, Robert's brother would. Ted was the oldest of three boys and the only one not in trouble with the law or controlled by drugs. He owned a construction business and hired his brother when Robert found himself unemployed yet again. He had a gruff exterior and rarely smiled, but he showed love for his children and went to church every Sunday. Maybe he would be able to talk some sense into my degenerate step-dad.

That night, I lay awake in the quiet house thinking about our situation. I had nearly tricked my body into falling asleep when something rustled next to my head. My thoughts immediately jumped to a ghost because paranormal activity was preferable to the reality my mind desperately wanted to ignore. I cautiously stretched my arm out and patted the bed, but the bed was empty. The scratching noise happened again by my left ear. That's when I realized it was something in the wall, not a ghost, not my imagination, but most likely a small rodent.

A few nights prior, I'd turned on the back porch light and spotted three or four well-fed rats with rope-like tails climbing through the trash bags. The rats were likely the cause of the noise in the wall. The weather was nearing freezing at night, and they were seeking shelter. I almost pitied their plight if I didn't hate rats so much. The only heat source was the wood-burning stove in the living room, and I was sure the rats were simply nesting in the walls to stay warm. This fact did not help me sleep at night as I envisioned them clawing a hole through the wall and feasting on my eyelids as I slept. I scooted away from the wall and hugged the edge of the bed. *We just survived a drive-by shooting*, I thought. *I'll be damned if I let some rats get the better of me now.* To block out the anxiety spiking my heart rate,

I keyed in on the conversation happening in the kitchen in hushed whispers and occasional outbursts of profanity.

"Can you believe his stupidity?" my mom spat out the words. I could just see the fury on her face as she brought her lit cigarette to her lips again and again.

"They do have a reputation for being crazy," Joy replied.

"He's trying to scare me off from getting that damn child support check."

"Ann, he can't do that around my kids. What if they'd been outside playing?"

"I know. I'm sorry." Mom hung her head, waiting for the ax to fall yet again.

"I hate to do this, but you're going to have to find somewhere else to live."

"I understand," my mother exhaled loudly. "Would you give me a couple of weeks at least?"

"Yes. You can stay until after Thanksgiving."

"I'll try to find something by then."

Everyone involved knew that living in Joy's house was a temporary arrangement. Mom made minimum wage at the factory, not enough for decent housing, food, and cigarettes. She worked for $3 an hour, hunched over a sewing machine that left her rolling her shoulders and curling and uncurling her fingers from the time she got off work until she went to bed each night. It was barely enough to cover food costs and daycare for my brother. I wondered how we would ever have enough money to get out of the hole that kept caving in on us. What was worse, she was too proud to ask for any real help. The state would make Robert pay to support his son, but my mom hadn't applied for welfare and wouldn't do so for another year until her pride took a back seat to dire necessity. Robert's actions were incomprehensible and had cost us the only place we had left to go. We had a few weeks to save money and find other housing. Instead of my usual anger, I let numbness wash over me as I drifted off to sleep. I was too tired to muster up any righteous rage. I dreamt that night of rats in my bed, rats in my head gnawing great holes in the gray matter of my brain. One of the rats wore Robert's face and plagued me long after I woke the next morning.

Joy's nephew Mike, who lived up the road and drove me to and from school, often hung around. I sensed he liked me though he wasn't my type, and his presence repulsed me. I was unsure what kind of guy I wanted for a boyfriend, but it sure wasn't a to-bacco-spitting, shaggy-haired buffoon who spoke with abbreviated country grammar, almost as if he didn't have the energy to commu-nicate in complete sentences. However, he had a motorcycle, and that intrigued me. I wondered if riding a motorcycle was like riding my bicycle in South Carolina. I missed my ten-speed bike we had to pawn for money. I watched him from Joy's front porch swing as he raced down the road on the thing. Every time he went by, I longed to be on the back of the motorcycle, not to be close to him, but to experience the air whipping through my hair like I was floating away from my life.

I waved the buffoon down and asked for a ride. The night I threw my leg over the seat and settled on the back of the motorcycle without a helmet, I wasn't concerned about crashing and dying or incurring permanent brain damage. Those concerns flitted in and out of my mind like a hummingbird moving from flower to flower. Mike instructed me to hold on tight, pointing to his waist. I loosely wrapped my arms around his emerging beer belly as he pulled on the gravel road, revved the throttle a few times, and then gunned it.

"Faster!" I yelled.

He nodded and accelerated until wind-spurned tears splattered my cheeks. We were going so fast that I suspected if I spread my arms, I would fly away like seagulls soaring and dipping in the ocean breezes. I initially wanted Robert to return home and for our life to return to normal. It was all I thought about for months. I wanted my old life back, yet on the back of the motorcycle, speeding through the dark night, I realized that would never happen. My family had reached a point of no return. My childhood had been far from normal, but those years in Monroe had been ideal in my opinion. I longed for something that may have been a fallacy anyway. Happy families were fictionalized on television because real-life families and relationships were messy and complicated.

The motorcycle ride fueled my dreams of striking out alone, away from all the drama, but I was too young, a mere child caught in the quicksand of adult decisions. I craved peace, solitude, and freedom, and for half an hour, I had it. I vowed I would be different. One day, I would change my life. Me, not relying on the kindness of others or some man. I opened the front door to Joy's house and caught sounds of a lively game of Uno being played by the adults and children. My reality was light-years from normal and my dreams, for now, were only fictitious longings.

# Love Is a Lie

"So, we're moving in with Ted and Marcia for a while."

I sighed as I watched my mom packing our meager belongings yet again. "Does this mean I have to change schools again?"

"Yes." My mother averted her eyes. She shoved jeans and her favorite Texas T-shirt with the longhorn symbol over the left breast into a bag.

I chewed on the corner of the only fingernail that remained intact on my right hand. Though I didn't like it, I had adjusted to my new reality of living with strangers and in strange places.

"Did he set it up?" Robert was a villain in my eyes, his name no longer worthy of being spoken out loud.

"Your dad did call his brother and ask. They're letting us stay in Adam's room until we have enough money saved to get our own place."

"Why doesn't he help more?" The question had been circulating in my brain for months. I didn't understand how Robert changed overnight from a loving dad and husband to a deadbeat loser who staged drive-by shootings and refused to support his family. Did he wake up one morning and decide he was no longer interested in being a husband, father, and employee? I'm sure my mother also wondered, although we never really discussed it. Mom was never one to talk about her feelings. The answers to my questions came through her tone and facial expressions. I had extensive conversations with her in my head on the things I wanted to say, and I now wonder if she did the same. Mother and daughter, more alike than I wanted to admit at that time.

Mom answered my question about Robert's lack of assistance with a shrug. "I wish I knew."

Mom dropped to the bed and lit a cigarette to replace the one she'd snubbed seconds ago. We wouldn't ever get a satisfying answer to my question. My step-dad failed to pay child support for Jacob for years, until Jacob was an adult himself.

We were on the move yet again with little to sustain our family of three. The new school transition was easier this time because I was related by marriage to two kids who attended the local high school. Robert's niece and nephew were students there. I occasionally glimpsed them walking down the hall and smiled in greeting. My greeting was sometimes lost in the crowd of students changing classes, but at least I wasn't as out of place here. The cowboy hats, the ball caps advertising dip, and the exaggerated twangs of the kids from the county high school were replaced by students who wore jeans, khakis, alligator emblem polo shirts, and tennis shoes rather than pointy-toed boots. I suppose those years of my mother insisting

I dress in khakis and collared shirts prepared me for this level of familiarity. It always amazed me how student bodies at schools only miles apart behaved so differently.

Life at Ted and Marcia's house was a breath of fresh air. Dinner was always home-cooked, complete with meat, two sides, and a piece of bread, and served promptly at six o'clock. There were prayers before dinner, and everyone was asked about their days. The normalcy made my heart sing. It reminded me of how our family used to be before Robert left. I tended to stay silent and let the conversation swirl around me as I watched the family members' shared affection. I wanted my old dad, not the new one I no longer recognized. I wanted our former home and the old school I loved before my life imploded. I wanted it to be us laughing at the table and talking about our days, just like we did before he left. Even though we were staying with his family, he still wouldn't come to visit us.

The more I wanted to return to the way things were, the more I realized I couldn't manifest muddied dreams. My life was similar to riding the Scrambler, the classic fair ride, my favorite ride of all. The ride would start slow and then steadily pick up speed until my body would dig into the metal and my knuckles turned white. Being out of control, feeling the sense of flying through air was once fun, but not that year or the ones that followed.

After these nightly dinners, I helped Marcia clean the table and wash the dishes. I settled into the routine of helping her clean the kitchen while Mom took Jacob outside to play and have an after-dinner smoke. At the end of the clean-up, my aunt would pull me in for a warm hug and a thank-you. I lived for those hugs because they reminded me of ones I once got from Great-grandma Beulah.

One night in bed, before drifting off to sleep, Mom asked, "How do you always fit in so well?"

I was uncertain how to answer her question, which hung heavy in the darkness while I searched for the correct answer. I didn't fit in at school; I simply existed. I blended into the hallways' edges and back rows of the classrooms. I set the table and washed dishes at Ted and Marcia's house because I wanted to help. I was motivated to assist because Marcia always hugged me after cleaning up. I relished the love my mom appeared unable or unwilling to give lately. My mother rarely hugged me after Robert left. Looking back, I understand she struggled to love herself and had little leftover affection for me.

"I don't know," I answered. I had no clue because I was simply following what felt natural to me. I lived by instincts.

The silence stretched, and the apology nearly slipped off my tongue. I gritted my teeth until they ached. Eventually, Mom shifted and turned away from me in the bed. I somehow hurt her feelings while trying to spare them. I guess we had different sets of people skills. She chatted with strangers while I struggled. I blended into any situation by jumping into the mix and helping. I would ask Marcia what I could do to help. Mom asked if she *needed* help. I learned no one wants to appear needy but instead prefers to direct the offered support as they see fit.

Our lives settled into a more comfortable routine while we were living with Robert's family. He started to visit us, and Mom smiled again. Living in a secure home had a way of making my tight shoulder muscles relax. They sat on the front porch swing and talked while Jacob played near their feet. They went for talks in the car, and she returned hours later. I allowed a kernel of hope to take hold. I thought a reconciliation might be possible, but even if it wasn't, maybe I could actually finish high school in this town. There was a chance to have a symbiotic relationship with Robert, one where we all got what we wanted. After a few weeks of peace, Mom returned late one night to the room.

She emitted so much emotion the room grew warmer. Anytime she was that angry, without a doubt, Robert had probably fucked up her expectations, most likely some foolhardy daydreams of a reconciliation. I imagined the situation wasn't easy for her because everyone in the household expected she and Robert would get back together, me included. I had overheard Marcia tell Ted that very thing, the happiness leaking from every word. The problem was, Robert had changed his mind about being a family man. He tried it on for a while, but when it no longer fit, he cast us aside without a second thought.

Robert and his two brothers had some notoriety in their hometown. There was talk of their corrupt behaviors, including drinking, drugs, side women, and a chicken fighting ring. I saw the chicken cages a few times but never the actual fighting. Anytime my mom wrote her last name or mentioned she was Robert's wife, the bank clerk, store clerk, or new best friend from the laundromat would respond with awe, disgust, or a hint of jealousy. When my mom visited the caseworker for the child support issues, the woman always said, "Those Dopp Boys." I sensed Robert liked the bad boy persona, the whole big-fish-small-pond scenario. I may have imagined the false security of the last name. Still, we were never bothered, not even at the questionable hotel where we stayed when we first arrived in Wadesboro.

The Dopp Boys expected their wives to follow the unspoken rule to look the other way. These men weren't expected to walk the straight line of a committed marriage or law-abiding ways. But my mother wasn't that type of wife. Soon the drives with Robert ceased, and she started going on dates with a nice man from work who picked her up in his sensible gray four-door Honda Accord. He wore crisp button-down shirts and sharply creased jeans, a pointed contrast to Robert. I never understood the creased jeans part. Taking an iron to denim is a travesty, but Mom appeared to like his company. She briefly introduced him as Tom with no last name. I took this as another indication our life might be moving forward.

Tom invited my mom to a New Year's Eve dinner at his parents' house. I bathed Jacob and went to bed early. I had used the alone time that evening, before the dawn of the new year, thinking about the changes we endured and wishing for a better year ahead of us. When we were still an intact family, we used to sit around and watch the New Year's countdown with Dick Clark. We talked about what we wanted for the new year: for me, it was a new bike, more books, and to make straight A's because I loved the praise I received from Mom, but later on because I simply enjoyed being the best. I also asked for braces to fix my teeth. Mom had said something cheesy about having everything she wanted, and Robert had nodded his head and smiled as he agreed with her and pulled us in for a hug.

We said those things on December 31, just one short year before, and then toasted sparkling grape juice as the ball dropped. I never imagined where we'd end up, staring down the barrel of 1985 with little hope for change.

Mom returned early that evening, hours before the ball dropped at midnight. She sported flushed cheeks and nervous energy, signs I'd come to recognize as drinking way too many cups of coffee.

"What happened?" I asked, pointing to the clock.

"I passed out," she answered a little breathlessly.

"You what?"

"Passed out. Toppled right out of the chair while eating with Tom's family."

I was shocked and didn't know what to say. Nothing like this had ever happened before. "Well, crap."

"Language."

I rolled my eyes under the cover of darkness. *I didn't say shit.* Although I said it many times in my mind, along with other choice words. She slid under the covers and hugged a sleeping Jacob.

After a few moments of silence, she spoke. "I think I might be pregnant."

I braced as the tectonic plate of my messy but improving life shifted.

"Tom's?" I silently wished for it to be this uptight but gainfully employed man's baby.

Her long, drawn-out pause told me everything I needed to know. "No. It's Robert's."

*Well, fuck.*

My mom gave birth to me when she was nineteen years old. It was a complicated pregnancy. Afterward, the doctors told her that she might never have children again. Almost thirteen years later, my brother Jacob was born. And, by the time I turned fifteen, I would have another sibling.

*What now?* I squashed the question that popped into my head, the one I asked too many times in the past six months that felt more like six years. The ball drop at Times Square hadn't even ushered in the new year yet, and already it was shaping up to be another shitshow.

I wondered how she could bring another child into our struggling family. I choked back the anger and frustration until my throat burned. I was blindsided. I wasn't allowed to date boys until I was sixteen, but she went about life without considering the consequences of her actions. I prayed that night, not to a god, because I had a hard time believing in one of those, but praying for strength and guidance from my great-grandma Beulah. In the wake of Mom's poor decision-making, I needed her more than ever.

# Straight Ahead

O n the second day of school at the third high school I'd attended in five months, I sat on the edge of the hard yellow plastic cafeteria chair, trying not to bleed on the seat. I looked around and studied the fifteen other students pretending to read textbooks. I felt the unwelcome and unexpected menstrual gush right after the bell rang. Scoffing at my schedule, which indicated the cafeteria moonlighted as a classroom in our underfunded school, I threw my half-eaten peanut butter and jelly sandwich in the trash and moved three tables down to join my class for study hall. Apparently, study hall seemed a viable option when the school didn't know what to do with a new student and hadn't received academic records yet. As an adult, I've tried to remember the school's name or even the town in South Carolina where we'd landed that time, but it's a blank. Despite my efforts, I'm only left with the memory of my anger and disappointment.

After burdening me with her heavy secret, Mom had loaded us into the car, and we struck out for some other South Carolina border town. The move seemed furtive and shameful, like we were making off into the night like thieves. I tried to push my anger aside in the car as I reminded myself how much I loved my mom and brother. It's a wonder to me, the human ability to hold both love and boiling anger in our hearts at the same time.

Mom's pregnancy betrayed our alliance. We struggled enough to take care of one child between the two of us, like I was an adult in this situation, though I was still six months shy of fifteen. Because I was treated like an adult with grown-up responsibilities, I allowed my supposed adult mind the freedom to have opinions and hold grudges when the alleged adults fucked up. I never thought human life was a mistake, but to bring a new baby into our chaotic and unstable situation was problematic.

When I was much younger, Robert watched boxing matches on television. I would plop down beside him on the couch, studying the two men as they danced around the ring, feigning and dipping in a dance of aggression and strategy. Eventually, one fighter wore the other down with body shots or completely took the other by surprise with a left uppercut knock-out. I always rooted for the underdog. I yelled and sent telepathy through the screen, encouraging the man to get off the ropes, fight back, or get up off the mat before the ref counted to ten. Most of the time, my telepathy had no effect other than making me feel like I tried.

The television cameras would capture the dazed expression on the fighter's face, their eyes widened in shock at their predicament. All of their training had resulted in defeat. The difference between the winners and the losers in those underdog matches was the fighter squaring his jaw, inhaling deeply enough for his ribs to be outlined, and coming off the ropes swinging. Most of the time, that fighter would win the match, or at least not find themselves unconscious on the mat, while the loser would close his eyes and drop his head before taking a devastating body shot. The match's victor didn't always win by the scorecard, but damn, that fighter was a winner in my mind. I secured my wins by always continuing to fight.

That day in the cafeteria surrounded by strangers, the thought of having to stand up out of that chair had me against the ropes, like the fighters on television. I squished my butt cheeks together to staunch my flow and silently damned my body and my mother for betraying me. I couldn't sit there and continue to bleed freely. I scanned the room to see if anyone noticed the new girl sitting alone. Starting at a new school was still awkward and terrifying, but I'd grown comfortable with flying under the radar unseen. Fortunately for me in that moment, when my body declared a mutiny, I approached the study hall teacher unnoticed. I pulled my T-shirt down in the back just in case anyone looked up.

"Excuse me."

"Yes," the woman in charge of study hall answered.

"May I have a hall pass to go to the restroom?"

My mother would've been proud of my use of "may I" instead of "could I."

She eyed me briefly before she handed me a rectangular laminated piece of construction paper. I clutched it in my hand as I headed to check the damage, grateful she promptly returned her attention to her book.

The girls' bathroom at this backwoods school didn't have those metal boxes holding pads or tampons on the wall. A woman could find those dispensers in every bathroom across the United States, even in run-down gas stations in long-forgotten, backroad towns. But not at that school, where my future stellar reputation as a popular girl would forever be sullied by a bloody Carrie incident, because there weren't any goddamn feminine hygiene products in sight. I had to find a solution or die of shame. I grabbed paper towels, wet them, and headed into the stall to assess the damage.

As I vigorously scrubbed my soiled panties, with the blood-stained crotch area of my jeans, I analyzed my options. The car wasn't currently running, and my mom had no phone because we couldn't afford one. I couldn't believe my body was so traitorous, much like the adults in my life. There was another hour or so until the end of the school day. I would have to return to study hall and eventually leave my seat to ride the bus home. I pulled and tugged on the roll of one-ply toilet paper until it resembled a thick, make-shift cast on my hand. I slipped a thumb under the paper cast, dislodged it from my hand, and stuffed it into my panties. I pulled up my jeans, did a couple of squats, and wiggled until my make-shift pad felt more seated in my crotch.

I hoped the temporary fix would suffice because if anyone noticed, I'd probably keel over from embarrassment and beg my mom to never make me return to school. I handed the pass back to the teacher and resumed my seat. I sat on the chair's front edge and leaned back, so my spine slumped in the middle, and I didn't create any additional mess on the seat. I twirled a pencil between my fingers and pretended to do algebra equations while in fact I was hyper-focused on how I was going to get on the bus without anyone noticing my bloody pants. Most of my high school career was spent figuring out ways to remain invisible.

By the time school was over, I'd successfully made it home to yet another cramped trailer without bloodying any more seats. I slammed the door once but felt like reopening it just to bash it again and again. My anger boiled as I clenched my teeth to prevent hateful words from spewing. It was all Mom's fault for putting us in this position. If she hadn't done more than just talk to him, she wouldn't be pregnant. If she'd just continued working, we would still be in Wadesboro and not back in yet another shithole South Carolina town. Her whole life, Mom mistook flight for a solution. She chose to leave without telling him she was pregnant with his baby. I blamed my mother for everything that happened to us—Robert leaving, my slew of new schools, our financial struggles, and now another baby on the way. Somehow, the early arrival of my period was her fault as well.

"How was your day?" Mom asked from the kitchen, where she sat with her afternoon coffee and a cigarette.

"Not great. I hate this school, and I hate this town."

"And me?"

I paused too long before answering. "No."

She nodded slowly and eyed me as she saw through my lie. "Why are you so angry with me?"

I shrugged, not trusting my voice.

"One day, you'll stop hating me."

*Doubtful.*

I looked around the small two-bedroom trailer taking in the plaid couch, the green shag carpet reminiscent of Jacob's poopy diapers, and the wood-paneled walls. I wondered if this was what my life would continue to look like. At least this trailer wasn't in a trailer park, but we were in the middle of someone's backyard like a tin can afterthought.

"I'm going to my room to do homework."

"Okay. I'll start dinner in about an hour." She returned to reading her romance novel with the long-haired, shirtless guy holding a buxom woman on the cover.

I preferred reading mysteries. I tried reading some of Mom's romance novels a few times when I was really bored and had depleted my books. I quickly grew tired of the damsel in distress always needing to be saved by a man; same storyline, interchangeable names. Once I discovered Mary Higgins Clark, Stephen King, and Dean Koontz, I never picked up another of my mom's romance novels. I shook my head as Mom's eyes devoured the words on the pages. I wondered if she truly believed some intelligent, rich, handsome man would swoop in one day and pluck us from this shitty situation. I highly doubted a man was ever the answer in life.

Jacob trotted after me and tried to follow me into my room. I put my hand on his chest and lightly pushed him back across the threshold. I shut the door, taking care not to slam it, and locked the brass-colored doorknob. I changed clothes, rolled the dirty jeans and panties into a ball, and stuffed them into the pile of dirty clothes on the closet floor. I lay on my bed, which was part of the pre-furnished trailer package price. I never thought about it at the time, but now, the number of used mattresses I slept on all those years makes me shudder. God knows what the previous owners had done on those mattresses. I know for a fact I slept on several cesspools of sweat, tears, piss, and sex fluids because those were the types of things adults did on mattresses. Simply, yuck.

I turned on my radio/cassette player and recorder that I received from Mom and Robert on Christmas of '83. It was my prized possession for the past two years and would remain my coping mechanism until I left home. I tuned in as "Careless Whisper" floated from the speakers. Mom was right; a part of me did hate her. I had initially hated Robert for leaving us stranded, but the feelings shifted to the immediately available one. My anger wasn't always focused on the appropriate target, and a lot of times, when Mom angered me, I internalized it. I used it to scold myself relentlessly for making careless mistakes. I never wanted to repeat any mistake my mother made. I would never be my mother.

The time in South Carolina appeared to be a regrouping of sorts. Since my mother was never one to talk about her feelings, she spent her days trying to figure out solutions. While we bided time in this town, she actually applied for welfare assistance. She hated taking hand-outs, as did I. Using paper food stamp bills like bad Monopoly money was more embarrassing than my bloody pants. I spent many hours walking to and from the small country store to buy food when the car wasn't running, which frequently happened with that old

Caddie. I even found I enjoyed the solitude that walking provided. During those hours, I wasn't required to babysit my brother or sit and play cards across the table from the woman I didn't like much at the time. I took to frequent daydreaming during those trips to the store as I kicked my way through the loamy soil along the roadside.

I daydreamed about all sorts of things. In the early days of 1985, I wanted Robert to find us. Once he found us, he'd be overjoyed to have another child, and we'd become a family again. The only problem was he seemed happy to not have a family or pay child support for my brother. During one of my grocery store trips, I realized that the fantasy I was perpetrating was no better than Mom's romance novels; I never fantasized about Robert swooping in to save us again.

I began to daydream about what I could do to save my family. I recognized my mom wasn't the enemy I liked to envision. She was a woman who had lost her way in her fantasy of what she assumed was a good marriage. She was a human who'd made some mistakes and was betrayed by her heart and a man she thought was the love of her life. Robert became my new antagonist for not taking financial responsibility for his son and leaving us. Supposedly, an antagonist isn't all evil. Everyone has some redeeming qualities. For Robert, I couldn't think of a single one.

We left South Carolina sometime in April 1985, after we spent three months in a town and walking the halls of a school I couldn't name. The only sign I remembered was for a church. The Ebenezer AME Zion Church sat on a hill with its pristine white building and perfectly manicured dark-green lawn. I think it only spoke to me because it oozed peacefulness. It reminded me of the church building I frequented with my great-grandparents when I was much younger. Mom's pregnant belly grew to about the size of a partially deflated volleyball as she pointed the wheel of the DeVille toward Mooresville, North Carolina, the town where I spent the first nine years of my life. Mooresville held all of my good memories and a few bad ones too. Little did I know then that I would leave that rural town at eighteen once and for all without so much as a look back over my shoulder at the place that had raised me.

# Sunshine and Sweat

I swiped the sweat from my forehead with the sleeve of my T-shirt as I struggled to push the borrowed lawnmower through the grass as tall as my knees. I finished the last strip of tall grass, exhaustion and thirst taking a back seat to the pleasure I felt looking at the uniformly even lawn. When I arrived at the house a couple of hours prior, the yard had been in dire need of cutting. I knocked on the door, necessity overriding shyness. The widow agreed to pay me for cutting her yard, telling me her husband had passed away a few months prior, and she had no one else. I considered cutting her yard for free, but my family needed the ten dollars. The first few weeks back in Mooresville had been financially tight. Same story, different town. I took to walking the neighborhoods in Mooresville, looking for unkempt lawns and offering to mow them for a nominal fee. There was something relaxing about tidying up an overgrown yard.

The yards along this section of the area known as Mill Hill were slightly larger than the smaller lots along the interior streets.

My great-grandparents' old house was just around the block. My great-grandpa worked for Burlington Mills for thirty-plus years. As an employee perk, they'd sold homes to their employees and took their mortgage payments directly from their checks. When we returned to Mooresville this time, Mom cruised by their old house at least twice a week. We held our memories in a choke-hold, grief and regret growing like a bubble between us, crowding the car and pressing us into our respective car doors. I wondered if she was looking for answers to our present in the past. Maybe I was, too.

Whenever I saw that house, my heart would ache for my stern but loving great-grandma Beulah. When I was a child, there were toys scattered in the backyard—bikes, balls, a small kiddie pool and chairs for Great-grandma Beulah to sit and watch all the grandkids playing. She wasn't a woman who suffered fools. I guess that came with growing up in a large family during the early 1900s. She would allow me to sit on her kitchen table barefooted and eat handfuls of Boo Berry cereal straight from the box while she baked persimmon pies. I never saw her allow my cousins the same leeway. I know now I was treated differently because I didn't have a father, but regardless, I thrived on her attention.

That house held so many memories of a time when I was cared for. Now I was my own keeper and expected to do the caring when all I really wanted was for someone to hold me and tell me it was going to be okay. When I was about four, I busted my knee open on the sidewalk that ran in front of their house while chasing my cousins, who were around my age to a few years older than me. We'd grown up together at my great-grandparents' house while our moms worked. Mom carried me inside as I cried out in pain, my knee cap throbbing and blood running down the front of my shin. Mom rubbed my arm and placed warm lips against my sweat-drenched forehead. My great-grandma directed Mom to hold me still while she poured iodine on my cut. Quite the trio, we were—three generations of Hendron women fighting and scraping to carve out a little space in this world for ourselves.

If I had more energy and didn't have to push the mower four miles back across town to the relative stranger's house where we were living, I might've walked by their old house just to have the memories play out in my head like a classic movie. Instead, I knocked on the widow's front door. She handed me a crisp ten-dollar bill I almost hated to fold and shove into my sweat-laden jeans and a glass of iced lemonade.

"Have a seat, hon. Take as long as you need to cool down."

I stuffed the cash in my front pocket.

"Thank you, ma'am."

I dropped to the front steps because I didn't want to leave grass and sweat on her white porch swing. I was about half finished with the lemonade when I heard the music from an approaching vehicle blaring the notes of my current favorite song, "Walking on Sunshine." The song was the quintessential feel-good ditty. I always cranked it up and sang at the top of my lungs, though I was not a good singer. The music grew louder, and the car turned on the street in front of me. I immediately recognized my cousin, Tina, my Uncle Patrick's youngest daughter. I shrank back into the porch shadows and watched as she and her friends bobbed their heads to the beat. I didn't want her to see me even though it was unlikely she'd recognize me. I hadn't seen any of my cousins in over eight years or my Aunt Rosie in over five. I suppose I hung onto memories of the people I once thought loved me like Mom did to the small cardboard box she protected like a safe of money, but was instead full of black-and-white and color photographs of everyone from her parents and siblings, aunts, and uncles to grandparents, and all stages of my life from birth to around the time Jacob was born.

Sitting on the widow's porch that day, I longed to be a part of the fun they were having, so carefree and happy. Tina turned right at the stop sign. She was going to my great-grandparents' house. Aunt Leigh told us last year that when they died, their house was willed to my great-aunt Rosie since she was widowed and still had children living at home. Her siblings, my grandma Bobbie and their brother, Patrick, had their own homes at the time and saw it best to sell their stake in the house to their sister. I felt a thrill of elation when I saw Tina turn in the direction of the house. If Aunt Rosie still lived there and not a stranger, I had a chance to once again walk through the rooms.

I wasn't sure anyone in our extended family realized we were back in town, and I wasn't ready for any family interactions. I was a little surprised to discover I still held a grudge toward our family, my elephant memory reminding me they turned their backs on us when we needed their help the most. Though Aunt Rosie probably didn't know we'd been turned away by her sister, Grandma Bobbie, I still didn't trust the family to help even if we had asked. Strangers' kindness was more prevalent in my life.

I drained the glass and placed it by the front door. I pushed the mower I'd borrowed from Louise across the railroad tracks that divided the town. I pushed it past the teenager-filled pizza joint, past the Harris Teeter on the corner where my cousin David bagged groceries, and on toward Louise's house.

Louise was the latest Good Samaritan Mom had befriended at a laundromat. She took us into her home, letting us live in her front bedroom. I couldn't fathom Louise's depth of kindness that allowed her to open her home to a pregnant woman with two children. I helped Louise with chores and mowing her lawn while Mom took responsibility for cooking meals as partial payment for giving us a place to stay. I got the sense we helped Louise as much as she helped us. She lost her husband some years before, and her children lived out of state and didn't visit except for holidays. Their pictures stood on the table by the front door, and every time I passed them, I wondered why they didn't come to visit such a kind woman.

When Mom registered me at the fourth school of my ninth-grade year in early May, I was disappointed to learn that in Mooresville, ninth grade was still considered junior high. I was forced to spend my school days with seventh- and eighth-graders. Not only that but I was forced to take home economics class yet again. I was a pissed-off teenager with little motivation to make any effort in my classes anymore. I just wanted the ninth grade to be over. The pleasure I once took in learning had been entirely stripped away.

A few years ago, I found my old freshman year report card. I showed my husband and daughter the proof that I made a D in home economics class, which they falsely assumed was a lie because

I'd fooled them into thinking I was competent at everything I tried my hand at. We shared a laugh as I shared the memory of my teacher shaking her head and walking away because I couldn't get the hang of using a sewing machine, and even when I got the mechanical beast to operate, sewing a straight line was a challenge.

When I got to Louise's house after school one day in late May, Mom was gone from her usual spot on the living room sofa where she read books while Louise watched soap operas.

"Where's my mom?"

Louise sat in her recliner in the corner of the living room. She puffed on a cigarette while Jacob played on the floor with blocks.

"Don't you worry. I had to take your mom to the hospital."

"Why? What's wrong?" Blood pounded in my ears, and I dropped beside Jacob and waited for her response.

"She had some contractions. The doctor decided she should go to the emergency room in Winston-Salem."

My mom was only six months along. As angry as I'd been at her for bringing another child into our fucked-up family situation, I didn't want anything bad to happen to my unborn brother or sister. My stomach knotted.

"When can we see her?"

"She said she'd call when she gets into a room."

As it would happen, my sister was born three days later, barely topping the scale at three pounds. The medical staff tried to stop my mom's contractions, giving my sister more time to develop, gain weight, and improve her respiratory functioning. But that little girl had it in her mind to enter this world on her own terms and so that's what she did, damn near giving all of us heart attacks in the process. Mom named her Hannah, a name she'd already decided on if she and Robert ever had another child. I didn't get the significance, but I loved the name. My sister lived in a Neonatal Intensive Care Unit inside an incubator for nearly two months before being transferred to a hospital closer to home.

During that time, Mom tried to visit Hannah in the NICU most days, but Winston-Salem was an hour away. Since we were dependent on public assistance at that time, there was little money for gas. But my mom had gotten better at swallowing her pride, and she approached different social service organizations requesting gas money to make the drive. The times I was able to go with her, I'd hear the nurses call my sister a miracle baby. Being born so premature, she could've had any number of medical issues. My sister was a fighter, and a resilient one.

During one of those visits, one of the NICU nurses walked me through the sterilization process so that I could be in the room with my baby sister. We began by scrubbing my hands with a soapy lather. Then I stuck my arms through a gown she offered and donned a face mask. Lastly, I slipped paper booties over my grass-stained tennis shoes, the only ones I owned. My nerves and excitement overrode the humor I felt when I caught a glimpse of myself in the mirror. I looked like a frizzy-haired clown impersonating a doctor. My glances skidded off the other babies in the incubators, too afraid to study the various IV lines and monitors attached to their fragile frames for too long. The babies looked more alien than human.

The nurse stopped in front of an incubator with my sister's name written on a paper card adorned with a grinning stork. She appeared to be asleep, eyes closed. The bright lights shining on her protective incubator made me think of a movie I watched once about aliens, only this movie was about babies who were born too soon. The nurse nudged me forward and told me to not be afraid to touch her, that babies need as much human touch as possible. I eased my hand inside the incubator opening and touched her foot, barely the length and width of my thumb. My roughened thumb and forefinger caressed her purpled smooth skin along her left foot and leg, the only portion of her lower body free of monitors and lines. I ran a finger over her wrinkled, matchstick fingers. They curled in response, and I choked back a sob that nearly escaped my mouth. It was in that moment I vowed to always protect her, this baby who beat the odds.

I didn't get to hold or rock Hannah until she was three months old. She'd finally been detached from all the wires and tubes and observed in the regular nursery in a hospital closer to home. The last obstacle she needed to conquer before coming home was gaining weight. She'd lost about a pound and a half in the NICU and had to weigh six pounds before they discharged her. The first day I held her, I washed my hands and slipped on a surgical gown and paper booties. The nurse smiled as she handed me my little sister. I smiled down into her bright blue eyes and felt fathomless love. I rocked her for a good hour as she slept in my arms. I was nearly fifteen years older than her. I was, and still am, a lover of underdogs. I already loved and admired Hannah for her fierce determination to live. My mom knew how to create scrappy daughters, a virtue that failed to translate to her sons. But that's a story for later, and I've gone and gotten ahead of myself.

To me, Louise was a guardian angel who saved us, an older, chain-smoking version of Mom. I think Mom saw Louise as a mother figure, giving her the support and unconditional love her own mother could never muster. To show Louise how much she appreciated her kindness, Mom gave Hannah the middle name Louise, her high regard for the woman forever etched on official documents. I heard them talking one morning at breakfast about what would happen once Hannah came home from the hospital.

"You can stay here, still."

"We've imposed on you enough."

"You're no imposition."

Mom chuckled, "Of course we are."

I peeked through the doorway of the kitchen from my perch on the living room floor where I'd been playing trucks with Jacob to see Louise's reaction.

Louise coughed and wiped the corner of her eye with the heel of her hand, all the while holding a lit cigarette.

Her voice cracked as she said, "You always have a home with me."

Mom covered Louise's hands with hers, "I know, and I thank you."

After that morning, Mom spent time scouring the newspaper for rental properties that would fit into the meager public assistance budget. She finally found one. We moved to a one-bedroom, one-bathroom trailer in a small park on the outskirts of town. It was furnished and cheap, our two requirements for living accommodations. It reminded me of the trailer in South Carolina where I'd been prepared to shoot an intruder with my BB gun. We moved our few belongings into the space, and Mom put me to work washing all surfaces with lemon-scented disinfectant cleaner.

Our new home was fourteen by forty feet, just under six hundred square feet of living space. I didn't have a tape measure, I simply walked it off one day when boredom and curiosity colluded. Back then, a tiny house wasn't a trendy, eco-friendly badge of honor. It simply meant you were poor. I already knew I was poor; the trailer park we moved to was a blaring and obvious reminder. The trailer had a small kitchen in the front; a two-person table along the wall next to the front door; a living room with a couch, also known as my bed; an armchair; a short hallway with a laundry closet; a bathroom; and a small bedroom Mom shared with my brother and sister. As an adolescent girl in the process of exploring her individuality, I craved my privacy and missed having my own room.

Beyond the close living quarters, I hated the stigma associated with living in a mobile home. The knowing looks I caught from classmates when they asked where I lived added to my shame. Slurs like "trailer-trash" and "white trash" enraged me, mostly because they confirmed my worst fears about myself. Even though I was living it, I felt like I was somehow above our situation. I knew our financial situation didn't dictate my worth as a human, but no one else outside my family seemed to understand that.

People tend to associate class with moral value, though I've met good and bad people at every socioeconomic level during my lifetime. There's a sick irony to the modern phenomenon of hailing people who travel and live out of their van as adventurers and countercultural revolutionaries, yet those who live modestly because it's all they can afford are generally met with derision. Though their external situations look similar, those who live in trailer parks are unfairly presumed to be less intelligent and have lower human value.

The year I started tenth grade was a bit of a blur. I'm not sure I ever rightly passed ninth grade, but the system ushered me along regardless. My transcripts read:

Days present at Mooresville Junior High: 29

Days absent: 16

Lowest grade for the year: 70, a D in home economics [shocker]

Highest grade: 84 PE/Health [again, shocker]

Physical fitness wasn't my strong suit, but all the walking and mowing must have given me a leg up. In regards to the rest, like my chronic absences and abysmal attempts at sewing, I can only assume it was a pity promotion.

Shortly after my sister arrived home from the hospital, I had just started the new school year. I walked to the main road on the first day to catch the bus. It was a good quarter of a mile to the main road, and most days, it seemed even longer as I walked past an enormous brick building with the words "Brawley Seed Company" painted in huge block letters. I had always despised riding the bus when I was a child, every day facing the anxiety in my stomach over whether there would be an empty seat or if someone was willing to share their bench with me. It hadn't gotten much better over the years, and when I climbed on board the bus, I willed myself to get smaller as multiple pairs of eyes followed my progress down the aisle. I hunched my shoulders and lowered my gaze to study the floor littered with broken #2 pencils and Zebra gum wrappers. Always the new kid with nowhere to safely call home.

If Mom ever realized the hellscape she created for her introverted daughter with our constant upheaval, she never let on. But it forced me to adapt quickly to change, a skill that would transfer well into my adult years. During that first week of tenth grade, an upperclassman befriended me. Laura approached me while I was eating lunch alone at a table outside. I suppose I looked like a lost puppy, and something in her wanted to save me. Laura introduced me to her friends, a group of potheads who accepted me, no questions asked. They waved to me in the hall, invited me to eat lunch with them, and occasionally allowed me to join them for a post-lunch smoke session in a deserted stairwell. They offered to give me a hit, but I turned them down. I hadn't yet discovered the cruel ecstasy of using substances to momentarily dull my pain, but I would. Oh, I would.

Laura drove a lime-green pickup truck that she revved whenever she was stuck behind a car in the student parking lot that wasn't moving as quickly as she wanted. It made her a complete badass in my mind. One day she asked if I wanted her to pick me up and give me a ride to school instead of riding the bus. I immediately agreed. I didn't even care if she thought I was a charity case. Laura smoked cigarettes like a coal-powered train engine, and I swallowed my aversion to the smell by cracking my window. Smelling like an ashtray was a worthwhile tradeoff for skipping the bus. Pretty soon, I settled into a routine of riding to school with Laura and walking the mile and a half home in the afternoons. I used the time to mentally prepare myself for what came after school.

It was my duty to babysit my siblings once I got home, which pushed my homework to a later time, usually after dinner and baths. I wasn't too upset because attending school had become a chore rather than the joy I'd experienced before my family life went to hell. I found it hard to learn, adapt to a new school, or even make friends when I felt trapped and ashamed of my living situation or worried about if we'd have enough food. Mom told me to always hold my head high no matter what. It must've been easier for her. My head and shoulders struggled under the weight of our circumstances.

I tried to stay out of the trailer as much as possible to avoid my baby sister's crying or the responsibilities that inevitably fell to me if I sat still too long. Mom liked to use me as a second parent, dropping the babies into my arms and taking some "much needed quiet time" as soon as I got home from school. To shirk these duties, I volunteered to walk two to three miles round-trip to the store to buy Mom cigarettes or pick up formula, milk, and cereal. By then I'd overcome my aversion to using food stamps. They were still the paper kind in 1985, a glaring scarlet letter that folks took one pitiful or disgusted look at and decided they knew something about me. Both were looks I rejected. Instead of turning bright red with shame when I'd been forced to cash in food stamps for gas money in the past, I now boldly glared at anyone who stared as I paid for our food with fake money. I don't know when or how the shift happened, but I dared someone to make a comment.

My other reason for wanting to stay out of the trailer was because we had a roach problem. Mom noticed them when we initially rented the trailer and used a bug bomb to fumigate before moving in. She cleaned religiously, always had. No matter where we lived, the place was always spotless. We shared a hatred of anything creepy-crawly. I hated bugs then, and I hate them still to this day. I let silverfish, spiders, snakes, or ants live outside the walls of my home, but once they cross the drywall barriers, they're dead. I annihilate them without remorse. I'm sure some good must come from some bugs, but I could never think of one for roaches. Mom would buy those Raid roach canisters, and on a Saturday morning at least once a month, I loaded Jacob and Hannah into the car while she went inside and deployed toxic bombs in both the bedroom and the kitchen. Mom would rush out the front door with a cloud of poison on her heels, fall into the driver's seat of the car coughing and gagging, light up a cigarette, and drive us to the park for a few hours while the chemicals handled the infestation.

When we returned to the trailer, the acrid smell would burn my nostrils, so we'd open all the windows before bringing the kids back inside. There was always one blessed roach-free night, but the vermin inevitably returned to reclaim the dark recesses of drawers. By the next day, the bold fuckers had taken to crawling in plain sight, and we were back to squashing their innards on surfaces all over the trailer. Mom would always say it did little good to be the only clean trailer when everyone around us failed to keep a clean house. I didn't know for sure if our neighbors kept dirty places, but I could see the trash-filled trailer of the legless, drunken neighbor who leered at me whenever I walked outside. I imagined the roaches loved the stacks of black trash bags I could see piled up in his kitchen as he sat in his open doorway pounding Natural Light beer and silently wished they'd take up permanent residence there instead of our house.

Regardless of our roach-infested living situation, I was finally settling into my new high school, though I hoped we would find a new place to live soon. I had a friend in Laura, I was being asked for help by fellow classmates with studying, and it felt like I could sustain this new routine. My high school color was blue, my favorite color, and I was already picturing what it would be like to wear a Blue Devil class ring. The sense of normalcy and belonging I so desperately longed for was just within reach. And so, it makes sense that Robert, in his typical maelstrom of chaos and disruption, would show up at our front door one hot autumn day in late August, just when we were getting into a rhythm. I never did find out how he found us since we'd moved so much that year.

But when Mom opened the door and demanded to know how he'd found us, he grinned triumphantly and replied, "You'll always return to Mooresville."

# Voices in My Ear

The warm September night air rushed in through open windows while laughter and music filled the car. I gleefully tipped back the wine cooler my cousin Melissa offered. At first, I hesitated, but I eventually caved to the pressure to be like them, to cut loose and be free for just a few hours. My first sip of alcohol was sweet, the wine cooler a jolt of pure sugar. Even though I hated the taste, it boosted my self-esteem. I wished the night wouldn't end. Mom had agreed to an 11 p.m. curfew because I was with family. It wasn't the wine cooler making me feel loose and bubbly. Being away from Mom and my siblings made me drunk with freedom. Well, okay, maybe it was a little bit from the wine cooler. Tina raced through the back roads around Lake Norman, a large man-made lake just north of Charlotte and in Mooresville's backyard. We drove the roads before Nascar and Charlotte's elite migrated to our area and built million dollar mansions along roads that were once lined with fields and farmhouses.

Tina drove since she was a senior in high school, and my cousin Melissa, who was only a month older than me, sat beside me in the back seat. We couldn't talk over the wind rushing through her open windows. They were technically my second cousins, but we'd grown up together in great-grandma Beulah's house since we were around the same age. I wanted to spend the entire night rocketing through the dark, sucking down the mixture of sweet, slightly damp air. A part of me worried we'd get pulled over. How would I explain underage drinking? Would I get in trouble? I took a deep breath, stuck my arm out the window, and weaved it through the air. But I was feeling brave, so I decided I didn't care if I got caught. It was the most fun I'd had in over a year.

"Do you want to go back to your house?" Tina called to Melissa over her shoulder.

"Yes!" she yelled.

I grinned like an idiot in the darkness. It would have been the first time back inside my great-grandparents' old house since I was seven years old.

That night in 1985 when I walked into my great-grandparents' old house, I stopped in the kitchen first to say hello to its new owner, my Aunt Rosie. She pulled me into her full bosom for a bone-crushing hug I welcomed with all of my body. She smelled like honeysuckle perfume the older women in our family seemed to favor and flour from the cakes she was baking as a side hustle. For some reason, at this point in my life, Mom had stopped hugging me as often. I wasn't sure if she thought a fifteen-year-old didn't require as many hugs or if my simmering anger concerning her decisions would burn her if she came too close.

"Good Lord, Dawnie, you should have come by sooner."

"She goes by Sandra now," Melissa yelled from the living room.

"You will always be Dawnie to me," Rosie said as she smiled. "Tell your mom to come see me soon."

"I will." I left the kitchen with one last glance and followed the laughter to the front living room.

When I was younger, Beulah had used it as a formal living room. I had only ever used it to traverse the house to sit on the front porch and swing while listening to summer afternoon thunderstorms. I couldn't remember ever having guests sit in the front room. We'd always watched her soap operas in the den that adjoined the kitchen, her in her recliner and me in my kid-sized rocking chair. I joined my cousins in the living room, dropped onto the end of the couch, and focused on watching whatever my cousins were watching. My face reddened with embarrassment when I realized it was a soft porn movie about some woman named Lady Chatterley. I looked around the threshold to see if my aunt heard what they were watching. I suppose she'd been too busy baking or possibly didn't care since we were all teenagers. I knew my mom would've lost her mind if she knew I was watching that kind of movie. She gave me hell for watching MTV back then, once we could finally afford cable television.

After some moments of watching the on-screen figures and then averting my eyes to study the tips of my tennis shoes, I tapped my cousin's arm and asked if she could take me home. My mother had given me a curfew of 11 p.m., and arriving an hour earlier seemed a much better option than watching the movie that had been playing. On the way out the back door, I asked my aunt for soda to wash away any remnants of the wine cooler in case Mom got too close. I gave her one last squeeze around her waist. Aunt Rosie and her sister, my grandma Bobbie, were polar opposites when it came to emotional availability.

The following Monday at school, I just knew my cousins would acknowledge me in the hall after our fun-filled Saturday night. I had a great time hanging out with them. We laughed, reminiscing about the days we played hide-and-seek and doctor. Or the time they chopped off my hair in their basement, and my mom flipped out when she saw my shoulder-length locks reduced to a choppy bob. I spotted Melissa standing at her locker with a group of friends. I raised my hand in greeting, and she met my eyes briefly before turning toward her friends without acknowledgment. I guess my memories were better than hers.

The hurt I felt was masked by all the excuses I made for her ignoring me—I knew she was just trying to fit in herself, and maybe she hadn't seen me in the crowded hallway. I plastered a smile on my face and chatted with the cheerleader who sat beside me in biology and assisted the softball player who unwisely asked for my help with an Algebra II problem. I settled into my classes and learned to converse with anyone who would make me forget how lonely I felt.

A few weeks after my joyride with Tina and Melissa, Robert showed up for another visit. He'd been twice before, each time driving a different vehicle. The first time he drove a black pickup, the second time a blue and white pickup, and the third time a black Trans Am.

"What's the deal with these cars? Where's the truck you had last time?" I asked.

Robert stepped closer to where only I could hear his response. "I borrowed this one," he winked.

I had a pretty good idea "borrowed" meant stolen.

"Isn't that dangerous, *borrowing* cars?"

"Only if I get caught. Anyway, I torch them when I leave here."

He smiled a wide grin, the grin I found reassuring as a child that now left me uneasy and angry.

"Be careful with my mom," I snapped and walked inside the trailer.

Mom handed me Hannah, and I made sure to wrap both arms around her wiggly body. One week earlier, I'd held her snuggled against my body while I heated a bottle on the stove. I thought I'd perfected the one-handed hold with her head tucked into the crook of my elbow and my grip on her thigh. It had worked well for us so far, but on that particular night, she turned into a greased pig. Somehow when I turned her away from the stove to switch off the burner and pluck the bottle from the boiling water, she slipped right out of my grasp and landed on the floor. Hannah's cries were only outdone by my bawling as I picked her up and rushed her to my mom in the living room. Mom checked her over closely as I stood shaking.

"She's fine," Mom announced after checking my sister like she inspected a pack of cube steak for too much gristle.

"Oh my god, I thought I hurt her."

"Sandra, she's okay."

I buried my head in Mom's shoulder and left a trail of snot and tears on her T-shirt. Hannah had stopped crying by that point and looked around wide-eyed and curious. Mom recounted the story of me dropping Hannah for many years. I don't know if her rationale was to show how tough Hannah was or how her eldest daughter, who had taken to not showing her emotions, had cracked open. All I know is my brother Jacob once said he wished I'd dropped him when he was a baby and maybe he would've turned out like Hannah.

The day Robert pulled up in the black Trans Am, he followed me inside the trailer and asked Mom to take a ride with him so they could talk. I had the distinct thought that it was a poor decision on her part. My shoulders tightened like a maxed-out tow rope stretched too thin as I watched them back out of the driveway from the small kitchen window. Nothing good ever came from Mom going anywhere with Robert. I then looked to Hannah's angelic face and relented some. To keep my mind off my anxiety, I did everything I could to stay busy that evening. I fed Hannah a bottle and fixed Jacob and me a dinner of cheesy rice with the block of welfare cheese we'd waited hours to pick up at the National Guard Armory. I eventually gave them baths and put them to bed. This supposedly innocent talk had extended for too many hours for my liking, and I ran worst-case scenarios as the minutes ticked away on the wall clock. Around 10 p.m., I heard a car door slam. I peeked through the curtains covering the kitchen window and saw Mom exit the passenger door of a police cruiser, thankfully uncuffed.

"What happened?" I ambushed her as she came through the front door.

She rubbed her eyes and dropped her purse beside the chair.

"Robert's been arrested."

"And?"

She tapped a cigarette out of the pack and lit it before answering.

"He apparently stole that car. He turned around in the gas station parking lot by the What-A-Burger and burned out. A cop flipped his lights to pull him, and Robert led them on a chase."

"He took you on a police chase in a stolen car? What's wrong with him?"

She exhaled a puff of smoke and added, "He got caught when we crashed."

I smacked my forehead, collected my pinball thoughts, and asked, "You crashed?? Never mind, I guess you're okay. If you were a passenger in a stolen car, why'd they let you go?"

"Robert took the blame, said it was his fault and that I didn't know the car was stolen. Asked if we would call his brother to let him know what happened."

I was still focused on running down all of the worst-case scenarios. My anger pendulum typically swung between Mom and Robert, but that night it landed hard on Robert. He could have seriously hurt my mom with his recklessness. I cringed at the thought of her being gone.

She lit another cigarette and asked, "Can you run out and call them for me while I shower?" She handed me a quarter like she knew I had no choice.

I snatched the quarter and exited into the starless night. The closest pay phone was up by the corner where I caught the bus. I hopped on my new-to-me used 10-speed bike I'd purchased with grass-mowing money and took a leisurely ride, letting the cool night air lift my hair away from my sweaty forehead.

My mom used to say women from the South don't sweat; we glisten. Of course, that's some bullshit. My head, especially my nose, would break out with beads of sweat anytime I became nervous or worked too hard.

When I called Ted's house, Lynn answered. I relayed everything Mom had told me like a good puppet.

"Oh honey, how's your mom?"

"She seemed fine. She's not hurt."

"Thank God."

I nodded like she could see me through the pay phone. I shivered, unsure if it was shock or the fact that hot, angry tears threatened to spill over my lower lashes.

"Well, I have to go."

"We love you, honey. Hug your mom for us."

"I love you, and I will."

Mom left the trailer early the next day to return with the local newspaper. The car chase had made page two of the news. I observed her clip the article and throw the rest of the newspaper in the trash can without a second glance at the actual news.

Mom had been perusing the Sunday paper for years, clipping coupons and stuffing them in an envelope for later use. Mom was the original coupon queen. She cut and saved the stolen car police chase article like a special coupon for a buck off Tide laundry detergent.

Years later, I sat in her dark basement, going through boxes with her husband Wayne's permission. The process felt invasive, delving into her memory boxes. She'd kept all of the homemade Mother's Day and birthday cards I'd made for her since 1976. She had a Ziploc bag with my picture and a Mother Mary medallion even though she wasn't Catholic. At the bottom of the box, beneath the stacked cards and photographs, were three newspaper clippings: Beulah's death announcement, my grandpa Ralph's death announcement, and the article about the goddamned police chase. I tossed the last item into the trash because I didn't need a memento. I lived through that night and everything that came after.

# Things May Get Better

From the tinny speakers of our old Gremlin, George Strait's voice crooned about how a woman looked so good in love as Mom drove us across the flatlands of eastern North Carolina. I hated the sad tone Mom's voice took on when she sang along with the lyrics, and it made me wonder if she'd ever been truly in love. I certainly had no clue about the kind of love he was singing about, but I definitely knew the kind that had left my mom an empty shell of a person, the kind of love that left us hungry and broke. And if that was love, I wanted nothing to do with it. We spent hours traveling to visit Robert at the Caledonia Correctional Institute. Mom bundled us into our car and used our limited funds to see him at least twice a month. I wondered if it was out of misplaced guilt or if she thought his recent visits meant he wanted to work on their marriage since they were separated and technically still married. I didn't know or care and simply tried to keep my composure after listening to my siblings cry on and off throughout the entire six-hour drive.

The evening he took Mom for a ride in the stolen Trans Am, Robert was arrested for driving under the influence, driving on a revoked license, and possessing a stolen car. When he'd been sent to prison in November of 1985, it was for those offenses and additional charges of felony, breaking and entering, and larceny. Too bad the internet wasn't around then, because I would've blown up his con long before he had the chance to take my mom on yet another joyride.

In December of 1985, we pulled into the prison parking lot, and the first thing I noticed were rolls of razor wire topping the chain link fence. We waited in a makeshift line behind other families who'd traveled for visitation day. The guards opened a gate, allowed a group of family members to enter, closed the gate behind them, and then opened a second set of gates that led to a large metal door. We inched closer to our turn to enter the gates of the prison. I wondered what else I could do instead of feeling tired and anxious about this little family reunion. I'm unsure why at fifteen I felt I had to be the one to do something, but the thought kept plaguing me. Maybe it was the lack of confidence I had in the adults in my life to make the right decisions. Maybe it was my dissatisfaction with my current life welling up like a volcano throbbing and pulsing molten lava just below the surface. Or maybe, the thoughts pounded like a drum beat in my head that I was better than this, meant for more than this, and they were finally reaching a crescendo.

Once inside the prison walls, a guard searched the contents of Mom's pocketbook and diaper bag. We walked through a set of metal detectors, and a guard ushered us to a visitation area that looked strangely similar to my school cafeteria. Who knew architects used the same designs for both children and criminals?

We had an awkward visit for about an hour in which Jacob refused to sit still or talk to his dad. Mom and Robert kept everything civil, and he mostly talked about appealing his sentence. I didn't understand how a criminal could appeal something when caught red-handed. Apparently, the number of stolen cars attributed to Robert's hands was the sticking point. We shuffled back through the gates, the reverse operation taking mere minutes, and we were back in the car for another six-hour drive home.

Robert had a habit of trying to escape, multiple times. He'd laugh about his escapes when we visited like it was some kind of game for him. His recounting of the attempted escapes involved taking off while out on work release. The best story was when he tried to escape using a prison guard's horse. Fortunately for him, he had a way of charming the prison officials and he never wound up shot for his efforts. The Division of Prisons eventually moved him to a prison in the mountains due to his attempts, and he was no longer outside on work release.

While Robert was playing prison roulette, I started paying more attention to the morning announcements at school, including job opportunities for students who wanted to make extra money. The announcement directed students to see the school counselor for additional details, and on a whim, I decided to stop by one day during lunch. I ended up snagging a one-day job that involved stuffing envelopes for a business in the town's industrial park area on a Saturday. On another weekend night, I did some babysitting for a family with three small children. I realized I liked my siblings better than other children, who were headache-inducing monsters. My siblings could also give me a splitting headache, but I loved them, so it was different. I decided I'd no longer take babysitting jobs for others no matter how much money it paid.

Around this time, my mother got a third-shift job working at a plastics factory. Our arrangement turned into me watching the kids overnight while she worked. She made minimum wage at the factory because that's the wage high school dropouts could attain. She worked forty-hour weeks at a backbreaking job. When she got home in the early morning hours, her hair and clothes were covered in tiny pieces of white plastic. I asked her what she did at this job. She replied with a shrug and said something about running machines to make some sort of plastic pieces. It wasn't the work that mattered to her; it was a means to an end. Living paycheck to paycheck afforded us a roach-infested one-bedroom trailer in a neighborhood hidden on the outskirts of town surrounded by people with evil intentions if their black eyes and leering grins were to be trusted.

Mom was a proud woman. We received welfare checks when she was pregnant with my sister, but they stopped when she returned to work. She always did love working, even if it meant getting paid minimum wage and being covered in plastic. She was fueled by the friendships she'd strike up with her co-workers and rattled off stories about them on the weekends over breakfast. I did homework as soon as I got home from school so I could focus on caring for my siblings while Mom slept for a few hours before getting ready for third shift. I cooked dinner, gave my siblings a bath, and tucked them into bed. Sometimes, I fought back the tears as I kissed their foreheads, wanting to give them a better life but not knowing how. I can only imagine how Mom must have felt.

I felt stuck in a rut like when I was mowing a steep backyard and no matter how hard I pushed, the mower tires slipped and spun as I tried to thrust it up the hill. I eventually ceased trying to go straight up the hill, and instead mowed it sideways in a series of switch-backs. Any situation, no matter how seemingly insurmountable, has a solution. I observed my mom spinning her wheels making plastic pieces for $3 an hour and wondered how we would ever change our course. Where was the solution that would actually create some upward mobility for my family?

Adding to our stuckness was the fact that Mom would take what little cash she had left after bills and use it for gas money to visit Robert in prison. We could have used that time and money for so many things, but instead Mom kept returning to the dried-up well hoping for I don't know what. But something started to shift when we visited him in the mountains. I sensed that her resolve to continue the visits was waning. One Saturday afternoon on the way home, she complained about how she could make better use of her time cleaning the house or doing laundry. It wasn't long after that she finally filed for divorce. Driving long distances over the rolling Blue Ridge mountains and conversing with the ancient spirits of that land has a way of guiding a person to the dawn of epiphany, and

Mom must have come face to face with her own reckoning. Lord knows she certainly put in the hours. It's only right she received something in return. I wanted to congratulate her out loud or ask what changed, but I kept quiet, fearful that if I questioned her process, she'd change her mind and stay with him. I hoped we were done spinning our wheels in the futile and destructive patterns of the past.

In the spring of 1986, there was an announcement at school about job openings at Mitchell's nursery. I thought I was a shoo-in for this job since I had plenty of experience with children. I thought maybe at this point I was ready to try babysitting other children again. I stopped by the counselor's office and inquired about the job opportunity during my lunch break.

"So, Sandra..." She chuckled when I asked about the nursery job working with kids.

My face turned red, and I felt the sweat bead on my nose because I could tell by her tone that I was way off base.

"Mitchell's is a plant nursery. They need help weeding and fulfilling orders on Saturdays."

I flashed a toothy smile and said, "I can do it, Ms. Allen. I mow yards and do all sorts of yard work on the weekends. I'm a fast learner."

Miss Allen took off her glasses and stared at me for a long minute. I knew she underestimated my slight frame. According to the physical fitness class, I barely weighed more than ninety pounds in the previous semester. I was a strong five and a half feet tall string bean.

"I really need this job. My family needs this job."

"Okay, I'll call my contact over there and tell them you'll be by Saturday at 9 a.m. Don't be late or make me regret this."

"Thank you so much, Ms. Allen." I began to feel the tides shifting. I could make my own money, some real cash that would ease our daily stress, like releasing the valve on a pressure gauge.

"You're welcome. Just stop by on Monday and let me know how it went."

That Saturday morning in mid-March arrived, and Mom reluctantly gave up sleeping as soon as she got home from work to drive me to the nursery. She promised to pick me up at four o'clock. She waved as she backed out of the parking lot, and I suddenly felt alone and nervous. I knew I was a hard worker, but I feared I had screwed up this opportunity my school counselor had arranged. What if I damaged the plants or said or did something that wouldn't allow me to return to the job? All this doubt before I even stepped through the front door of the nursery office. I now realize my worth and my value at that time hinged on what others thought about me. It would take years before I could look at my reflection in the mirror, trust my abilities, and know I was enough.

My first real job consisted of picking weeds from quart-sized landscape shrubbery. The sun bathed my neck and shoulders as I plucked weeds in long rows of quart-sized black buckets. Pulling weeds was not that challenging, but the repetitive pluck and toss allowed my mind to wander. The smell of sun-warmed mulch filled the air, and the weeds dyed my fingers green. I was the only worker pulling weeds. I noticed the order fillers were older boys from school, and I appeared to be the only female besides the owner's wife. I now understood the school counselor's hesitation. It wasn't about my size; it was that I was a girl. I took my thirty-minute lunch break and pulled weeds with renewed vigor when I returned to the shrubs.

I returned to my guidance counselor's office during lunch the following Monday.

"I spoke to Mitchell's." She paused, and I held my breath, terrified she would confirm my worst fears and tell me I was fired. "They want you to return on Saturday."

I smiled and nodded, relishing the feeling of being appreciated for working hard. Positive reinforcement like that wasn't something I'd experienced much. Mom told me I needed to sweep the floor again because I missed a dust bunny or to rewash the bathtub since she saw a soap line. It felt as though I never did clean the house to her stringent criteria; the nursery job was my first experience being commended for my work, and I felt high on the praise.

After school let out, I passed the row of buses, turning up my nose as I sauntered down the sidewalk toward home. I had always despised the school bus rides. It reminded me of a smaller microcosm of the cliques I witnessed during the school day. The mile-and-a-half walk home turned into a two-plus-mile walk home most days as I zig-zagged through neighborhoods, and it allowed me additional time to think about ways to escape our situation. No Prince Charming was swooping in to save us, no biological dad coming to my rescue. Mom and I had each other, and we had to be our own saviors. Those forty minutes were the most peaceful moments of my day, and I even looked forward to walking them in the pouring rain.

The following Saturday, I was assigned a new job at Mitchell's. Rather than pull weeds again, I helped load the truck with plant orders. I was now grabbing the same quart-sized landscaping containers I'd snagged weeds from the previous weekend, three in each hand as I carried them to the box truck. The containers were heavy, some heavier than others depending on the amount of retained water. The black plastic containers left white indentions in my fingers. On my trips to gather more pots, I massaged them, the blood returning to my fingers just as I grabbed another six pots.

A couple of older high school boys were also loading the truck. They took turns pretending not to see me and starting playful arguments with each other, such as who had the biggest penis, while I approached with plants. I wondered why this was ever a topic of conversation in the workplace. I discovered boys and men seemed overly concerned with my impression of their penis. I saw more cocks than a chicken farmer before I ever had sex. For some reason unbeknownst to me, men would proudly whip them out and show me, and when I wouldn't give them a reaction, right back in the pants it went. It's as though nine months in the womb playing with the thing leads to a lifelong preoccupation.

My mother picked me up at four o'clock, and I handed her my check from the previous weekend's work.

She frowned. Not the reaction I was hoping for. "That's not much for all the gas and time it takes for me to bring you here and pick you up."

"I enjoy working here, Mom." I couldn't tell her how much being outside and away from the depressing trailer was good for my sanity. It was like I'd tasted freedom only to have it snatched away.

Our unspoken deal was with every yard I mowed, all money earned went back to supporting the household. I worked, handed over my money, and never considered keeping it for myself. I hadn't asked for anything from those checks from Mitchell's. I just wanted to continue working there.

Then she dropped the bomb I'd been dreading. "I think next week should be your last weekend."

Open and shut. I knew the topic wasn't up for discussion, so I stewed on Mom's ruling on the drive home. It reminded me of the time in seventh grade when she forced me to quit the school newspaper because my grades slipped from all As to As and Bs. After all, I spent my free time writing, not focusing on my pointless homework. I realize now my mother thought she was doing what was in my best interest. Coming from a long line of practical women, her verdict on the nursery job boiled down to basic math—the amount of money I brought in after taxes wasn't worth the time or gas it took her to drive me back and forth. She also lost my babysitting duties on a Saturday, her precious time to rest and recharge for the coming week.

Since she worked the night shift and needed the weekends to sleep rather than chauffeur me back and forth for a measly $20, I grudgingly acknowledged her choice though I didn't like it. I kept thinking there had to be another way to improve our situation. In my mind, the correct answer wasn't to stay at the trailer for another two and a half years while I finished high school. After all the plotting and stewing, I realized it was time for me to make a change.

Ms. Allen shoved her glasses over her graying blonde tresses and stared through me. "You're only fifteen."

"I know, but my family needs me." I smiled broadly, something that always came naturally to me despite all I was dealing with at home. I dazzled her. "I turn sixteen in about a month."

I couldn't explain to my counselor that I knew in my soul this was the correct answer to help my family forward. I wouldn't tell her the truth that Mom had no idea what I was trying to do.

"I'll have to do some checking. I'll call you when I talk to the superintendent's office."

Less than a week later, I sat across from Ms. Allen, signed a couple of documents, and left my stack of books on the corner of her desk. I walked out of Mooresville Senior High School just after lunch. On that day, I was officially a high school dropout. Dropping out of school had proved less complicated than the prospect of telling my mother.

The lightness I felt in my chest walking through the high school's front doors was soon replaced by a school of minnows in my stomach being chased by a predator bass. I knew in my gut that my decision would change my life trajectory; I wasn't sure Mom would see it the same. My first of many adult decisions started that day. I do not regret it. I would never suggest anyone else do it, because education is one of the most essential things in a person's life. It was my choice, a leap of faith, and my way of having some control in my life.

Mom constantly spouted this saying: *There's more than one way to skin a rabbit.* I don't have a clue where she heard it. She clearly never skinned a rabbit in her lifetime. I learned there's always more than one way to approach a problem. Quitting school at fifteen was my temporary solution to skirt the gray area of my muddied life.

# Talk to Me

"How could you quit school?"

I shrugged my shoulders and thought she should've been happier than this, more pleased that I'd taken steps toward some sort of action instead of just slogging through the same mess.

*You quit and left home at sixteen.*

"What were you thinking?" My mom lit yet another cigarette off the one she'd smoked to the filter. She squashed the ember in a bed of red-lipped regrets and leveled ice-blue eyes in my direction. We were sitting at the small table in the kitchen, the amber-colored ashtray serving as the demarcation line.

I turned my head away from the smoke cloud and thought I should've practiced my explanation more. I studied her face, the deep lines running along her cheeks that acted as parentheses for her thin, downturned lips. Her deep forehead wrinkle led straight to narrowed eyes filled with disappointment and anger. I squirmed in the kitchen chair, trapped by her scrutiny. I remained quiet, my unspoken words and quelled rebuttals relegated to a notebook I buried between T-shirts.

I wanted to ask her why she was so angry with me when I was the only person standing by her side. The husband she'd chosen when I was five had deserted us. The same loser was sitting in the state prison serving his sentence for taking her on a joyride just last year in a stolen car that ended in a police chase. I pushed the peanut butter and jelly sandwich I'd had for lunch from the back of my throat and studied my clenched hands resting in my lap.

"I asked you what you were thinking?" She ducked her head and pinned me with her gaze.

She didn't want to know what I was thinking because I was always thinking. My brain was a hamster on a wheel constantly analyzing ways out of welfare cheese and food stamps. I'd explored all of the scenarios out of this trailer in this run-down park with a leering, drunken double-amputee neighbor, out of this bone-tiredness I had from feeding, bathing, and caring for my younger siblings while Mom worked a third-shift job and I struggled to keep up with homework.

*I think you put men above your children. I think you can't get us out of this mess alone. I think you treat me like an adult until it's convenient to insist I'm a child and say I don't know what I'm doing. I did this for me, so the hatred I'm feeling stops growing. I sometimes cringe at the harshness of my thoughts.*

"I don't know. I was trying to help."

I looked longingly at the red and green plaid couch. My bed. It had been part of the fully furnished listing for the one-bedroom, one-bath when we'd rented the trailer last year. The thick woven fibers of the couch housed our dirt and grime, but it also held years of funk from past residents. Even though I buried my head in my pillow at night, I smelled the pungent scent of Raid bug bombs and other mysterious smells I tried not to identify for my own sanity. And despite that, all I wanted to do was curl up in it and sleep until she left for work.

"I thought," the words croaked sideways and stuck in my throat as I swept my hand across the small kitchen barely bigger than my outstretched arms. I inhaled deeply and cleared the blockage, "I thought I could actually help get us out of this situation."

"By doing what exactly?" Mom tapped a mauve-tipped fingernail repeatedly on her pack of menthols.

"By working. By getting a job. Two full-time paychecks are better than one."

She stared through me. Mom's lips parted as though she was about to reply before snapping into a thin line and studying me again. I met her gaze defiantly. I refused to back down now. Hell, I couldn't change my decision. I had plotted and planned this high school exodus for weeks. I despised lying, but I'd lied anyway and told my school counselor that my mother knew and supported my decision. I'd given all of my textbooks back to the school. Ms. Allen, my counselor, had taken the stack from me and said, "I know you'll finish school and go on to do great things with your life." I teared up and had to look away from her support, or else I would've been full on snot-streaming-down-my-face crying.

These were the words I wish Mom had used with me now. Instead, she scowled and shook her head. "You're only fifteen."

"I'll be sixteen soon," I proclaimed like the next month mattered. "I promise I'll go back. I'll get my GED." *I won't end up like you.*

Mom jerked her head back like I'd jabbed her nose. I worried I'd said the last words aloud. Part of me wanted her to fight for my remaining childhood. But our roles were already reversed, and no amount of wishing on my part could right our tragedy.

A shriek erupted from the living room. Three-year-old Jacob and toddler Hannah were playing several feet away. My brother spoke little more than a few words. He'd refused to talk much since he stopped watching and waiting for his *da-da* to return. I rose and walked over to assess the situation. Hannah had taken Jacob's Hot Wheels car and promptly put it in her mouth. I gently pried the car from her clutches, wiped the drool on my jeans, and handed it to Jacob. I ruffled his blond curls and corralled Hannah's colorful plastic blocks into a pile at her feet. I dropped a kiss on Hannah's mop of brown curls before I reclaimed my seat across from Mom at the table.

We had to find a better place to live than this tin shoebox. I longed for my own space again like my bedroom at the brick ranch house. I wanted the life I had then. I dreamt of being able to close my bedroom door and get lost in a book or listen to the poetry of my favorite singers for hours on end. The fantasy I played in my head before bed sometimes felt so far away.

"How could that school just let you quit without calling me or anything?" Her words held more resignation than indignation. Her shoulders slumped and she pressed back into her chair, one arm crossed against her body while the other pulled the cigarette to her mouth.

*Maybe because we can't afford a phone. Maybe because I told the principal and counselor that you knew about this decision and supported me. Maybe, just maybe, someone recognized my desperation and took pity on me.*

I shrugged and looked away. My silence had a way of nullifying her. She'd asked me multiple times over the past year why I blamed her, why I hated her. I'd reassured her I didn't, yet I'd learned that my silence in the face of her questions or lectures would halt the conversation and fuel her insecurities. I felt frustration, disappointment, and anger, but I loved my mother and my siblings. I loved her despite all of the questionable decisions of the past year, the depth of that love only equal to the hatred I felt toward being poor.

I despised wearing thrift store clothing and longed to pick out my school clothes from a catalog, even if that catalog was Sears and Roebuck. I endured the pitying or outraged stares of other shoppers when I paid for groceries with food stamps that looked more like Monopoly money than anything that held real value. I was sick of washing my hair with lemon-scented dish detergent just so we could put extra gas in the tank to go visit a felon in prison who didn't care about us. I simultaneously loved my family and hated my life.

I had to change my circumstances. Me. I had to save myself. If, in the process, this also saved my family, so be it. I had finally made a decision commensurate with the adult I'd been playing for too long. I returned my mother's gaze. I affixed the smirk I'd perfected when I was feeling my most stubborn. She placed her cigarette in the ashtray and crossed both arms over her chest. I thought I caught a flash of sadness, but I discarded the observation. I'd already spent too much time trying to gauge and manage her moods. For once, I wasn't preoccupied with making her feel better. This decision, this day, was for me. I'd lost hope that she'd prioritize my needs.

"I'm going to lie down for a while before I go to work. Watch the kids." She stood and crossed behind me, laid a hand on my shoulder, and gently squeezed.

I leaned back until my head touched her stomach. A tear escaped my clenched eyelids as I inhaled vanilla, baby powder, and cigarette smoke. I needed more, but that day I took what she gave.

I knew there wasn't some all-knowing god waiting to answer my prayers and set our lives right side up. Instead, I prayed to the only saint I'd ever known asking for guidance, insight, a break, a sign, anything to show me my life would get better from this point forward. I begged my dead great-grandma Beulah for the strength to help my family overcome the hardships in our future, but as life goes, our troubles were only just beginning.

# Rise and Struggle

In late May of 1986, a couple of weeks after quitting high school, I got my first real job working 4:30 a.m. to 10 a.m. as a biscuit maker at Hardee's. It was the only opening they had at that time, and I took it. I didn't like waking up that early or doing what I considered then to be an old person's job, not that I knew what a biscuit maker was supposed to look like.

At four o'clock in the morning, I jumped on my red 10-speed bike and pedaled the two miles to my job. The pitch-black morning was like another world; everyone was sleeping, and the landscapes that flew by me were quiet, eerily quiet. Once daylight rose, the streets were busy, packed with people and traffic noise, so I relished the silence.

I liked to imagine what other people were dreaming about as I pedaled past dark houses. I wondered what their lives were like because, at that time, I imagined everyone else's was better than mine. I wasn't under the illusion that I'd be doing this for long. I had exchanged my books and classes for piles of dough, using my hands to roll and cut, culminating in a tray of biscuits ready to shove into the oven for twelve to fifteen minutes until they were golden brown.

Biscuit making was a nonstop moving-intensive experience with the demand for biscuits dropping off around 9:30 in the morning. Ironically, I had never liked biscuits very much. Yeast rolls were my favorite bread item. I only ate biscuits when they were drenched in sausage and gravy or with strawberry jam.

Hardee's was able to give me about twenty to twenty-five hours any given week. Mom voiced her displeasure with me being out so early in the wee morning hours, plus twenty hours a week really didn't make much of a dent in the mountain of our financial needs. Suddenly, she was okay with me working more. I asked my manager for more hours and was told I'd have to be a cashier if I wanted to get more like thirty-six hours a week. I took it since it would mean about fifty more dollars on my weekly paychecks. I continued to mow the grass on the weekends, sometimes pushing my lawnmower for miles just for an extra $10 to $20. My life as a high school dropout was just as I'd imagined, waiting for the next bad thing to happen.

The revelation of Robert's criminal stupidity shed light on the reality of what my mom had been dealing with, and I felt some of my resentment toward her dissolving. I was entirely Team Mom after the stolen car incident, and when she told me in late May that she was filing for divorce, I wanted to shout my excitement. There was a resolve in her eyes that I hadn't seen in years. She told me it was time because Robert would never change and she needed to move on.

While Mom and I were mending our relationship, at least on a surface level, we continued to butt heads over layers of conflict. One day after work before she left for her night shift, I was relaxing on the couch, aka my bed, watching music videos on MTV. She walked out of the kitchen and stood in front of the television screen.

"Why are you so lazy?" she demanded with misplaced venom in her voice.

"What?"

"You're always laying around."

*You mean* lying *around?* I bit down hard on my tongue and blinked back tears.

"Whatever." She stormed off to her bedroom while I had a full-blown verbal jousting match with her in my head.

*Me, lazy? I work all the time. If I'm not working in fast food hell, I'm babysitting YOUR kids, and that's stressful enough. But because I'm taking a moment to rest in the afternoon, now I'm lazy?*

I'd like to say I was able to brush the comment off and go back to watching TV, but I wasn't. I let her words sink deep into the recesses of my brain, the spot where I stored all of the offhanded, hurtful comments she probably thought little about after they were spoken. But her bullshit activated the fighter in me, and I was determined to prove her wrong. I used my pain to fuel daydreams about a different life. My sixteen-year-old brain had already reconciled my experiences with a defensiveness meant to keep anyone else from hurting me or taking advantage of me. I would never let a man screw up my life. I definitely didn't want marriage or children in my future. I dreamed of being a successful, independent adult with the freedom to travel.

I'd own a tastefully decorated loft in downtown Charlotte with a big comfortable bed where I could take naps and watch music videos as long as I damn well pleased.

Eventually, Mom moved from the second shift back to the third shift for a better pay rate. I got a new job working the drive-thru at McDonald's since the Hardee's manager was determined to keep me around twenty-five hours a week regardless of my job title.

Later that summer, a new family moved into the neighborhood, a woman and her daughter, Julie, who was around my age. Mom encouraged me to befriend her. She was worried I was too absorbed in my daydreams and books when I should have been going out and being social. Nothing I did during this time in my life satisfied my mom. She was critical and unhappy with the life she'd built for herself, and I made an easy dumping ground.

Julie was a high school dropout as well. I'm sure Mom would've eaten her words about befriending her if she'd known the shenanigans we got into together. One night, while Mom was at work, Julie brought over a bottle of Boone's Farm wine and urged me to try it. I hadn't drunk anything since the single wine cooler in the back of my cousin's car last spring, but it wasn't for lack of interest. I grabbed the bottle and scrutinized the label as if it would provide some guidance to my decision. After sniffing the bottle and smelling the sickly sweet grape jelly scent, I took a swig and immediately coughed up a lung. It tasted like a nastier version of Dimetapp that made my throat burn. Within minutes, the bottom of my right foot started itching. I don't know if it was a true reaction to the nastiness of the wine or my anxiety at drinking that caused it.

Julie laughed as I removed my sock to reveal a bright-red sole, and I furiously scratched it. I worried the rash would spread to the rest of my body, and I'd have to explain what happened to Mom. She offered me more, and I shook my head, telling her Boone's Farm was not for me.

"Maybe you should go. I don't want my mom to find out I drank."

I hadn't seen Mom drink alcohol since Robert left the first time, back at the house in Monroe. I didn't want to explain my allergic reaction to Boone's Farm because she already thought me lazy apparently. I didn't want her to think I was heading down the path to alcoholism. *Mom would be so disappointed. I couldn't disappoint her again when all I wanted was for her to be proud of me. Fuck...why do I care so much?*

"You need to relax." Julie then reached into her pocket and removed a hand-rolled cigarette. Only it wasn't a cigarette; it was a joint, like the ones I'd seen my friends at school smoke. Julie lit it, took a couple of puffs, and extended it toward me.

I studied the smoking joint pinched between her fingers. This was a crossroads moment, but of course I didn't recognize that in the moment. All I knew was that I had a decision to make, and I didn't want to look like some goody-two-shoes with no knowledge of the world and all its pleasures. I reached for the joint, took a couple of puffs, and violently choked on the smoke. I felt like a fucking rebel that night; I was on top of the world, making my own choices for my life. I waited for the much-anticipated buzz and mellow elation to kick in like Julie promised to help me relax. But after about ten minutes, I still felt nothing. I was disappointed. I'd watched my pot-head friends at school look delightfully blissed out after toking on a joint, yet nothing for me.

I even tried smoking pot a second time a few weeks later, convinced that the first time was a fluke. But after watching Julie turn into a giggling mass on my couch while I remained stone-cold sober, I decided pot just wasn't my thing. Now, wine coolers were a different matter. My friendship with Julie grew by default since she was the only one around my age where we lived. We had little in common other than drinking wine coolers after my siblings went to bed and talking about boys. She introduced me to her boyfriend's friends, dead-eyed, restless young men with skin browned by the sun from their days picking produce for local farms. They worked long hours so they could send money back to their families in Mexico. None of them could speak more than a few English words, so our communication was limited. But I understood their prematurely hunched shoulders burdened with the weight they carried for their families. Four or five of them shared the trailer next door to Julie and her mom. Luckily for us, they were all over the age of eighteen, so they bought the booze when Julie asked.

I was too naive to know that people don't usually do things for free, especially hungry men who buy alcohol for underage girls. A guy named Jesse took a liking to me. I practiced kissing with him, which I saw as a major improvement from my only other experience awkwardly locking lips at a basement party. Jesse was another form of distraction, but when he suggested I should let him touch my breasts to help them grow, I ended it. I had no desire to let anyone get that close to me. I had no interest in sex because I knew that meant there was the possibility of getting pregnant, and I certainly wasn't trying to become a teen mom. Mom had never had the sex talk with me, even though I was well over sixteen. She'd simply trusted the North Carolina educational system would provide the necessary information in health class.

Julie suggested a few weeks after I broke up with Jesse that we host a party at my place since Mom was working the third shift and the kids would be asleep by nine o'clock. I agreed because I didn't want to lose my only friend in the trailer park. The term "friend" seemed a very loose interpretation of our relationship, given that drinking and boys were the only things we had in common other than our age. She was clueless about music or books, which were the true passions in my life. But hell, she was a warm body, and I was in need of companionship.

Julie invited her boyfriend and a couple of his friends to the party, and we all squeezed into our tiny trailer, playing poker and throwing back wine coolers like bottles of water. Somebody lit a joint, and I quickly yelled at them to extinguish it. The last time Julie lit one in the trailer, I freaked out and opened all the windows, frantically airing out the living room. But as soon as Mom walked through the door, she took a deep inhale, sniffing the air like a bloodhound. A strange look passed over her face, and the next night under the cover of darkness, she asked me if I was doing drugs.

I never liked lying for any reason. I don't see the point, and I don't like it when someone lies to me. Honestly, I have a hell of a guilty conscience because for some reason Mom had me believing I was supposed to be this perfect child who matured to sainthood. I took a minute to answer, ensured my voice was modulated correctly, and then I promptly lied to her. I think this was the only time in my life I lied to my mom. I knew in my soul if I told her the truth, her hurt would be infinitely greater than living with my lie. I'd already disappointed her by quitting school, and I refused to break her trust in me anymore.

Now, it wasn't a full-on lie because though I had smoked pot twice, I was no longer interested. The guilt of this lie fresh in my mind, I didn't want Mom smelling it and thinking it was me. I opened all of the kitchen and the living room windows and waved my arms like a human fan. Julie approached from the kitchen and handed me my third wine cooler. She put her hand on my shoulder and told me to calm down. It seemed she was overly concerned with me relaxing or calming down. *Am I really that uptight?* I downed the contents too quickly, and my head felt like a detached helium balloon. I dropped onto the couch and watched everyone else laughing and talking. I often found myself watching others live their lives, as if I was an outside observer, never fully present in my body.

When I woke up on the floor sometime around 2 a.m., everyone had left. I felt an irritation on my neck like a nasty rug burn. I checked my neck in the yellow glow of the bathroom mirror, and I saw a big ass hickey that I didn't even remember getting. I'd never had a hickey on my neck, but I'd seen plenty around Julie's neck. I thought they were disgusting. I was suddenly queasy with the realization that my body had been marked without my consent or memory, leading me to panic about what else I didn't remember. I pulled my jeans down and grabbed my panties: no pain, no blood, my virginity was still intact. Thankfully the only thing that had been violated that night was my neck.

I took the bag full of wine coolers out of the trailer and put them in the big trash can outside. I went into the bathroom and stripped off all of my clothes, turned the shower to the hottest setting, and stepped under the scalding water. I scrubbed my body with the soapy washcloth three times before I rinsed and the hot water ran out. I debated putting on one of my mom's turtleneck sweaters, but instead, I crashed on the couch, too tired to hide the evidence and too tired to close my eyes.

When Mom got home from work that morning, she immediately spotted the hickey and lost no time badgering me for answers.

"Did you have sex?"

This was Mom's go-to question. I never really understood her preoccupation with my sex life, which went on until well after I left home. She was always accusing me of having sex. I don't think she understood my absolute aversion to being pregnant or making the incorrect decision with a man. I refused to give anything of myself to a man because I had a healthy distrust of them, especially after my lapse in judgment last night. And, I'd seen firsthand how it had worked out for her.

"No," I replied groggily through my hangover haze.

"How did you get that then?" She pointed to my neck.

I shrugged and scowled. My mom usually left me alone when I got the angry teenager look.

"You'd better be careful."

"Got it."

She didn't need to lecture me. I'd already decided I was done with the boys and the wine coolers as I'd lain awake for those hours until she got home. I vowed to never let myself get out of control again. I knew better. I blamed myself for someone else's actions. I felt dirty and ashamed because I'd let another man take advantage of me. Despite my vow after all of Mom's boyfriends, Robert, and our pervy neighbor, Jim, I'd let my guard down and fucked up again.

After the party incident, I went back to spending my time reading, watching television, and babysitting my siblings. I avoided Julie and the trailer of Spanish-speaking guys since I couldn't know with certainty which one of them had decided to take advantage of an unconscious girl. I blamed Julie for not having my back, and cutting her out of my life was easier than I'd imagined. More than blaming Julie or the man responsible, I blamed myself. I had used the alcohol to numb my pain and to make me feel momentarily carefree during a time in my life when everything felt like a disaster. I told myself I knew better.

After the kids went to bed, I played my Roseanne Cash *Rhythm and Romance* cassette tape. I played that tape over and over for hours. I have no idea why I loved it so much other than the pain in her voice that matched the depth of mine. After a couple of weeks of playing the tape, I pushed the incident into the dark recesses of my brain and focused on moving forward. I moved forward, but my compartmentalized shame festered.

# Growing Together

At the end of that year, Mom changed jobs again. She had grown tired of being covered in white plastic confetti from her factory job, so she changed directions and got a job at Baucom's nursery in Charlotte. It seemed quite a change for her because she had never been one to work outside or do any sort of yard work. It was more money per hour, and she enjoyed watering the indoor plants. She was very good at keeping potted plants alive and thriving, their shoots branching out of pots and onto tabletops and windowsills. She kept spider plants throughout my childhood, the kind with purple-green leaves that dangled down in tendrils. Its real name was spiderwort, but she called it "the wandering Jew," a colloquialism no longer appropriate but still widely used in certain regions. She had other plants she called the Devil's Ivy (pothos) because she said the plant could survive anything. She was correct about the pothos. Check any gardening website, and it'll confirm the plant is perfect for anyone who struggles to keep a houseplant alive because it can thrive in any condition and just keeps growing vines.

To my surprise, Mom loved her job at the greenhouse. I was sure she'd quit within weeks, but instead, she thrived watering and talking to plants all day long. I used to tease her about dropping used coffee grounds into the soil and whispering to the plants' leaves, but I guess she did have a technique with them. I marveled at how easy it was for her to give praise to an inanimate object, while I was left desperate for an encouraging word. I suppose she was giving them what they needed to grow, but I was no longer a child in her eyes. I had perfected the art of acting like I didn't need anything from her, and I was way too stubborn to admit I still needed her loving attention.

Since my mother was working a first-shift job, she asked that I watch the kids. Reluctantly I agreed because it was what my family needed at that time.

"How long until we can put them in daycare?" I asked, hopeful this was a temporary situation but dreading the possibility that it wasn't.

"Probably a couple of months. Just until I can save some more money," she replied.

A couple of months seemed like an eternity. My brother and sister climbed from the furniture and jumped from said furniture onto each other. They also indulged in screaming and slapping matches so intense, it made me fear stepping between them. I put them in time-out a lot. I loved them dearly, but the constant sibling rivalry

and bickering wore on my teenage nerves. I found myself threatening to spank them more than I'd like to admit.

Mom seemed much happier at the nursery job than the one she'd
had at the plastics factory. She smiled more often, making the atmosphere lighter around the house. Since I watched the kids during
the day, as soon as she got home from work, I quickly asked if
she needed me to go to the store. I'd ride a couple of miles to the
Harris Teeter on Main Street to buy her a carton of cigarettes, a
gallon of milk, and a loaf of bread that we always seemed to need.
In 1987, anyone under eighteen could still buy cigarettes without
any questions. I looped the plastic grocery bags onto my handlebars,
ensuring they were properly balanced, and biked back home like
this. Sometimes, I could even ride with three or four bags on each
handlebar. I was proud of my ability to juggle groceries and ride a
bike. This was an impressive feat for someone who hadn't learned
to ride a bike until she was twelve.

My bicycle was showing considerable wear and tear by this point,
and the bike desperately needed new brakes. Brakes were low down
on the list of things we could afford, and I wanted daycare for my
siblings more than bike brakes. When I needed to slow down or stop,
I'd lift my right foot and place the inside corner of my sneaker sole
on the rear wheel to slow the bike. I was soon in need of some new
tennis shoes, especially after one afternoon when I braked too hard
and a chunk of the rubber sole flew off.

I loved my broke-down bike, but I began eyeing our car more and
more, wishing I could hop in the driver's seat and take off to where
I needed to go. I had my learner's permit, but I didn't have enough

driving experience to take my driver's license test. Mom refused to ride with me after a little incident involving me pulling out into oncoming traffic. She'd been in the passenger seat sedated from a dental procedure, but not too sedated to yell at me or remember the sight of an oncoming car on her side.

By early spring of that year, Mom found a daycare for the kids and helped me get a job at Baucom's. I was an order puller. Suppose a truck needed a thousand daylilies to deliver to a store. In that case, I'd get on an electric cart, which everyone called a donkey, and collect the plants from the storage area. During certain times of the year, such as fall, mum season, or poinsettia season, I'd wear a belt around my waist with plastic bags attached to it. I'd pick up a plant and drop it in the bag. It would then detach from my waist, much like produce bags from the grocery store. I'd stack them on trailers attached to donkeys, and a team of employees would transport them by cartloads to the warehouse, where they would eventually be loaded onto the trucks.

I'm not sure if it was being exposed to all the greenery or spending time outside, but this was by far my favorite job to date. It beat working fast-food jobs, hands down. I didn't have to be friendly to rude customers, and I soaked up the perfect mix of sun and physical activity to keep my body and soul happy. Mom worked in a different nursery area, and occasionally I'd catch a glimpse of her and wave, though we never ate lunch together. It was probably better for our relationship to keep our distance at work.

After work, we'd meet at the car, and on the way to pick up the kids, we'd discuss our day. It felt comfortable and effortless between us once again. There was no anger on my part toward her for poor decision-making, no nasty looks or unease. We were simply equals working toward a better life. By April, we had saved enough money to leave that tiny trailer in Mooresville. We moved into a newer trailer park in Concord, an up-and-coming town about thirty minutes southeast of our old place. The trailer park in Concord was much larger, and most of the trailers there had been built within the previous five to ten years.

Life in the new trailer took on some normalcy. I had my own bedroom once more. I wasn't sleeping on a used couch, afraid of bug infestation or insects breeding under my skin and then bursting through like some alien larvae while I slept.

A man Mom worked with asked her out on a date, the first real date she'd been on in over two years. I even had a guy my age ask me out as well. He approached me one day in the breakroom, his shoulder-length red hair frizzier than mine, freckled face red from nerves or being fair skinned and working outside. His voice quavered and my heart went out to him. I still wasn't very trusting of the opposite sex at that point. I wondered why I should trust men when my trust had been broken multiple times. I studied him for an uncomfortable amount of silence before I agreed, partly because I needed a friend my own age and partly because I didn't want to hurt his feelings. At no point was there any attraction, which should have clued me into a potential problem.

Neal was an unassuming kid, though, and I got no vibes of any ill will. He drove a deep-purple Volkswagen bug with large dual exhaust pipes and loved listening to Pink Floyd and smoking pot, though never when I was in the car because he knew I didn't like it. We went to the movies and the county fair, and Neal even took me to Carowinds, the sprawling amusement park built on the border of North and South Carolina, for my seventeenth birthday. When he came in for a kiss while we waited in the line for the Scrambler, I turned and presented my cheek. I knew then I would never kiss Neal because I simply had no desire to lock lips with the guy. The attraction just wasn't there no matter how much I enjoyed his company.

When he dropped me off at home that night, I told him that I didn't think we should continue dating. He nodded agreement while staring out the driver's window. While I was happy to be without male companionship and the societal pressure of intimacy, Mom started letting her new boyfriend sleep over. One night I was getting a glass of water after a bad dream. The kitchen sink was in line with my mother's bedroom. The door to Mom's bedroom was cracked open. Her boyfriend was stretched out on top of the sheets, the street lights illuminating his naked figure. Didn't he realize or care that she had children in the household? And why didn't Mom put a stop to it? I had questioned her taste in men for years and was hoping this wasn't just another degenerate who would use her up and leave her behind. I dropped the glass into the sink and returned to the safety of my room, locking the door behind me.

My prized possession, my AM/FM/cassette player and recorder I'd received for Christmas when I was thirteen, was my safety blanket. I'd wait for the Casey Kasem countdown and carefully record my favorite songs for the ultimate mixtapes. The night I'd seen Mom's naked boyfriend, I turned on my mixtape and let the music lull me back to sleep. I'd moved on to some newer music after moving to the new trailer. I'd given up my Rosanne Cash phase and had taken to listening to The Pretenders: "Back on the Chain Gang," "Don't Get Me Wrong," and "Middle of the Road." But "Brass in Pocket" was my favorite song from the band, even though it was released years earlier. There was something about the lyrics that made me feel more confident, a feeling I had in short supply.

The summer I was seventeen, I found I enjoyed my job at the nursery so much that I wasn't really thinking about going back to school. They'd just promoted me to the vital position of starting seedlings in the special greenhouse. I was the apprentice of a not very friendly woman who didn't appreciate having to teach someone else her trade. I got the distinct impression she preferred to work alone. While my supervisor said the job was central to the nursery's future plant growth, I missed the days of filling orders and being outside. Instead, my days consisted of carefully monitoring the development and watering of new seedlings in a greenhouse with a constant temperature at eighty-five degrees and a hundred percent humidity. For someone with thick, wavy hair, a mere ten minutes in the greenhouse resulted in me looking like an exasperated witch standing over a failed cauldron experiment. When I climbed into the car in the afternoons, Mom would spend the first fifteen minutes of the ride home complaining about her day. I wondered how long it'd take before she moved to a different job.

Her sudden job dissatisfaction seemed to coincide with the fact that her boyfriend broke off their hook-ups to date a young red-headed girl who'd just started at the nursery. I judged the new girlfriend to be about my age, while he was clearly in his late thirties or early forties. I couldn't understand what would make an old man want to date a woman young enough to be his daughter. Mom was more pissed off than hurt by his new girlfriend. We never discussed her feelings about it, but I assumed she was not in the race to find another man in her life. Of course, this didn't stop her from trying to fix me up with someone, a new obsession of hers I didn't share.

A couple of weeks after the break-up, she hit me with this conversation on the way home from work.

"I met a new woman today." Her eyes sparkled like she had a secret. I knew that look well.

"Oh, really."

"Yeah, this is her first job after getting out of prison." Mom nonchalantly dropped this bit of information as if we associated with ex-convicts all the time.

"What?"

"No, she's nice."

I gave her a side-eye. "Please don't tell me you invited her to live with us. I like being alive."

Mom laughed, saying, "No, silly. She has a son."

"Oh. I see."

"Hear me out. His name is Kip."

I shoved a hand over my mouth, but not before a snort-laugh escaped. "Kip? Sounds like a frat boy name."

"You need to learn to give people chances before judging them."

Properly chastised, I said, "Sorry, Mom. So, the moms think we should go out?"

"I told her you're sweet, and apparently, her son took care of himself while she was in prison."

I wanted to ask her what my sweet nature and this young man's strong survival instincts had to do with compatibility. Instead, I swallowed that response and asked, "What'd she do?"

"Drug possession and writing bad checks."

I shrugged. At least it wasn't a violent crime, I guess. She told me he was eighteen, and I agreed to go on one date with him if it would make her happy.

"I just want *you* to be happy."

"I can tell you dating some guy isn't the key to my happiness."

She rolled her eyes as she merged onto the highway. My mom was born in an era when women still believed the right man was the golden ticket to a happy life. I assumed her experiences with men would've taught her the opposite, but she never did learn. I suppose that's why she never seemed truly happy in her lifetime.

The next Saturday, Kip rolled into my driveway with his convertible red two-seater. I didn't recognize the car's make, but I assumed it was a foreign model given its graceful curves, unlike boxy, sharp-edged American cars most people in North Carolina drove. Men may not be the key to happiness, but I'd gamble my life that car was. Kip was a couple of inches taller than me, light-brown hair trimmed close to his head, and he wore Chino shorts, a pink polo shirt, and loafers. When Mom took in his look, I could see the wheels turning as she pictured our future children in fully monogrammed matching outfits. She was always a sucker for collared shirts and khakis.

Before he closed my car door, I knew that he was not interested in my gender. I also knew he probably hadn't come to terms with it just yet. Our first date consisted of a round of minigolf filled with plenty of laughter and conversation, followed by a country road jaunt at fast speeds. Kip just wanted to talk, and I'd never felt so at ease with the opposite sex. It was the first time I had the perfect date.

When I got home, Mom asked about the date.

"It was fantastic. We're going to the movies next Saturday."

Mom grinned over the cover of the women's magazine she was reading. I knew she saw her version of my future, but I welcomed Kip's companionship that felt safe and easy. There was something reassuring in spending time with someone my age who wasn't interested in wanting anything from me other than conversation.

Mom had decided to quit the nursery. Her decision, not our decision. This left me the sole breadwinner in the family while she looked for something else. We moved back to Mooresville in September 1987, to yet another old trailer; this one was apparently less expensive to rent than the one in Concord. Mom sat me down the weekend we moved and told me I'd be responsible for driving back and forth to Charlotte since she would watch the kids during the day while I worked.

"I only have a learner's permit. What happens if I get caught?"

"Don't speed or get in an accident, and you won't get caught."

*Why didn't I think of that? So obvious.*

That Monday morning brought a new level of freedom and a slight thrill of breaking the law as I pulled out of the driveway without a supervised driver. I stopped at the gas station down from our trailer to fill up on gas and grab a breakfast of champions coffee and six-pack of donut cakes for one dollar. I drove down I-77 south toward Charlotte. Back then, traffic was light. Now that Charlotte is one of the fastest growing cities in the country, everyone and their mom travels the highways leading in and out of the city at breakneck speeds. My commute in 1987 was only about twenty to twenty-five minutes. Nowadays, I do everything in my power to avoid this road for fear of sitting in bumper-to-bumper traffic for an hour or more, all while dealing with average Joes who think they're auditioning for the NASCAR circuit.

My date night the next Saturday was something I was looking forward to. I wasn't sure how Kip would like to drive to Mooresville from Concord, but I figured we'd explore the roads around my hometown before the weather got too much colder. Kip was always prompt, at least ten to fifteen minutes before an agreed-upon time. On that Saturday, when he didn't arrive at six o'clock, I was concerned. The first hour, I worried he'd been in a wreck. By eight o'clock, I realized I'd been stood up. And on the following Monday morning, I knew our companionship was over by how his mother avoided me in the break room. At first, I was hurt and sad because I genuinely enjoyed his friendship. I suppose he may have realized after several dates that he wasn't into me. I knew I did nothing wrong and just wished him future happiness.

By October, Mom had met a new guy, Wayne, through one of her newly made friends next door. She went next door to Joy's trailer and played cards on the weekends. She came home one Saturday evening talking about going on a date with a friend of Joy's. I had finally reached a point in my life where my feet felt steady instead of mud-surfing down a rocky ravine. I had no interest in dating, and I was the happiest I had been in a while having worked at the nursery for well over a year and content to simply work, read, listen to music, and watch *Scooby-Doo* with my siblings on the weekends.

When Mom told me she was going on a date and a week later she invited this scruffy man to move in with us, I could only shake my head in disbelief. *Here we go again.* I felt something shift in my soul. I didn't have the words to verbalize my disappointment, realizing once again that Mom would never not have a man by her side because she never trusted she was enough.

It's a wonder more women don't swear off men entirely, opting instead for female partners or a life of perpetual singlehood. I was keeping a running tally of all the things I'd do differently than my mother once I had my freedom. I vowed not to trust anyone who didn't prove they deserved it.

# I Love Rock and Freedom

U p to that point in my life, my mother's love had always made up for the consequences of poor decisions she'd made. Our bond of knowing we could rely on one another for just about anything was about as thick as the welfare cheese I'd once used to make macaroni and cheese. My mom's job turned into chauffeuring Wayne and me back and forth to work, him because he'd lost his license for a DUI ticket and me because our car was "broke-down."

They were picking me up from work one day in late November after I'd worked overtime to fill orders for poinsettias for the Christmas season. I climbed into the back seat of the wagon with Jacob and Hannah and let out an exhausted breath. There's no greater hell than working retail during the holidays. My mom shifted in the driver's seat and fixed me with her stare.

"Wayne and I think you should quit this job because it's not worth the drive. You can get a job closer to Mooresville making the same."

She turned and stared out the windshield. Clearly, I had no voice in the matter.

I stared back at her eyes in the rearview mirror as she concentrated on backing up.

I felt rage begin a slow simmer in my belly. *Who the fuck does he think he is? When did it become Wayne's decision what I do with my life? I'm grown.*

"But I like my job here."

"You'll find another one." She looked in Wayne's direction for support. He remained silent and stared straight ahead like the road was suddenly more interesting than the conversation.

I stared at the back of their heads and wondered whose idea it really was for me to quit my job. Wayne was a tall, thin man with a beard as full as a mountaineer and scraggly hair that reached almost to the tops of his stooped shoulders. His unsmiling demeanor reminded me of a human version of Oscar the Grouch from *Sesame Street*. Mom told me he reminded her of the country singer Alan Jackson. I don't know what she saw, but she was clearly delusional. I had deemed Wayne nice enough up to this point. He was a painter by trade and went to work every day, which seemed like a winning trait and just what Mom needed.

I was confused why she'd let him live with us so soon after meeting him; then again if male companionship was her ticket to feeling whole, I guess it made sense to her. Some people are completely satisfied to be alone because the silence does not haunt them. My mom wasn't one of those people.

Wayne was eleven years younger than my mom. This made him only ten years older than me, and this age difference felt strange. He wasn't a father figure; I already had one of those even though he didn't act like much of one, even before he was incarcerated. But Wayne also wasn't a friend, and I never knew how to behave or feel around him, so I mostly stayed silent. He'd done nothing to stir my ire, until today. Ripping the job I loved away from me was a massive overstep, and I resented his entitlement to mess with my life.

I dared him to meet my eyes, but his gaze refused to meet mine so I crossed my arms and stewed all the way home, that inner simmer growing to a slow boil. Once again, decisions were being made for my life without my contributing thoughts or opinions, much less my consent. I bit the hardened skin around my nail beds and tasted dirt. The taste was bitter like my impotent anger, now roiling and threatening to spill over the edges of the neat little container I kept it in. I felt and acted like an adult, but I was still only seventeen and always at the whim of the adults in my life. I spent more time in my room and even less time interacting with my family after that night. Something in me closed up shop.

One afternoon a few days later, I was lying on my bed weighing my options for my future. I had to get out. My options were limited to a job in fast food, yet again. I preferred the warm, pungent scent of my sweat mixed with soil. I'd take that smell a hundred times over rather than the smell of stale grease on my skin. The last time I'd worked at McDonald's, I'd nearly bit my tongue in half as customers cussed, yelled, and treated me as though I was dumb because they had to wait an extra two minutes for a fresh burger or fries. Customers aren't always right; sometimes they're just entitled assholes. I had daydreamed for hours, strategizing ways out and wondering how long this moron would be sticking around. If he meant to make this a long-term stay, I needed to hit the bricks as soon as I turned eighteen. Unfortunately, I gave all my money to Mom for the family and had zero savings of my own. I was six months from turning eighteen and felt stuck.

"Sandra!"

I jumped off my bed and ran out of my bedroom looking for Mom, the desperation of her cry startling me to action. She called out again, the sound coming from the hallway bathroom. I opened the door and saw her sitting on the commode, holding her stomach with one hand while the other gripped the edge of the countertop. I entered the room just as her eyes rolled back in her head, and she toppled off the toilet. I rushed to her side and saw the toilet bowl was filled with blood.

Crouching beside her on the floor, I tried to speak, but all that came out was a stifled croak. I cleared my throat and tried again. "Mom?"

I brushed her hair from her eyes, and they fluttered open. I exhaled pent-up breath. I was only a split second from running to the phone and calling for help.

"Help me to the bed," she said weakly.

"Are you okay?" I kept my panic in check for her sake.

She leaned against me as I walked/carried her down the short hallway toward her bedroom in the rear of the trailer. I was already a couple of inches taller than her, and while I barely weighed a hundred pounds, I was strong from working at the nursery. I laid her head back onto the pillows and gently lifted her legs onto the mattress.

"I'm fine." She struggled to nestle her head into the pillow.

"You don't look fine." Her skin was bleached pale as a sheet and glistening with cold sweat.

"Can you get a warm washcloth and clean me up? I just don't have the strength right now."

I raced to the kitchen and stood there, briefly paralyzed by rare indecision. The kids were too busy watching cartoons and had no clue what had happened. I opened and closed cabinet doors. The only pail in the household was used to mop the floors, and I refused to use it to clean her. Grabbing a mixing bowl she used to make biscuits, I filled it with warm water and snatched a washcloth from the hall closet on my way to her bedroom. I paused a moment at the end of the bed, taking in her nakedness from the waist down. I'd watched Mom get dressed from my earliest memories. Seeing her naked wasn't anything new. She'd taught me early in life not to be ashamed of nakedness. But that day, she was barely conscious, bright red blood staining her upper and inner thighs.

I fought embarrassment and lightheadedness at the sight of all that blood. Wrestling competing feelings, I gently wiped the blood from Mom's legs until she was clean once more. I erased the evidence so she wouldn't have to face it when she woke up. Grabbing a pair of clean panties from her dresser, I slid them over pale and listless legs. I pulled the covers up to her chin and placed a kiss on her forehead before I grabbed the bowl of water.

I poured the contents down the bathroom sink and watched the bloody water circle the drain through a veil of tears. Many people have mistaken my tears for over-sensitivity throughout my life. I cry quite easily. My body cries when sad, when I laugh too hard, and especially when I'm nuclear pissed, as I was that day. I couldn't believe she was trying to get pregnant again. Not after having Hannah so prematurely. Was she trying to kill herself by satisfying some man's desire for her to sire his child?

I returned to the room and rubbed her arm. She smiled weakly and said, "Thank you."

"Why are you doing this?" I demanded.

"He wants a child of his own."

I shook my head but didn't ask what she wanted because I already knew—she wanted whatever Wayne wanted, or at least that's what she told herself. Why did she continue being a vessel for a man's wants? I wanted my self-assured mom back, the one who'd stood her ground as a confident single woman. As I sat there keeping my opinions to myself as usual, I thought back to a night just six months prior when I'd glimpsed that version of my mom once again; it lived in her still, and I'd been relieved to see it.

We'd gone to a bar and grill after work at the nursery with some co-workers. Our co-workers had ordered a beer at the bar and dropped onto barstools to sip at frosty mugs with suds on top. Mom and I spotted the pool table in the back, and she'd already shimmied off in that direction. The one game my mom loved to play more than cards was pool. I racked the balls while she sauntered over to the monstrous jukebox against the wall. She dropped a quarter in and Joan Jett's "I Love Rock and Roll" blared inside the room. We sang along at the top of our lungs, ignoring the men who had gathered to watch the game, while she proceeded to skunk me. She whooped and grinned as she dropped the eight ball in the corner pocket, and I smiled instead of scowling because I'd lost. There she was, the woman full of the zest for life who didn't take shit from anybody, always playing the odds. I'd lose to see her win any day of the week. Mom did it all for a man; I did it all for her.

I lay beside her in the bed and stroked her head as she drifted in and out of sleep. I pressed the inside of my wrist against her forehead to check for a fever.

I whispered to the cold and unforgiving universe a desperate plea. "I love you, Mom. Don't leave me."

"I won't," the universe whispered back from the rumpled sheet-covered form beside me.

When I was sure she had drifted off to sleep, I returned to the kitchen for the bleach cleaner and wiped the blood of my unborn sibling from the bathroom surfaces. I washed my hands under hot water until my skin turned red and then put all of the dirty clothes in the washing machine. Just like that, it was over. I headed into the living room, where Jacob and Hannah were laid out on the floor watching cartoons. I pulled them in for a tight hug, happy they were unaware, and watched Tom chase Jerry across the television screen. We never talked about it again. Not a word, like if it was unspoken, it never happened.

With only one car running and the job search taking longer than I'd expected, we were forced to move out of the trailer and into a motel room in town. It was one of those motels that advertised weekly rates, comprised of two full-sized beds, one small bathroom, and cable television with thirty nonsense channels that didn't redeem the sub-standard surroundings. It reminded me of the rundown motels in Albuquerque and Statesville, a sorry excuse for a home I hoped to never revisit. I couldn't erase the thought on repeat that we were going backwards. I couldn't go back, I wouldn't go back—my only option was forward.

I couldn't help but wonder then what would've happened if Wayne hadn't entered our lives. Would we have wound up living in the same questionable motel listening to late-night screaming matches of the other occupants? I wasn't sure of anything, and at seventeen, I felt like cinder blocks were being stacked on my shoulders. I was starting to crumble under their weight. I thought I'd go insane if I didn't get out of that room, out of that town, and far, far away from my family.

# Faith and Fast Food

I grudgingly kicked off 1988 by returning to Hardee's, this time working the drive-thru. The walk to and from work was about two and a half miles each way, forty minutes to an hour, give or take, based on my motivation level on any given day. Feeling stuck in a situation with no way out was, and still is, one of my greatest fears. My mind couldn't focus. I imagined being swallowed up by thick river mud, struggling not to drown in fear and frustration. I searched for any kind of sign or way out. Some days I chose to walk different routes back to the motel to break up the monotony and get a change of scenery. If I walked by the water tower, I could see the old plastics plant where Mom used to work and passed the tunnel road where I'd flashback to the first time she'd driven me there as a child. I'd been about five, shirtless and sprawled across the back seat smoking a candy cigarette pretending to be Mom as she'd stopped inside the big metal tunnel.

She turned in her seat and looked at me with that signature sparkle in her eyes. "Scream as loud as you want. I come here whenever I need to."

I studied the back of her head for a minute and then let out a loud "Woooooooooo."

"Do it again. See how good it feels?"

I smiled and nodded slowly as she laid on her horn and screamed, "AHHHHH" at the top of her lungs.

The sounds reverberated; we felt the vibrations in our bones. I'm sure the folks living close to the tunnels did not appreciate the noise, but Mom always seemed in a better mood after doing it. By the time I was seventeen, the tunnel road was dark, untouched by sunlight and framed by kudzu vines looking to choke the entrance and exit. The little voice in my head always warned me from taking a detour on foot to enter the dark, wet tunnels even though I longed for a place to release my pent-up frustration.

The other way to the motel from the Hardee's required me to pass the National Guard Armory that was tucked between a seafood restaurant and a lawn equipment store. I acknowledged its existence most of the time but never really paid attention to the sign out front. I'd been inside the building once, right after Hannah was born. We'd gone there one morning to wait in a long line to pick up a brick of welfare cheese, a little bigger than a big block of Velveeta. At that time, I'd been impressed by the crisp camouflage uniforms and shiny black boots of the soldiers who walked past the line of needy people waiting for food. By the end of January, after nearly a month of passing by the armory, the sign's subliminal message had finally taken hold.

Instead of just passing by that day, I walked to the side door, opened it, and stepped inside before I lost whatever inertia had pushed me in that direction. I followed the country music to a small office that flanked the building's front. There was an older man sitting there, hunched over his desk reviewing paperwork. He had a bushy mustache and a potbelly that strained his faded camouflage uniform when he leaned back in his chair. He didn't look much like the other soldiers I'd seen a couple years ago or like the ones smiling back from the posters on the walls.

"Can I help you?" he asked.

"I just have a couple questions. If you have time. If not, I can come back some other time." The butterflies tickled my throat.

He motioned for me to take a seat in the sole metal chair across from him. I perched on the chair's edge and fiddled with my Hardee's hat.

"I saw your sign outside. About money for college, if I joined."

He nodded and then went on to explain that the National Guard served the people of the state of North Carolina. I nodded, sat up straighter, and scooted back until my spine flinched against the cold metal. He continued to explain that if I joined, my commitment to the National Guard would be one weekend a month and a couple of weeks of training in the summers after basic and technical school.

Sergeant Smith lowered his voice and leaned forward like he was imparting a secret. "You'd actually be better off joining the regular

Army. You'd get more money for college, and there are way better benefits."

"Really? How'd that work? I'm not eighteen yet."

"Are you in high school?"

"No, I dropped out to help my family." I hoped my decision to leave school wasn't about to bite me in the ass.

Sergeant Smith got a thoughtful look on his face. "Well then, if you're serious about joining, you need to get your GED and take the ASVAB."

"How much money for college?" I'd do what needed to be done if it got me out of this town.

"The last I heard, they were offering $24,000 for some MOSes."

I'd heard announcements about taking the ASVAB when I was in high school but had no idea what it meant. I had no clue what a MOS was. The acronyms were making my head spin.

"What's an MOS?"

"Military Occupational Specialty. Basically, it's the job you get based on your ASVAB score and the needs of the Army."

"And the ASVAB is a test?"

"Yeah, but it's a test you don't really study for. Based on your results, you get to pick your job. Stands for 'Armed Forces Vocational Aptitude Battery.' You'll get used to all the acronyms."

I nodded and let the information sink in. I rose from my seat and the chair made a horrible screeching noise against the linoleum floor. "Thank you, sir. I appreciate you taking the time to answer my questions."

"Take these pamphlets and let me know if I can help. Good luck in the future with whatever you decide." He shoved a handful of information into my hands, and my mind raced with what he'd told me.

I turned around at the threshold and asked, "If I want to take the ASVAB, what would I need to do?"

"Come back by and let me know. We give the test once a month, and our next one is two Saturdays from now."

I nodded and thanked him once more.

I knew if I continued doing what I was doing, I would go absolutely nowhere; that simply wasn't an option. I would lie awake at night terrified by the thought I'd never escape my situation. If I joined the military, I could earn money for college after four years, get out, and go to school for criminal justice. I toyed with the idea of being a police officer and eventually a detective.

While I loved writing, I had to get a good job that would provide a steady paycheck and never put me at the mercy of a man's whim. I always liked the idea of protecting and serving people in need. Joining the military could help me; it could help all of us. I strolled the rest of the way to the motel, deep in thought about how I would broach this idea to my mom. I'd wait until Wayne got home from work before I brought it up. He once talked about being in the National Guard. I was pretty sure he'd support the idea of me leaving. A blind person could see the dirty looks I shot at him, and the atmosphere in the motel would lighten up quite a bit once I was gone.

Mom would be the harder sell. I'd been her running partner. I had supported her my whole life either as a companion or co-parent. I wasn't sure she would be willing to let me go without a battle. She depended on me more than I wanted. The more she tightened her hold, the more I dreamed of leaving. I didn't have the words to describe our relationship then, but I now know we were enmeshed with too many years of her depending on me to be her friend, confidant, and parent. I needed space. I needed to be my own person.

After dinner that evening, I broached the subject of going back for my GED and then joining the Army.

I waited until I was drying the electric skillet before starting the conversation.

"Mom?"

"Yes?" She turned her head away from the mystery book she'd checked out from the local library just down the block.

"Can we talk?"

Wayne watched television, and Jacob and Hannah were sitting at the small table by the door playing with cars. Wayne didn't move his eyes from the screen, but I knew from his tilted head that he was listening to our conversation.

She placed a bookmark on her page and turned her full attention my way. We didn't talk very much, at least not about deep, thought-provoking situations. We had a kind of telepathy going on when it came to things like that. By the time we moved into the motel, our nightly discussions had centered around crazy customers at work and the latest entertainment news.

"I spoke to a man at the Armory today, and...I've decided I want to join the military."

She let the silence drag, and I felt like my stomach was in my throat.

Wayne stopped pretending to watch the news and turned his head to watch her response.

Just as I had predicted, hope shone in his eyes.

"Why would you want to do that?" she asked after a few eternal seconds.

She was questioning my motives, and I saw her point. It wasn't like my family had an infamous military legacy like the fictional Lt. Dan in *Forrest Gump*. According to Mom's stories, my uncle Junior had gotten himself kicked out of the Army for doing drugs. That was the extent of our family's military legacy. I knew of no one else serving.

I couldn't speak my truth for fear of hurting her. I loved that woman too much to tell her I felt smothered in her household. I knew in my heart if I didn't get out, I'd lose myself forever. Hell, I had no fucking idea who I was at the time or what I wanted from life, but I knew I wasn't a minimum wage fast-food worker. I also knew I couldn't live my life for her.

"Look, Mom, I know it may seem crazy. I can join for four years and get money for college. Just four years away, and then I'll be back."

She'd studied my face, looking for what, I didn't know. "What're you going to do? You're not even eighteen yet."

"Tomorrow, on my way back from work, I'll stop at the Mitchell Community College building and ask what I need to do to finish high school. That's the first step. Then I'll register to take the ASVAB."

"Well, I'd be happy if you were to finish school. I never wanted you to quit anyway."

"Oh, I remember." I smiled at her and felt our conversation had moved into a happier territory. The air shifted, drawing out my confidence. But she was just gearing up to stick the knife in and twist.

"I just don't think you have what it takes to listen to someone else. You don't like it when I tell you to do stuff around here."

The momentary happiness gave way to irritation as I realized she thought I wouldn't be successful. I was hurt and frustrated. She really didn't know me. I was fired up and ready to show her just how well I would do in the military. I mulled all the possible responses to her jab, opting for a charming smile and said, "I can do anything as long as I know it'll change our lives."

Mom nodded agreement, still not sold, but swayed by my logic. She returned to her book while Wayne told me about how the military had changed his life. I nodded along feeling the tide turn in my favor.

That day in February, when I walked into the Mooresville campus of the continuing education center of Mitchell Community College, I felt a wave of calm wash over me.

One of my favorite movie lines is from *Almost Famous*. Penny Lane, the self-proclaimed Band-Aid, and William, the wannabe rock reporter, are discussing his age. After several lines of back and forth jockeying over his age, he finally confesses his actual age of fifteen. Penny Lane looks at him and solemnly says, "Isn't it funny how the truth just sounds different?" I love many lines in this movie, but this is by far my favorite because it is so damn accurate.

Just as the truth sounds a certain way, a decision that's correct and true on the path of life strikes a certain nerve. Quitting school at fifteen and joining the Army at eighteen seemed like the right decisions at the time. I'd always relied on my gut and sixth sense to get me to that point. The feeling of inner alignment is like drinking the first sip of coffee on a crisp fall morning as sunlight pierces the treetops. Or like standing at the edge of the ocean, staring down the mysteriously vast expanse while the waves lap at my soul. Or like wrapping myself in a blanket of total calm, the "what if's" and "woulda, coulda, shoulda's" momentarily banished.

The day at the National Guard Armory had been my first sip of coffee. While Ms. Harris explained the difference between the GED and adult high school diploma, I felt a calmness I hadn't felt in a very long time. Since I'd turned fourteen, every decision in my life had been made by others without my consent or regard for my feelings. I knew I was technically still considered a minor, but I'd been straining at those reins now for many years. Freedom was finally within my sights. Somehow, with absolute certainty, I knew I was on the right path for my future.

Much to my absolute joy, I had to quit my job at Hardee's because the adult high school diploma required that I study all day. When I finished studying a particular subject, I took a test. It was like being back in high school, except I was only one of a few other students who spent the day with my nose in the books. Ms. Harris would make her rounds during the day. She would put her hand on my shoulder and tell me what a great job I was doing.

When I took the ASVAB, it seemed like a bizarre cross between any number of standardized tests I'd taken since the third grade and an IQ test. It was interspersed with questions about mechanics and electronics. I hadn't held anything larger than a screwdriver at that point in my life, but I was a quick study and hoped my responses represented me as such. After I finished the test, I walked out the doors feeling like I'd possibly screwed up my chances in an unwinnable contest. How would I know if I did well? I wasn't confident my military job would coincide with my interests. I knew whatever I did, I would only do it for a few years. And I acknowledged with confidence that the past three years ensured that I could survive almost anything for a sustained period of time.

# Who Will You Turn To?

It would be months before I got to pick my military job, but the ASVAB was done. In between studying for the subject tests to complete my high school education, we moved from the motel in Mooresville to another trailer park just about a mile from where my grandparents had lived in an area between Troutman and Statesville. It felt like another transition point, but I was happy to be clear of the rundown motel known more for drug addicts and prostitution than anything else. This trailer park was wasn't as bad as some we'd lived in, not as nice as others. I guess I deemed it in the lower middle class of trailer parks. Most of the yards were kept tidy and there were brick ranch homes lining the streets in and out of the back side of the park.

Every time we drove past the driveway leading to where my mother and her siblings grew up, I was filled with animosity toward the grandmother who turned us away. I couldn't help but think if she'd just let us stay with her, we wouldn't have bounced around everywhere. It was an early lesson that wasting time and energy on "woulda, coulda, shoulda's" was futile. It was easier back then to hold anger against a grandmother who hadn't been much of one. I needed a scapegoat, and she was a handy placeholder. I hadn't yet learned that people make choices in life based on their capabilities at the time. We needed $10 and she didn't have two nickels to rub together, literally and metaphorically. However, I'll never forget the deep hurt it caused my mom.

In April of that year, I walked into the recruiter's office in Statesville with all but one of my subject tests completed for my high school diploma. The ASVAB was in the books, and I was ready to permanently commit to joining the Army. My mother signed the permission form, and just like that, I joined the delayed entry program. I probably could've waited until I turned eighteen, but I wanted my decision to be a written commitment. I wanted a contract to bind me and to signal Mom that this decision—my decision—was permanent. I had an exit plan. Mom didn't sign with a smile; her approval was scratched out grudgingly, and then she dropped the pen like it was engulfed in flames. She had so much attitude that day. I reminded her that I was doing this for us, but I hid the truth that I was doing it solely for me. I needed space.

I spent my days in Mooresville at the learning center studying high school subjects and dreaming of being away from Wayne and Mom's constant arguments. I didn't know what the fights were about since they usually did it behind the closed bedroom door. I wondered what they could possibly be arguing about, and a small part of me wondered if it would affect my future.

When their voices got too elevated, I took my brother and sister for long walks around the neighborhood. A young blonde-haired twenty-year-old man who lived a couple trailers down would strike up conversations as I walked with my brother and sister. He'd come over and talk to me while I played ball with my siblings. I knew he liked me, but I didn't want him getting any ideas or attachments.

One day he asked if we could go to the park with my brother and sister, and with the children as my insurance, we walked around the pond and fed bread to the ducks. We went to the park a few more times, and eventually, I would leave my brother and sister at home. It was nice to talk to someone outside of my family, another adult. He thought we were more than we were, and I probably should have told him that holding my hand as we walked the trails was as far as it was going. I had no intention of letting him any closer than arm's length. I wasn't letting anyone get close enough to hurt me.

I was awarded my adult high school diploma on June 23, 1988, mere days before my eighteenth birthday. My diploma was delivered only weeks after what would've been my graduation with my class from Mooresville Senior High. I was ecstatic about the future, with getting out of Iredell County, seeing other states besides the Carolinas and possibly other countries. My journey, my story as an adult, was about to begin. In less than a month, I'd be on my way to basic training. I was still waiting on the recruiter to give me a report date to go to Charlotte to pick my military job and take the oath of service.

The excitement turned to trepidation a few afternoons later when Mom and Wayne's argument escalated to a concerning volume. I opened my bedroom door and stuck my head out to see if I needed to intervene. Jacob and Hannah were sprawled on the floor in front of the television watching cartoons, ignoring the yelling. I saw Wayne coming down the hallway from their bedroom, his face a deep red. He had an armful of my mom's clothes. I watched him toss her clothes onto the patch of grass in front of the trailer. I have often wondered how anger could cause people to act so irrationally. What makes people turn violent, verbally abusive, physically abusive? Wayne didn't get physically violent that day. I don't recall his words, only the fact that his face was contorted, at least the parts I could see under his scruffy facial hair, and he sounded crazed, screaming obscenities at my mom.

I'd been plenty angry over the years, but I never once considered turning violent to express it. I turned my anger inward, pushing it deep into the pit of my stomach and held it there, waiting for the right opportunity to use it as a jolt of motivation to change a situation. My anger and displeasure with my situation are what pushed me to change. It never allowed me to give up or give in when life's circumstances felt like they were too much to overcome. Anger and stubbornness wouldn't ever let me quit.

On that day when Wayne's anger was unleashed, I gathered the kids and buckled them into their car seats, and then helped Mom gather armfuls of our clothing. Everything else was left behind. The years we'd spent collecting household goods from thrift stores, the time and money we'd paid to carve out our life after Robert left, to make our life our own again, was wrecked by another fucking man. He stood in the doorway of the trailer and frowned like we were inconvenient castaways. I sat silently in the passenger seat at a loss for words as Mom backed out of the driveway, letting out her own string of curse words.

My mom could string foul words together like she was a professional curse artist. I now laugh at how she used to tell me not to cuss. She said I shouldn't use foul language because it made me appear unintelligent. Don't curse, don't drink, don't smoke, sit up straight. The one area of my life in which she never dared offer advice was regarding men. I suppose she knew I wouldn't have listened if she tried. Mom liberally expressed her opinions on people or situations but certainly didn't live under any pretense that she had a handle on the male species.

There are moments in life that cause a chain reaction, sometimes for good, other times disastrous. I swallowed my anger and a growing sense of panic like I'd never experienced before. My best laid plans felt like they were unraveling before my eyes, and I tried to feel compassion for how Mom was feeling in the moment. But try as I might, all I could think about was how these new developments in my mom's romantic relationship would once again affect me. Forced out of our home that day, we set off on a new path no one saw coming.

# Stand By

We drove around Statesville aimlessly, lost as to where to go or what to do next. The kids talked about their Ninja Turtle action figures, oblivious to anything outside their play world. I was happy they were so involved in play that they knew nothing about our plight. There we were, homeless, yet again. How in the world did we get to that point? Why didn't Wayne just leave instead of throwing out two women and two small children? I couldn't understand how a man could act so callously.

As we rode around in our car that day, left with nothing but a few changes of clothes and each other, I worried about what would happen. We only had each other and no money because Wayne was the only one working at the time. I'd just completed my high school education and was only weeks from enlisting and leaving for basic training. Guilt and anxiety gnawed at my guts, and I questioned how I could possibly leave them in that situation.

I sat beside Mom in the front seat and studied her profile. Her chin was set, no tears this time. I never asked what they argued about because I had no real investment in their relationship like I'd had with her and Robert. She pulled down a side street into a residential area. I saw a former church surrounded by a six-foot chain-link fence with green privacy shading woven through the metal. I could make out the outline of a playground around the back. Next to the church was another house, likely the former pastor's residence.

"What's this?" I asked.

"A shelter," was her clipped reply.

I didn't know how she already knew about the homeless shelter only miles from the trailer. I wondered if maybe she'd been researching it for a while, maybe after one of their other arguments. After her experiences with Robert, I knew she always wanted to have a back-up plan. I learned from the best.

As we approached the house's door, we were greeted by a staff member before we even knocked. We were processed into the shelter and informed we could stay no longer than two weeks. The shelter required that we help with cooking and cleaning. Everyone staying there had chores. We were also required to look for work daily until employment was obtained.

The staff member showed us to a room upstairs in the women and children's part of the home. It was a co-ed homeless shelter, though the men and women were separated by floors. There were two double beds in the room, indicating I got to share a bed with one of the kids. Hannah made the decision for me by jumping right onto the bed and grinning at me like we were just having a girls' sleepover. I ruffled her curls and gave her a hug. I loved both of my siblings equally, but my sister clung to me like a joey in a pouch. I was concerned about how she'd react when I left since she'd developed more of a maternal relationship with me than with our mother.

Mom once told me that one of my cousins had started rumors around town that Hannah was my child and not my mom's. I suppose people who are bored or have esteem issues must gossip to inflate themselves. Hannah's adoration was the cutest thing ever and came in handy when I wanted her and Jacob to stop fighting because she never wanted to disappoint me.

Hannah and Mom never had a close relationship. I attributed it to their lack of bonding, given that the NICU limited human contact so early in her life. She was connected to so many wires; my mom was only allowed to touch a hand or foot through the incubator the first few weeks of her life. Hannah somehow loved me unconditionally even though I didn't hold her for months after she was born. She sat beside me on the couch, glued to my side when we watched TV, and always requested I tuck her into bed. My feelings for her and Jacob were maternal, and I knew I would miss them when I left, but I also hoped my absence would allow Hannah and Mom to get closer. I didn't have the same concern for Jacob because he'd always been a mama's boy, one who she thought could do no wrong.

The first couple of nights living in the homeless shelter left me nervous, the kind of nervous that settled in my bones and kept me looking over my shoulder when I walked down the hall or entered the dark stairwell that led to our bedroom on the second floor. There were too many people, especially men, milling around. My distrust of men was well-informed from personal experience, but the ones roaming the shelter had an added air of danger. The shelter provided meals and a place to stay, but the job-finding aspect fell solely on the individual with little help from shelter staff. The always-hiring food industry came through once more.

Mom and I secured jobs as waitresses at the Waffle House by the interstate. We worked it out to where we were on different shift schedules, so someone was always with the kids. Of course, Mom made a competition of waitressing. She took great pleasure in teasing me about how I would never beat her tips when I refused to smile at the customers.

I only laughed at her jibes because I knew she was trying to goad me. Her competitive streak was as wide as the Mississippi and I'd once thought it possible to beat her at the card games or board games, but since about the age of eight I resigned myself to the fact she could outlast me in her quest to always win with games. I considered the tip challenge irrelevant, but I let her think I was buying into her game.

While at the Waffle House, she worked the first shift, and I mostly worked the second shift that ran from 2 p.m. to 10 p.m. Mom's gift for talking up strangers served her well in her job as a waitress. She could've taught negotiation tactics and communication skills at a doctoral level. I did not inherit this ability from her. I was shy and untrusting of people. I had a way of watching people and judging within the first thirty seconds whether or not they were a danger or if they were safe. I couldn't force a smile or be nice to creepy people for tips. It went against my nature and made me a terrible waitress.

The manager of the Waffle House approached me one evening at the end of my shift. He wore heavily embroidered cowboy boots, way too much cologne, and walked like he was trying to work out a wedgie. I couldn't take him seriously, and I feared one day he'd see the eye-roll aimed at his back whenever he walked away from me.

"Hey, how would you like to make more money?"

I eyed him cautiously and said, "Doing what?"

"Do you know the cooks here make minimum wage and keep a percentage of the cash register?"

"No." I didn't know that. "I don't have experience as a short-order cook."

"I have faith in you. You're smart, and I'll have Joe train you for a week before putting you on a shift alone, second shift mostly. It's our easiest shift. Light until about early evening. You miss the breakfast crowd and the drunks."

I thought about it for less than a minute before agreeing. I hated being friendly to rude customers and only getting a quarter for waiting on them hand and foot. At least this way, as the cook, I was guaranteed money.

"I'll do it." I slapped a smile on my face to make him think I was suitably appreciative.

On the walk back to the shelter that day, I rationalized my decision. It would only be for a short time. I was on borrowed time as a civilian, and I would be grateful for the extra money to help Mom find a new place. We had to leave the shelter in a little over a week, but I also worried about what my mom would do once I left. I had committed to joining the Army, but I sensed my mother thought

I could just walk away so I could stay by her side. My inevitable departure had been an enormous elephant in the room we didn't discuss on those nights we lay awake after the kids went to sleep.

The night before we reached our two-week limit at the shelter, I turned to her in the dark. I found it easier at times to talk to her when she couldn't read my face.

"What are we going to do?" I asked.

"Tomorrow, we'll move to the little motel by the interstate. We have enough cash to stay there for a couple of weeks."

"Then what?"

"I'll figure it out when we cross that bridge."

"Mom, I'm leaving soon."

"I'm aware. I'll figure it out."

The words snapped through the dark, stinging just like she meant. Not "we," as it had always been. She made it clear I was no longer included on her team.

Thinking back, my mom had taken that attitude with many of the obstacles we'd faced since Robert had walked out on us. I suppose this is one reason I overcompensated by turning into a control freak as I entered adulthood. I wasn't the kind of person to wait out a bad situation like a game of chicken with life. I don't mind change, but I also like to know that I have back-up options.

As we prepared to leave the shelter, my family packed our few possessions into trash bags because we still couldn't afford actual travel bags. We moved to the motel that primarily housed out of town construction workers and weary travelers along I-40. It had a swimming pool, which struck me as very funny since the deep-end view was the interstate and a car dealership. On the horizon, I could see the large Waffle House sign beaming against the skyline.

While Mom turned on cartoons and settled the kids into the room, I walked the short distance to work to continue my training as a short-order cook. As a Waffle House waitress, I stood in the area just outside the cook's station and yelled orders to the cook as we'd been instructed. It wasn't rude because there was always a ton of noise: clattering silverware being loaded and unloaded from the two dishwashers housed underneath the bar, the banging of plates, along with the crescendo of the customers' conversations. This yelling of orders was supposed to impress customers as the cook whipped out the food from memory alone.

Every Waffle House restaurant I'd ever frequented had been de-signed the same—long and narrow with the kitchen area in the center of the restaurant. After working at one, I haven't eaten there more than a handful of times in over thirty years. Waffle House wait-resses had a hard job because they were required to serve customers and ensure all the dishes were cleaned promptly due to the limited supply. The one perk of being an employee was getting one free meal while working. I took full advantage of the chocolate cream pie housed in the refrigerated case. And I loved the "scattered, smothered, and covered" hash browns. For those who've never eaten at a Waffle House, these are loose hash browns (scattered), not the version they have at McDonald's that come in sleeves, with onions (smothered), and *covered* with lots of cheese.

The other advantage of being a Waffle House cook was learning how to cook nearly any breakfast food. I learned how to flip over-easy eggs without a spatula and without breaking the yolk. I made fluffy omelets, waffles, and even a kick-ass Reuben from the oft-known Waffle House lunch menu. I can now feed an entire houseful of people breakfast without breaking a sweat. Sometimes, my nieces and nephew will yell their breakfast food requests and make me feel like I'm back in 1988 wearing that sexy yellow and brown uniform covered in coffee and grease stains.

The day we moved into the motel, I worked the 10 to 2 shift. I learned tips from the head cook, Joe, on memorizing multiple orders at once, even though the waitresses stuck the orders on the metal holder next to the griddle. Another part of the cook's job was that customers wanted a show with their meal. Who knew? The trick to cooking at the Waffle House was lots of oil, nimble wrist action, and laser-focused concentration. By the end of those four hours, my head and right wrist ached.

I walked into the motel room and dropped onto a bed without removing my shoes. I buried my face in the pillow and inhaled the strong bleach scent. I needed Tylenol, a Coke, and a nap to annihilate the tension headache.

"How is being a Waffle House cook?" my mom asked.

"I can tell you that I'm glad it's only temporary. It's harder than it looks."

"Can you watch the kids for a few hours this afternoon?"

"Why?"

"You remember Mike, from the shelter?"

"No."

"Kind of stocky. Curly dark hair."

I shrugged my shoulders. I knew who my mom was talking about because he'd been following her around the last few days we spent at the shelter. I was simply through with men falling all over her. I wanted to tell her to stop using men to boost her esteem, but I bit back the observation. She would've told me to mind my business anyway.

I have to remind myself that she was only thirty-seven at that time, still young, her face untouched by wrinkles. The more she used men to prop up her worth, the more I rejected a man in my life. I waffled between how much I enjoyed kissing a man or holding hands, and pushing away any sort of emotional or physical dependence on one.

"Well, anyway, he'll be by in a few, and we're going out to get something to eat."

Some people are evil, and it's clear when you look them in their dead eyes, while others hide their evil behind niceties and a smile. I just wished I'd been able to see the monster before he drove off with my mom that day.

# Dead or Alive

M y mother vacillated between wanting to assist lost souls and being one herself. The afternoon of her date with Mike dragged on past sundown. I attempted to keep the kids happy by letting them watch television as I failed to control my fatalistic concern. The last time she drove off in a car with a man, she got into a wreck and was almost arrested for being an accessory to grand theft auto. I paced the small room and, every few minutes, parted the stiff rubber-lined curtains thinking I'd heard Mom pull up. She'd left in her car. She was driving and in control, but I couldn't shake the fear that something had happened to her.

After another hour of nervous fidgeting, a car finally pulled up, but it wasn't my mom. The headlights illuminated the window, and moments later, I jumped at the sharp knock on the door. I peered through the peephole and saw a police officer on the other side. Hands trembling, I opened the door.

"Ms. Huffman?"

I nodded, expecting the worst.

"Your mom is okay, but there's been an incident. I need you to come with me to the police station."

I nodded again and mutely pointed to my brother and sister laid out across the bed.

"Of course, they can come too."

"It'll take me a few minutes to get them dressed."

"I'll wait outside."

The shock I felt at that moment made everything a blur. I've read about how some people remember every minute detail about a traumatic event, like the adrenaline brings everything into sharp focus. That wasn't the case for me, and I floated around the motel room completely disconnected from my body. One minute I was pulling on my tennis shoes, and the next I was standing beside the police car feeling dazed.

"Their car seats are in my mom's car," I said as I stood holding my brother's and sister's hands by the passenger side of the unmarked police car.

"It's okay, miss. They'll be fine buckled in the back seat."

This was the first and only time I've ever ridden in the back of a police car. All I could think the entire time was how it was somehow okay for the officer to break the law by not having small children in the required car seats. This thought struck me as funny, and I bit my tongue and slammed my hand over my mouth. I've always been the type of person who laughs at the most inopportune times, usually when I'm overly stressed or in situations that call for decorum. Usually, I will freaking lose it with deep belly laughs, tears, and snot running down my face. That night in the back of that car, I willed the hysteria away by reminding myself that the officer said Mom was alive and okay. She was at the police station and not at the hospital, or worse, at the morgue.

Being classified as fine or okay covers a wide spectrum of states of being. Someone can seem physically fine but be psychologically unstable. The casual observer would have no inclination of the inner workings of that person's brain. The police radio crackled, the only sound in the car as we pulled into the parking lot. Jacob and Hannah were too sleepy to question anything. The officer opened the back door and ushered us into a waiting room. The police station's interior looked like a doctor's office waiting room, not a place where criminals or victims were housed. And definitely not like any police station I'd seen on television. This station had four hard plastic chairs lined up against a wall, and a window with a uniformed officer sitting behind the thick glass.

"Please wait here," the detective pointed to the chairs. "Your mom will be out shortly."

I sat down, and both kids climbed into my lap. I buried my face in their hair and willed my racing heart to slow down. *She's okay. She's alive.* This was the mantra I kept running until she walked out from behind the glass seemingly hours later.

I took in her appearance. She was still wearing the clothes she'd worn when she left the motel room. I didn't see any blood or visible bruises. I wondered if this had been another one of those Robert incidents where she'd been released from police custody because they'd determined she wasn't guilty of anything other than poor choices in men. I wanted to grab her and give her a hug, but the look on her face told me she needed distance. She was still a million miles away.

"Do you want me to drive?" I asked.

"No. I can do it."

My mom lit a cigarette as soon as we were outside. I watched her profile closely as we rode back to the motel. Her hand shook slightly, and when she stopped at a red light, she readjusted her hands on the wheel until the skin stretched taut over her knuckles. When we were locked safely inside the room, and the kids were tucked into bed once more, she motioned me to the bathroom. She went over and turned on the spigots to fill the bathtub.

"What happened?" I asked quietly, although I already suspected. Why else would I be taken to the police station by a detective?

"He raped me." The words left her mouth in a whisper and sliced my heart wide open.

"That son of a bitch." Anger flooded my face. It felt as though I'd just shoved it into a hot oven. The pizza I'd eaten for dinner threatened to come back up.

"I'm going to be fine. We're going to be okay." She slipped off her clothes and sank into the hot water. My fist clenched and un-clenched as I took in the bruises on her back and arms; the light purple marks stained her pale skin

"Did they arrest him?"

"Yes, he's in custody."

I wanted to wrap her in my arms and protect her. The long line of men who'd played the villain in our story scrolled through my mind like a movie reel on repeat. I flashed back to the time John had tried to rip her head from her shoulders at the dinner table. I cursed Robert for abandoning us and ultimately putting us in this situation. I vowed to never forgive Wayne for kicking us out of the trailer and forcing us into the homeless shelter. The rage I'd been slowly and consistently brewing in the cauldron of my belly threatened to burst through the seams of my skin. And as for this most recent fucker, the rapist—I went to bed that night dreaming of ways to end his life if I ever found him.

The morning after my mom was assaulted, she woke like it was any other Sunday. She snuggled the kids next to her in bed, read the newspaper, drank her coffee, and acted like the previous twenty-four hours hadn't happened. She was supposed to waitress the first shift that day, but she called and told the manager she was sick. Of course, they told her to not bother coming back because missing a weekend morning shift was unforgivable.

I wondered about the safety of staying at the motel. I didn't want Mike to come back. I didn't have any means to protect my family if he returned to exact revenge for his arrest. I was also about a week away from leaving for the Army, and I knew I had to talk to my recruiter on Monday. There was no way I could abandon my mother now. Fortunately, after meeting with my recruiter and explaining what had happened, I signed a deferment to my enlistment. I breathed a sigh of momentary relief. I had three months to help Mom regain some semblance of normalcy before I left.

My mom contacted the battered women's shelter, and within a day, we were safely inside the chain-link facade of another former church. The sister shelter was quiet and controlled. The homeless shelter next to the domestic violence shelter was constantly busy with occupants and activity. At the quiet and controlled women's shelter, access was limited, and it felt safe. We moved into a room with bunk beds on the second floor. There were counselors available for the occupants twenty-four hours a day if needed. I knew I could leave for work and not have to worry about anyone harming my family.

I quickly discovered the Waffle House was bent on working the pool of short-order cooks into the ground. I was soon working double shifts and racking up sixty to seventy hours a week. Mom refused to relinquish control of the car for me to drive to and from work, though she didn't want to leave the safety of the shelter either. At the time, I was frustrated she wouldn't let me use the car, but I now understand—that car was her prized possession, giving her some semblance of freedom and control over her life. I wound up walking the two-plus miles to and from work.

At first, I enjoyed the walks, and I used the time to clear my head. Still, at the end of a double shift when I barely had the energy to walk a straight line, I harbored frustration that Mom wouldn't at least pick me up. But she refused to go out after dark, and for that reason, I couldn't fault her. I suppose those summer days of walking helped me with tenacity and the ability to do anything if I put one foot in front of the other and kept pushing. I told myself the walking was preparing me for the future road marches my recruiter kept telling me to expect when I arrived at basic training.

The majority of the following month spent at the shelter consist-ed of me working and sleeping. Mom's assailant had been arrested the night of the attack and released on bail the following day, pend-ing a court date. The district attorney's office informed her that she needed to buy a pair of black slacks and a nice white dress shirt to take the stand as the court date quickly approached.

On my day off, she piled us into the car and drove over to the JCPenney in the old Signal Hill Mall to find the appropriate court clothing. We walked around racks of dress clothes while she sec-ond-guessed every piece of clothing she touched. After inspecting a handful of white shirts by holding them up to the fluorescent lights, I said, "Mom, I'm proud of you for testifying." I wanted her to find her strength. "I know what you're about to do is hard."

I'd seen some of it four years prior when Robert left us. I'd seen in her the determination to keep going when all seemed lost. I needed her to find her strength before I left. I feared she would see my leaving as the greatest betrayal yet. I begged my guardians and God to give her the strength to fight because both of our lives depended on it.

She nodded and turned her head away, but not before I saw her blink away tears.

Back at the domestic violence shelter, she hung the JCPenney bag from the top bunk. For the next few days, I watched her come and go from the room. Each time her eyes lingered on that bag before she would turn and walk out.

After explaining the circumstances to my Army recruiter, my report date to enlist had been pushed to October. The trial date was set for the Tuesday after Labor Day. We were watching the kids play on the swings in the backyard of the shelter one late August afternoon when she turned to me and said, "I can't do it."

I played dumb even though I knew what she meant. "Do what?"

"They want me to get on the stand and go over every detail of that afternoon."

"That's ridiculous," I said. "Why would lawyers put a woman through the trauma all over again?"

"I don't know. I just...I can't."

My mom suffered through terrible social anxiety. I'd grown accustomed to calling people for her for years when it came to any sort of business over the phone. She was personable in one-on-one situations, but if it involved public speaking or writing, forget about it. I had learned to write my own sick notes for school by the second grade. I'd produce a beautifully written note explaining that I had missed a day of school due to a stomachache or a headache, my go-to ailments, and she'd sign her name to the masterpiece. I suppose this was one reason she harped on my cursive penmanship in the first grade.

When she told me she couldn't testify that day, I understood her unwillingness to relive her rape in a courtroom full of strangers. Part of me was angry that the bastard who hurt her would walk away. I've always wondered why the criminal justice system perpetuates the victimization of those who've been assaulted. Why has no one figured out a more humane way to use victims' testimonies for prosecuting assailants?

A few days after her decision, Mom asked me to call Robert's brother and wife. I raised an eyebrow, but dropped a quarter in the pay phone and punched in the numbers I'd memorized all those years ago. Ted and Lynn told us we could come stay with them, without hesitation, without questions. Ted and Lynn were our saints on earth. I have nothing but love and appreciation for their support during those years. Robert was still serving prison time, and even though he and my mom had been divorced for years, we were welcomed back to Ted and Lynn's loving home like family.

The day we left Statesville, I sat beside Mom as we headed to Wadesboro, not knowing what was coming next. I knew I had the grit to look adversity in the face and come out the other side with my head and fist held high. I owed much of that to the woman beside me who could've crawled under the bedcovers and quit at any point over the past several years. Yet she drove forward looking for a way to persevere when all the odds were stacked against us.

# Here We Go Again

The last time we stayed with Ted and Lynn, I'd been fourteen. I didn't feel as though four years had passed based on their reception, but I was a different person. Lynn was barely over five feet tall, but her hugs felt like I was being enveloped by a giant. Some people's hugs are timid, given with reservations, a quick embrace, a pat on the back—but not Lynn's. They were all-enveloping and full of unconditional love. We stayed in their son's old room, no questions asked. I'd always wondered how Robert could be related to Ted, a hardworking businessman without a legal history. I couldn't make sense of why he always bailed Robert out no matter how much trouble his younger brother caused. Robert stole from his brother and his company multiple times, and they kept letting him back into their lives. That's how I know Ted and Lynn were bona fide saints.

We'd been at Ted and Lynn's house for about a week when Mom realized that the school year was about to start, and she had to register Jacob in kindergarten. In the craziness of our lives, we'd temporarily forgotten he was five years old. I accompanied Mom to the school and waited outside with Hannah as she signed paperwork and made plans to leave him with his new class for the day.

I watched as my sister attempted to climb the flagpole while I sat on a bench. She jumped, grabbed the pole, wrapped her legs around it, and tried to pull her stick-thin frame higher. I watched her get about five feet off the ground and slide back until her feet were planted. She spat into the palms of both hands and climbed once more, crying out in frustration if she didn't get higher with each attempt. Hannah always had excessive amounts of energy and an undeterrable drive. I felt proud that she'd inherited our determination and spunk.

After Mom finished at the school, we headed to the Hardee's in town so I could apply for a job. I wasn't much for working at Hardee's again, but I knew any amount of money would help my family. I had less than a month before I reported to the MEPS station in Charlotte. October 12 was the day I'd been given to arrive at the Military Entrance Processing Station. Once I underwent a physical exam, my recruiter told me I'd pick a job and either go back home and wait for my report date or immediately ship off to basic training. Everything depended on the needs of the Army. By that point in my life, I can't say I even cared what I'd be doing in the Army. I just wanted something different.

Mom told me every chance she got that she thought I'd probably ship out right away. She was always spouting the worst-case scenario around the topic of me and the military. She also claimed they'd probably send me to the other side of the country. Sometimes people refer to being torn between two lovers, as if their heart warred with itself by reaching in opposite directions. In my case, I was torn between being the emotional support for my family and being my own person. I lay awake for hours that month begging for guidance from a wiser mysterious voice in the sky. In actuality, my nights felt like the gray static that came on after the late-night news.

I spent my days working the counter at Hardee's, those few weeks flying by in a blur. Recently, I came across a picture of my mom and me sitting on Lynn's couch. My hair was already chopped off short in preparation for my new military life. I appeared to be toying with a combination lock while ducking my head into my mom's shoulder. I remember the excitement I had at that moment, at the thought of my upcoming adventure. I was thrilled at the prospect of seeing and doing new things and never again working at a fast-food restaurant. Mom flashed the camera a wry smile, her tired eyes fearful of what life would become once I was gone. At the time I was too wrapped up in thoughts of my future to consider hers.

One day in late September, I pulled into the driveway and saw a familiar station wagon. I opened the door, and Saint Lynn was sitting on the couch talking to Wayne like he was an esteemed guest. I was confused about how he'd tracked us down. I wondered if she'd called him. Then I remembered I had spoken to my blond-haired friend, David, the previous week. I had given him the phone number. It was nice talking to someone outside my family, but he must've passed the number along to Wayne. I smiled at Lynn and avoided Wayne's gaze. I strode back to the bedroom to change out of my greasy clothes and ran into my mother.

"What's he doing here?" I snapped.

"He said he's sorry. He said he made a huge mistake throwing us out and wants us to come back." Mom examined her nails.

I willed her to meet my gaze without any luck. I wasn't sure how my mom would ever consider going back to him after all that had happened, but instinctively I knew she would. Most likely because I was leaving.

"Does he still live in the trailer in Statesville?"

"No, he said he's going to work on getting us a new place. He said to give him about a week."

I nodded and stripped the brown polyester shirt off my clammy skin. Sweating was always my fight or flight response, and that day found me ready to fight. I felt more torn than ever before. I knew she needed someone by her side if I wasn't there, but I still harbored a shit-ton of animosity toward Wayne for his part in our situation. I honestly don't know how I still had room for love in my heart with all of the hatred I harbored toward men in general back then.

I barely acknowledged Wayne that day. In actuality, it took years for me to fully trust his intentions with my mom. While I never regarded Wayne as my father figure, he did earn my utmost respect when he stayed by Mom's side until the day she took her last breath.

After Wayne left Ted and Lynn's house that day, Mom said he'd begged her to come back to him. He promised he was a different man. He told her he loved her. He said all the things that women in abusive relationships have heard for centuries. Mom believed the words, or at least acted like she did for everyone's benefit. After that week, we left Ted and Lynn's and headed back to Mooresville, back to Wayne, and back to another motel room. I was less than two weeks from reporting to the military and told myself I could survive anything for that amount of time.

# Shattered Dream

The Sunday morning before my scheduled trip to the Military Entrance Processing Station (MEPS), I awoke with sharp pains in my stomach. These were the types of cramps that signaled something was forcefully exiting my body, although I wasn't certain of the exit point. I feared I would get sick from being enclosed in the tiny motel room that measured no bigger than a ten-by-fifteen-foot space, which housed three adults and two children. Jacob had come home sick from school on Friday, likely some illness he'd contracted at elementary school, the modern-day Petri dish. For a moment, I wondered if Mom had intentionally infected me with his germs while I slept just to keep me from leaving. My mind ran away with images of her pressing a germy cup to my lips so I'd be forced to stay in my bed.

Mom smiled like an angel, but I wondered if she was using subterfuge to block my enlistment. I spent the next two days sipping ginger ale and water, and vomiting undigested saltines into the commode. I stumbled back to the bed I shared with my siblings and tried to force more liquid down my throat in hopes it would stay put.

When Sergeant Allen, the recruiter, picked me up on that Tuesday afternoon, I managed to weakly hug my family goodbye. I caught a glimpse of my face in the bathroom mirror just before he arrived, and I could have sworn I was the color of the off-brand ginger ale I'd been drinking. During the drive, my recruiter told me I'd stay overnight at a hotel in Charlotte. I'd have to be at the MEPS by 6 a.m. to do my physical, pick my job, and take the oath of service. I would either leave for basic training or be given a later date to report, depending on the MOS (military occupational specialty); in civilian terms, it meant my new job.

When we arrived at the hotel, I noticed it was much nicer than any motel I'd previously stayed in. The hotel was full of people enlisting in all branches of the military. The recruiters remained in a separate wing of the hotel to ensure they had peace and quiet and to avoid the late-night, last-minute displays of affection between teenagers and their lovers experiencing separation for the first time. The second floor had a party atmosphere, similar to the kind of excitement I'd seen on the *MTV Spring Break* specials I'd watched. Teenage girls squealed and ran along the corridors releasing nervous energy we all shared at the prospect of leaving our current lives and embarking on an adventure like no other.

The hotel sponsored an enormous dinner buffet. Since I'd spent the previous two days puking, I decided to stick with mashed potatoes, a splash of gravy, and a couple of yeast rolls. I washed my meal down with a glass of extra-sweet iced tea and was pleasantly surprised when the food stayed down. I looked longingly at the meatloaf but knew adding spicy, greasy meat to my stomach would be a disaster. After dinner, I returned to my room, where my randomly assigned roommate for the night asked if I wanted to go to a party a few rooms over. I declined because Sergeant Allen had already warned me against doing anything stupid the night before I enlisted, including drinking, drugs, or breaking the 10 p.m. curfew. I hadn't done any drinking or drugs in over two years and had absolutely no desire to possibly fuck up my future, not when I'd made it this far. I was on the cusp of leaving North Carolina and starting my adult life, and nothing was going to stand in my way.

The next morning, we all piled onto a white bus with a bluebird painted on the side. We were driven inside the gates of a squat brown building, typical government architecture as I would learn much later in life. I knew October 12, 1988, was going to be a great day. I could feel it. That morning, I was called into a room where a man dressed in slacks and a sweater sat at a desk perusing an open brown folder. He pointed to a small screen on the other side of the room.

"Have a seat. These are the job openings that fit with your ASVAB scores," he said monotonously, unwilling or unable to look me in the eye while talking to me. I wondered what had beaten him down.

I took a seat in front of a black screen with amber-colored words and peered at a list of job names, many of which I didn't recognize. Many I refused to do because of my aversion to the sight of blood. I'd really wanted to join the military police force, but those positions weren't open. I scanned the list again and chose the next available job I thought would be the best for my future.

"I'll take the air traffic controller, I guess."

I had no idea what the job entailed other than sitting in a nice, comfortable flight tower. Hopefully, the job included an opportunity to travel to foreign countries. The man annotated my choice in my file and printed a paper I was told to sign.

"Go back to the waiting area, and they'll call you for your physical next."

I spent the next several hours doing duck walks; yes, picture me squatting and waddling like a duck. I had my first gynecological exam, which was deeply uncomfortable for a number of reasons; hearing and eye tests; and some psychological questions toward the end of the physical to evaluate my mental and emotional proficiency. I was instructed after every test to return to the waiting room and listen for my name. Hurry-up-and-wait seemed to be the theme of my day. I spent my time between tests in a big, open waiting area filled with rows of chairs and televisions positioned around the room.

"Huffman." Finally, my name was called.

"Yes, Sergeant."

My recruiter sat down next to me and twisted his cap onto his knee.

"What's going on?" I'd seen people I'd duck walked with in the medical wing already taken back for travel and oath-taking hours before.

"You're underweight. They won't take you. You're only ninety-nine pounds, and you have to weigh at least a hundred and two to enlist."

"That's really a thing?" I couldn't believe what I was hearing.

"Yeah, it's a requirement. You have to come back next month and you have to gain three pounds during that time."

"I can do it. I just had a stomach bug last weekend."

"Just focus on eating three calorie-dense meals a day, plus snacks." He patted my shoulder and smiled. "Really pack on the calories."

The ride back to Mooresville lacked conversation. The car's atmosphere was filled with country music blaring from the speakers and the occasional muttered expletive from Sergeant Allen directed at a neighboring vehicle on Interstate 77. I felt like a deflated balloon. When I was much younger, Mom would blow air into a balloon until the air strained against the rubber, threatening to pop. She'd then release the balloon, and we'd giggle as the balloon flew around the room propelled by its air. That's how I felt on the ride back to the motel where my family waited, not knowing I had failed on my first attempt.

When we got back to the motel, I exited the car, waved to Sergeant Allen, and knocked on the door. I got the sense my recruiter couldn't wait to be done with me, and I couldn't say I blamed him. I'd unintentionally been a pain in his ass since I signed my delayed entry paperwork in April.

Mom opened the door and immediately enveloped me in a tight hug. When I told them what had happened, Wayne said the solution was to drink protein shakes. He seemed intent on me starting that very night, and soon he was back with a large container from the local vitamin shop. For the next six weeks, I drank the thick vanilla protein powder mixed with whole milk and ate every fatty food my mom could cook on an electric skillet. Wayne was dead set on helping me attain my goal, so he said, and bought me another big plastic container of protein mix each week.

I didn't walk anywhere for fear of burning precious calories, so I spent my days watching *Regis and Kathie Lee* and playing cards with Mom. I spent my nights dreaming about not living in a motel room with my family. Instead, I focused on my future, the future my recruiter said awaited once I passed my physical.

After eight weeks of basic training, I'd then attend my advanced training for my military job. After that, I would be assigned to my duty station. My recruiter had said I'd probably have a roommate, but I'd have my own space. I dreamed of my own space often. I didn't even care if I had a roommate; this was just one stop on my way to owning my own home after my service in the Army. Images of my future loft in Charlotte danced in my head. It was my motivation every day.

November 21 finally arrived. My recruiter picked me up from the motel and chauffeured me back to the same hotel in Charlotte. He stood outside my door that night and reminded me of the exact instructions as before. Around ten o'clock, there was a knock on the door. I peeped through the hole and saw my recruiter. I wondered if he was trying to catch me breaking curfew. I opened the door, and my recruiter shoved a handful of bananas toward me.

"Eat all of these between now and five o'clock in the morning, and don't take a shit."

I grabbed the bananas, offered a smile, and said, "Got it."

He turned and walked away while shaking his head.

My second time arriving at MEPS wasn't nearly as exciting as the last time. I was concerned. I'd eaten all of the bananas and figured I never wanted to see another one. I used to love eating peanut butter and banana sandwiches, but I couldn't touch the things for a long time after this. I didn't want to think about any other options besides the Army. I didn't want to think about the possibility of being stuck in Mooresville. I had no plan B.

This time the list of available jobs was much shorter. It must've been the fact we were approaching the holidays. The only one that really seemed to call to me was a defense artillery technician. I had no idea what I would do in this job, but again, I was desperate and only planned to do it for four years. I was using the military just as they were using me; it was a symbiotic relationship. I'm sure the government was well aware of how enticing up to $24,000 for college was for enlistees. They weren't oblivious to enlistment incentives that helped them reach their quotas in post-Vietnam America.

After going through a battery of tests for hearing, vision, and weight again as part of the physical exam, I found myself in the waiting area once more. I didn't want to focus on what would happen if I wasn't accepted this time. I started wondering if maybe this wasn't what I was supposed to be doing with my life. Perhaps the weight obstacle was a sign. I was always big on signs.

"Huffman, let's go."

"No, again?"

"You weighed 101. One pound off the mark."

"Dammit." I smacked my forehead with my palm.

"I know."

Walking through the parking lot to the car, I asked, "Was this my last chance?"

"No, you get one more chance. The doctors are giving you two weeks, but after that, if you don't weigh 102 pounds, you'll be deemed unacceptable for military service."

*Unacceptable? I'm fucking acceptable. Actually, I am* exceptional.

"I've tried everything to gain weight." I climbed into the passenger seat and stared straight ahead, afraid my frustration would spill down my cheeks.

Sergeant Allen turned toward me and said, "Look, just enjoy Thanksgiving with your family. We'll go back in two weeks. It either happens, or it doesn't, but stop worrying."

I sat in silence on the ride back. Total resignation suited my recruiter much better than agitation. I was certain his recruitment numbers wouldn't tank because of me, but I knew it didn't help. The two weeks leading up to my final shot with MEPS found Mom happier than ever. She started smiling a lot more, and I cautiously returned her smiles. I suspected her good mood was because she thought I would get rejected by the military and stay by her side. I became grouchier with my siblings, unintentionally projecting my frustration and fear of being trapped at the motel in Mooresville forever.

I was beginning to wonder if I'd ever escape my circumstances for new adventures, new roads to travel and explore. As the final trip to

Charlotte approached, I made a concerted effort not to worry about the outcome. I told myself that if I didn't get into the Army, I would simply find another path to attend college. I'd work somewhere, just not in fast food. I'd go to community college and then transfer to a university. I recognized there were multiple ways to reach a life goal if I evaluated all avenues and options. If life closes one door and slaps multiple padlocks on that bitch, the goal is to find a skeleton key.

On the afternoon of December 4, I packed my gym bag with a few changes of clothes and my toiletry items.

"Do you think the third time's the charm?" Mom asked as she sat puffing a cigarette at the table by the window.

I struggled to answer without hurting her feelings. How could I say I hoped it was without making it seem like I was happy to leave her and the kids?

"I don't know, but I do know I'm ready to find out so I can plan for what's next instead of being in limbo."

She nodded, stared down at the brown carpet patch by the door, and then turned back to reading her book.

I wasn't sure it was the response she'd hoped for. I wanted to tell my mother that I wasn't abandoning her but saving myself. My voice refused to verbalize those sentiments.

# Fast Car

The night before my last attempt to enter the military, I settled into my room after a dinner of McDonald's cheeseburgers and fries picked up from the restaurant about a mile from the hotel. The same hotel where I'd stayed twice prior in my hopes of joining the Army and leaving North Carolina behind. We'd arrived earlier, around 5:30, and now I sat by myself in the room savoring every bite. I mean, it wasn't the best cheeseburger I'd ever eaten, but it was nice to eat a meal in peace, without Wayne grumbling about the idiots he worked with or the kids hitting, kicking, or screaming at each other. Still, the dull ache of loneliness spread through my chest. I knew if I was actually able to join the Army this time I would likely miss the familiarity of my family in the coming days. Until then, I pushed them and my concerns from my mind as I watched the nightly news followed by an episode of *Jeopardy*.

There was a knock at the hotel door at curfew time, just as I was nodding off to sleep. I rubbed the sleep from my eyes, checked the peephole, and opened the door. Sergeant Allen, my recruiter, stood there in his all gray Army sweatpants and sweatshirt, looking more human and less intimidating without his uniform. I expected another bunch of bananas and a lecture about not going to the bathroom. Instead, I got this nugget of advice: "Get a good night's rest, Huffman. Don't worry about tomorrow." Sergeant Allen offered a rare smile before turning and walking away.

I shook my head and stared into the cold, quiet night air. Because it was only weeks before Christmas, the number of recruits at the hotel was at an all-time low compared to the other times I'd stayed there. I wondered what this meant for Christmas if I was to be in basic training. I would've rather spent my favorite holiday with family, but I cared more about turning my dream of escape into reality. The quiet of the evening meant I didn't have a roommate to try to entice me with socializing or partying. I lay in bed in my T-shirt and panties and watched syndicated television shows more for the background noise than for any interest on my part. Instead, I thought about my past and my future. I'd been accused of daydreaming since as early as I could remember, but daydreaming and thinking about how to escape my dire circumstances had me poised to finally change my life.

I drank cups of hotel coffee and ate a bag of peanut M&Ms while I played out what I wanted to happen the next day. I had to weigh enough. I wouldn't use the bathroom before the physical or exhale while being weighed. And as silly as that sounded, going back to that motel room in Mooresville was not an option. That night I dreamed of my future home, the loft in downtown Charlotte, and how I'd be a famous writer or a detective or maybe both. If I had a chance to leave and learn to be my own person, I knew I could attain those things.

The next morning I woke refreshed and ready for the day, eating a bowl of Raisin Bran and an apple from the hotel's continental breakfast. Sergeant Allen met me in the lobby to chauffeur me to the MEPS at 0745 sharp, 7:45 a.m. if I was going by civilian time. On the way, he sang along with some twangy country song on the radio that I didn't recognize. I tapped my foot to the rhythm, even though country music was still not my favorite. My mood was upbeat, and I was willing the universe to be different today—nothing but positive thoughts. Out with the worry about things I couldn't change.

"This is it, Huffman."

"Yes, sir."

He let the "sir" reference slide. When I'd first met him at the recruitment station, I'd called him "sir," and he'd hit back with, "I work for a damn living. Call me Sergeant." Southern manners die hard.

In the central waiting room, I sat and listened for my name. The uniformed nurse called me back to the area of the building for my physical exam once again. I duck walked to prove all my lower body joints still worked properly. Afterward, a doctor checked me out from head to toe once more, thankfully forgoing the pelvic exam since I'd just been there two weeks prior.

My eyes focused on the metal physician's scale in the corner. The doctor waved me over. I climbed onto the metal scale and stood tall and still in my underwear and socks. I watched as the doctor slid the counterweight to the one-hundred-pound mark. He then tapped the small weight to 101 as the weight beam teetered to the left. I inhaled and trapped my breath in my diaphragm, too afraid to exhale before he pushed the weight once more. He tapped the small weight over to the 102 notch, and the weight beam teetered, not balancing but also not falling to the right side of the scale.

"It looks like 102 to me." The doctor grabbed my folder and wrote the number on my physical form.

I smiled broadly. It was actually happening! Almost as soon as my smile stretched across my face, it faltered. After months of waiting, I was actually enlisting in the Army. The reality of it hit me like a loaded knapsack.

I returned to the waiting room and barely warmed the chair seat before I was called into the office where I would pick yet another job the Army had available. As long as it didn't have anything to do with cooking or customer service, I could do it. I crossed my fingers for a better selection than I'd had the last time.

I scanned the shortlist of jobs on the page until my eyes locked in on one near the bottom called "watercraft operator."

"Excuse me, sir?"

"Yes, recruit."

"What does a watercraft operator do?"

"Hang on. I'll grab you the videotape."

I figured he was being nice since there weren't many recruits to keep him too busy today. The man rummaged around his desk before producing a VHS tape that he then slid into the VCR next to the screen. "We just got this one the other day."

On the screen, I watched as a bizarre cross between a boat and something that resembled an aircraft with propellers in the rear of the boat skimmed across the water. It appeared to travel at fast speeds. My pulse quickened, and I grinned. Watercraft meant I'd have to be stationed around the water. Even though I had no idea how to swim, I adored being around water. I thought of my one trip to Myrtle Beach and how I wanted to be close to ocean waves once more.

"I want to do that."

"Great," he said, looking down at my folder. "You're going to be an 88K10 watercraft operator."

"A what?"

"Eighty-eight kilo ten. Just remember, watercraft operator."

I returned to the main waiting area while people behind the closed doors finalized my travel plans. I waited for my ticket, the location of my basic training station determining either plane or bus. My name was called, and I entered a room where they fingerprinted me for my FBI file in case I died. Finally, I was called to the travel office to receive my bus tickets and a stipend for food on my one-way trip to Fort Dix, New Jersey.

As a child, I'd been all over the South, from South Carolina, to Texas, to New Mexico—but I'd never been north. My nervous excitement waned, and I was left with the after-effects of an adrenaline dump and an early morning alarm. I was told the next step to finalizing my enlistment was to take the oath. Sergeant Allen had instructed me on my first trip to MEPS that I was to repeat after the person conducting the ceremony when taking my oath. It seemed easy enough, but I was still nervous I would screw it up.

I was using the military as a step to the next phase of my life. I was uncertain how I would feel about taking some oath. It seemed proper and final, but if it would move me to the next stage, I was willing to repeat the words.

A woman stepped out of a wooden door and said, "If your name is called, please come forward."

A group of five enlistees filed into a dark-paneled room that housed a row of flags in stands at the front. There was a flag for each branch of the military and the American flag. A red-haired man dressed in camouflage, with a congenial smile and who reminded me of a grown-up Opie from *The Andy Griffith Show*, instructed us to approach and line up in front of him. I studied the black pin on his collar that looked like a capital "I" and I tried to remember the rank from the chart hanging on the wall in the waiting area. My mind drew a blank, and I hoped this wasn't an indication of my inability to understand military rank.

He asked us some questions about doubts, coercion, and if we were sure about joining. I figured not many people turned around and walked out, but I guess they had to ask. Looking back now, I wondered if they asked those same questions during the Vietnam Conflict with men who were drafted. I imagine not.

"Please raise your right hand and repeat after me."

"I, Sandra Huffman, do solemnly swear that I will support and defend the Constitution of the United States against all enemies, foreign and domestic; that I will bear true faith and allegiance to the same; and that I will obey the orders of the President of the United States and the orders of the officers appointed over me, according to the regulations and the Uniform Code of Military Justice. So help me, God."

After those words left my mouth, the strangest thing happened. It was as if this decision was no longer only about my escape but was also about me being a part of something greater. It was as though when I spoke the words, they entered my bloodstream and gave me a sense of purpose I'd been lacking since I quit school. I told Mom I'd send her part of my paycheck each month to help. I had that purpose of helping support her and my siblings. But this was different. It was as if speaking the words solidified my determination to change my life, to become someone different, someone I knew was more than a high school drop-out, a waitress, a cook, or a poor bastard child.

After waiting at the bus station for hours, I finally climbed onto that Greyhound bus and mentally prepared for the next fourteen hours I would spend traveling to New Jersey. I had called Mom and told her where I was going, although midway through the call, I had to clamp a hand over the receiver so she couldn't hear me choke back a sob.

All of a sudden, I didn't know what I was doing. I was never an athlete. I barely ran anywhere. I hadn't done a push-up since ninth grade, and even back then, it was done from my knees. I sat toward the back of the bus, surrounded by strangers and flush with doubt. Maybe Mom had been right about my "rebellious" nature. Maybe I wasn't cut out for this. Maybe I would fail after all. I was an eighteen-year-old woman in a man's military in 1988.

I inhaled deeply and shut down the voice of doubt. I could do anything a man could do and do it better. I'd already been through hell in my lifetime, and I knew I could withstand anything they threw my way in basic training. All I could do was put one foot in front of the other, try my absolute best, and never give up. I knew if I did that, I would get through what came next. It had always worked that way for me; this would be no different.

My survival and sanity required that I leave Mom's side. I shook with fear and excitement for my life, my chance to make the hard decisions and live with my consequences. My adventure awaited. I embraced the unknown that night, the night I sat on the Greyhound and watched as I left the Charlotte skyline and my past behind.

# The Story

On a sunny Monday in 2008, I rode in the procession of cars behind the hearse that carried Mom's remains in a baby-blue casket. We shared the favorite color of blue. Wayne, her husband, had chosen it as a last homage to the complicated woman we loved. I sobbed with a fist to my mouth like it would stop the tears that streamed down my cheeks as I watched the police escort stop traffic. We passed the tunnel road where Mom had driven me and her grandchildren to listen to the echo as she blew her car horn and yelled at the top of her lungs. We passed Gibson Furniture, where my cousin Melissa screamed shrilly when she first heard the news Elvis had died, and we passed the hospital where I'd been born and Beulah had died. The memories flooded my mind as I vacillated between numbness and unbearable sadness. The procession weaved through the residential area that flanked the cemetery. I watched people in their yards washing cars and playing ball with their children as I finally let the profound numbness settle in my bones. Her final resting place was just down the hill from her aunts, uncles, and grandparents. Mom's journey had returned her to Mooresville.

About seven years after Mom died, my friend invited me to her house for a group reading from a medium she knew. It was $100 each person, and the medium would channel messages from loved ones from the other side. There was a chance that a loved one wouldn't come through, and that was the crap shoot of doing a group reading. After a little thought, I told her I would come because I was curious. I was doing research for a book, and I believed the experience would help with authenticity. I assumed there was an afterlife, but I didn't necessarily believe I would experience it that day.

The afternoon I sat in my friend's living room with eight strangers, some co-workers I recognized from the office and others I didn't, and a medium sitting front and center. I studied the medium trying to sense if she was a fake. I was leaning toward fake. I spent most of the hour doodling in my notebook and doing inner eye rolls since the ladies in the group kept jumping at random phrases and objects. It was the oldest hoax in the medium book of tricks: vague suggestions to grief-stricken people anxious to hear from their loved ones beyond the grave. The medium relayed with her palm pressed to her head, "I'm hearing a 'S' sound, like a snake. I'm being shown a lazy Susan. This person is very adamant about a 'miracle baby.'"

I listened as the medium delivered messages from deceased loved ones to those around me. I wondered if she was that accurate or just an excellent guesser. I kept waiting because I could've jumped at the "S"; after all, my name is Sandra. My sister had been deemed a "miracle baby" when born three months premature. Still, I was a damn fine skeptic, and I waited for something nobody else in the group could claim was their message since they'd all jumped on the previous clues.

About the time I'd determined the experience was a sham, the medium relayed a message from beyond that sent chills down my body—the deceased loved one was showing her blue beer cans lined up in the fridge. At that moment, I knew with absolute conviction it was my mother. My heart stuttered, and I croaked out to the rest of the group that it was my mom and the message was meant for me. The medium full-on belly laughed and said my mom threw up her arms skyward like *Finally, Sandra spoke up!*

Those blue beer cans she mentioned had once occupied the entire bottom shelf of Mom's refrigerator in neat rows. She didn't drink them all by herself. Wayne helped, but she used them and cigarettes to take the edge off her anxiety and unhappiness. She'd done it for years leading up to her premature death at the age of fifty-seven, using that combination of grocery store drugs instead of prescription ones to numb her pain.

The medium said, "Your mother wants you to know you were like a mother to her. She said she's never been good with words or emotions. She carried a lot of grief and agony. She wants you to know she no longer has bad habits or hurts. She wants you to know she's hanging out with Louise, and she's okay now."

I nodded along to the message, to the things I'd known since childhood about my mom, as tears streamed down my cheeks. Hearing those words, words she never spoke while alive, pulverized my soul. I sobbed hysterically once I reached my car, unwilling to show my soft side to those strangers who'd gossip about it at work. I wished she'd said them while alive. I wished she'd healed before she died. I cranked the ignition, and the distinctive clapping and drums from Joan Jett's "I Love Rock 'N Roll" streamed through the speakers, not David Bowie's "Changes," which I'd been listening to when I pulled in. I pounded the steering wheel to the beat and cried the entire way home.

What I've come to realize is that at the most critical points in our lives, we are unequivocally, utterly alone—alone with the grief, joy, sadness, regret, and all of the other multitude of emotions resulting from the consequences of our decisions in life. In the aloneness, I learned to take responsibility for my life, my choices, and my happiness, regardless of external factors. I will always be thankful for Mom with all of her strengths and flaws, because without her, I wouldn't be me. And I'm damn proud to be Ann's daughter.

## THE END

# Acknowledgements

My love and appreciation to all who have been a part of this process, from my beloved sister to my friends who read many versions of my rough drafts and still answer my emails and texts. A special thanks to my editor, Claire Beerbower. You're the best. A warm thank you for the readers of this book. Time is one of the most valuable commodities in this world, and I appreciate you spending yours with my story.

# About the Author

Sandra Tow holds an MFA in Creative Writing from Queens University of Charlotte. She is an Army Veteran who learned to live out of a bag as a child, and she still enjoys feeding the traveling wanderlust. Sandra lives in North Carolina with her husband and three dogs, and enjoys spending her free time with her family, scouring antique stores for hidden treasures, and always seeking the messiest and most flavorful all-the-way cheeseburger her state has to offer. Read more at sandratow.com.